Praise for

Until Christ Is Formed in You

"Dallas Willard combined intellectual rigor with a deep commitment to spiritual growth in a way that is rare among recent Christian writers and thinkers. *Until Christ Is Formed in You* is a demonstration of the continued power and relevance of his work. The intellectual rigor of these essays pushes all of us to become the persons God intends us to be."

—**C. Stephen Evans**, University Professor of Philosophy and Humanities, Baylor University

"Finally—a scholarly yet accessible volume that explores the broad spectrum of Dallas Willard's remarkable contributions to the field of Christian spiritual formation! These well-rounded essays probe Willard's central themes by addressing the Holy Spirit's work until Christ is formed in us. An indispensable resource for theological educators, students, and ministry leaders!"

—**Diane J. Chandler,** Associate Professor of Christian Formation and Leadership, Regent University School of Divinity

"This book has something for everyone. Academics will enjoy the deep dive into philosophy and theology; spiritual directors, psychologists, and pastors will love the mystical and practical wisdom related to transformation. All lovers of Willard will enjoy hearing these men and women reflect on their mentor with the earnest desire to carry forward the heart of his message."

—**Theresa Clement Tisdale,** Professor of Psychology, Azusa Pacific University

"Those who have been captivated by Dallas Willard's writings on Christian transformation will find in *Until Christ is Formed in You* a rich presentation of clarifications, extensions, critical reflections, and interdisciplinary commentary by ten theologians, philosophers, and psychologists who have been touched by his person and work."

—**Robert C. Roberts,** Distinguished Professor of Ethics, Emeritus, Baylor University

"Dallas left us a rich legacy in his writings and in his students. Through the lens of their own experience and training, these scholars, whom Dallas identified as his fellow pilgrims, beautifully illuminate and respectfully critique Dallas's thoughts on complex themes of discipleship and personal transformation. As we seek to broaden the impact of Dallas's teaching, this academic treatment of his work is a great gift."

—**The Dallas Willard Family**

UNTIL CHRIST IS FORMED IN YOU

Dallas Willard and Spiritual Formation

Edited by

STEVEN L. PORTER
GARY W. MOON
J. P. MORELAND

Abilene Christian University Press

UNTIL CHRIST IS FORMED IN YOU

Dallas Willard and Spiritual Formation

ISBN 978-1-68426-090-4 | LCCN 2018005035

Printed in the United States of America

LIBRARY OF CONGRESS CATALOGING-IN-PUBLICATION DATA
Names: Porter, Steven L., 1970- editor.
Title: Until Christ is formed in you: : Dallas Willard and spiritual formation / edited by Steven L. Porter, Gary W. Moon, J.P. Moreland.
Description: Abilene : Abilene Christian University Press, 2018.
Identifiers: LCCN 2018005035 | ISBN 9781684260904 (pbk.)
Subjects: LCSH: Spiritual formation. | Willard, Dallas, 1935-2013.
Classification: LCC BV4511 .U58 2018 | DDC 230.092—dc23
LC record available at https://lccn.loc.gov/ 2018005035

Cover design by Bruce Gore | Gore Studio, Inc.
Interior text design by Sandy Armstrong, Strong Design

For information contact:
Abilene Christian University Press
ACU Box 29138
Abilene, Texas 79699

1-877-816-4455
www.acupressbooks.com

26 27 28 / 7 6 5 4

To Dallas Albert Willard (1935–2013), an unceasing spiritual being with an eternal destiny in God's great universe. We trust that your plans for what you will be doing five hundred years from now are well underway. We look forward to seeing your ongoing work in God's great kingdom, and we dedicate the work of these scholars to you and to the Risen Lord you serve.

CONTENTS

ACKNOWLEDGMENTS

One unanticipated blessing of knowing Dallas Willard are the many wonderful persons we have gotten to know through our common connection with Dallas. Dallas turns out to be quite the networker, which is a bit surprising for someone who would never have been described as a social butterfly. It was our respective friendships with Dallas that caused the three of us to join forces on editing this collection of essays. And it was a shared appreciation of Dallas that brought us into contact with Jason Fikes, who has graciously guided this book to publication at ACU Press. Moreover, each chapter author was drawn to participate in this volume due to their interest in Dallas and his work. We are grateful for their contributions.

Many of the chapters in this book first appeared in a special issue of the *Journal of Spiritual Formation & Soul Care* that focused on the spiritual formation writings of Dallas.[1] Much thanks goes to those who helped bring that special issue into existence, including John Coe, the founding editor of the journal, and Joy Bergk, the academic publications manager at Biola University. For some time now Biola University has been the primary underwriter of the *Journal of Spiritual Formation & Soul Care*, which speaks loudly of Biola's commitment to encourage Christian scholarship on important issues for the sake of the church and society. The special issue of

[1] See *Journal of Spiritual Formation & Soul Care* 3, no. 2 (2010).

the journal, and thereby this book, would not have occurred without the generous support of Biola University. Thanks also goes to Pete Hill, editor of the *Journal of Psychology and Christianity*, who gave us permission to print a revised version of John Ortberg's contribution to this book which first appeared in *JPC*.

The Willard family (Jane, Becky, and John) also deserve thanks for how caringly they have approached posthumous publications that are in some manner connected with Dallas. They have gone above and beyond in helping to ensure that Dallas's writings and ministry "fight on!"

Lastly, we want to acknowledge Dallas, to whom this book is posthumously dedicated. While we have each been profoundly touched by having known Dallas, we want to acknowledge here not so much his personal influence on us but rather the overall influence of his published work in spiritual formation.[2] Many have written in recent years on the nature of Christian life in the Spirit, but most of those writings gradually fade away and newer books arise to take their place in publishers' catalogues. But Dallas's books seem to be standing the test of time. For instance, it is not uncommon for any of the three of us to find ourselves referencing or recommending Dallas's book *In Search of Guidance*, which was written well over thirty years ago in 1984. The staggering and ongoing brilliance of Dallas's writings on formation can be accounted for by some uncanny mix of the right timing, his platform as a philosopher at USC, his vivid embodiment of his message, and his incredible depth of analysis.

Of course, it is important to realize that to praise Dallas alone for the quality and impact of his writing in spiritual formation is to quite literally miss the point of his work. Anyone familiar with Dallas's writing and speaking on formation is familiar with his definition of grace: "Grace is God acting in our lives to bring about what we do not deserve and cannot accomplish on our own." We know God is graciously at work in and through us when what is accomplished cannot be explained by human effort alone. Now, make no mistake, we are quite sure that Dallas *on his own* could have made a significant splash. But the quality and outcome of Dallas's character, personal interactions, thinking, writing, and teaching

---

[2] Each of us have reflected on Dallas's personal impact on our lives in our respective chapters in *Eternal Living: Reflections on Dallas Willard's Teaching on Faith & Formation*, edited by Gary W. Moon (Downers Grove, IL: InterVarsity Press, 2015).

make it abundantly clear that God's grace was at work in and through him. What has been accomplished both in and through this man defies a purely naturalistic explanation. Dallas is not, at the end of the day, the one to be honored and praised. If we take the views Dallas did so much to proliferate seriously, then what we can do is honor him for his having continued to do what he could to offer his body to God as an instrument of righteousness (cf. Rom. 6:13). In doing this, Dallas exemplified what he taught, harnessing a power beyond himself to accomplish great and eternal good in millions of lives.

So, Dallas, we do thank you for doing enough of your part that God, in his grace, was able to do "far more abundantly than all that we ask or think, according to the power at work within us" (Eph. 3:20). May the Lord see fit to use the writings contained herein in a similar manner.

PREFACE

"My little children, for whom I am again in the anguish of childbirth until Christ is formed in you!" (Gal. 4:19)

It is clear from Paul's letters that he was indeed passionately concerned for the spiritual formation of those he pastored. To the Galatians he admonished, "O foolish Galatians! Who has bewitched you? . . . Having begun by the Spirit, are you now being perfected by the flesh?" (Gal. 3:1, 3). To the flock in Corinth he wrote, "But I, brothers, could not address you as spiritual people, but as people of the flesh, as infants in Christ. I fed you with milk, not solid food, for you were not ready for it" (1 Cor. 3:1–2). And to the church in Ephesus, "In [Christ] you also are being built together into a dwelling place for God by the Spirit. For this reason, I bow my knees before the Father . . . [that] he may grant you to be strengthened with power through his Spirit in your inner being" (Eph. 2:22, 3:14, 16). Paul's letters make it clear that he was one who had tasted of the goodness of the way of Jesus, and as a result he was unrelentingly dedicated to do what he could to guide others into that transformational way of life.

We daresay Dallas Willard was equally passionate about the spiritual formation of those whom his life, work, and ministry had the opportunity to touch. We dare to say this because it was no doubt the same energizing Spirit that moved Dallas as moved Paul. In speaking of his ministry goal to "present everyone mature in Christ," Paul writes, "For this I toil, struggling with all his energy that he powerfully works within me" (Col. 1:28–29). Dallas struggled with that same energizing presence as he toiled to clarify the vision of life with Christ, the necessity of intentionality in being conformed to Christ, and the various grace-filled means of entering more deeply into the kingdom of the God and Father of our Lord Jesus Christ. Dallas, like Paul, not only embodied such a life but earnestly sought to instruct others in it. In so doing, he was not so much remarkable as he was what should be expected time and time again when the Spirit of Jesus takes hold of one's life.

Much, but certainly not all, of Willard's written instruction can be found in what is referred to in this book as the Willardian corpus: *Hearing God*, *The Spirit of the Disciplines*, *The Divine Conspiracy*, *Renovation of the Heart*, and *Knowing Christ Today*. These five books—Willard's pentalogy—along with *The Great Omission* and several posthumous publications are the best place to go for interaction with Willard's views on formation.[1] But as with any scholar, the reach of one's work is often extended, refined, defended, and re-articulated afresh by others. Due to the methodological breadth of Willard's writings in formation, these others include philosophers, theologians, biblical scholars, psychologists, historians, sociologists, and so on.

And yet, to date Willard's writings in spiritual formation have not received as much scholarly attention as might be expected (Chapter One of this book briefly explores why this might be the case). While many academic theologians, philosophers, psychologists, and the like have been heavily influenced by Willard's writings, his views have not received extensive treatment by scholars in their own academic work. While Willard's books might be referenced here or there, they are not often critically engaged.[2]

---

[1] To date, Willard's posthumous publications are Dallas Willard and Gary Black Jr., *The Divine Conspiracy Continued* (San Francisco: HarperOne, 2014), *Living in Christ's Presence: Final Words on Heaven and the Kingdom of God* (Downers Grove, IL: InterVarsity Press, 2014), *The Allure of Gentleness*, edited by Rebecca Heatley (San Francisco: HarperOne, 2015), and *Renewing the Christian Mind: Essays, Interviews, and Talks*, edited by Gary Black Jr. (San Francisco: HarperOne, 2016).

[2] There are, of course, exceptions. Gary Black Jr., for instance, wrote his doctoral dissertation at the University of Exeter, entitled "Returning to Protoevangelical Faith: The Theology and Praxis of Dallas Willard," a revised version of which was later published as *The*

Part of the barrier to academic reflection on Willard's formation writings is that he was not writing with an academic audience in mind. In fact, Willard was once asked in conversation whether he wrote for an academic or a lay audience. Dallas responded that he did not so much think about writing for this or that group. Rather, he wrote what he felt needed to be said.

It seems Willard left the makeup of his audience up to his audience and, no doubt, the Spirit of God. Perhaps because of this approach, Willard's books are difficult to classify. They are not typical of academic works in theology, biblical studies, or philosophy. Nor are they standard popular-level writings. And partly for this reason, his writings can easily be missed by both audiences. The popular audience finds it hard to slog through sixty-page chapters (see *Divine Conspiracy*) and the academic audience doesn't see enough footnotes.

The problem with this is that Willard's views deserve further discussion and elaboration among Christian academics and, it seems to us, the Christian scholarly world needs the influence of Willard's ideas. For instance, Willard's views on the nature of the Divine-human relationship, the transforming effects of the grace of God, the nature of God, the role of spiritual disciplines in character formation, the uniqueness of Jesus among the world's religions, the Sermon on the Mount, the significance of the body in habit formation, and numerous other topics possess unique insights that can be fruitfully explored and developed. When scholars take up Willard's concepts, theories, and arguments, they tend to have a positive effect as they infiltrate the field of study in question. This book offers examples of that positive effect.

In what follows, ten authors from a variety of disciplines engage, extend, and enact Willard's views on spiritual formation. By *engagement*, we mean the attempt to penetrate Willard's positions and arguments with philosophical, theological, biblical, or other relevant tools. In engagement, we are trying to understand more carefully and critically what Willard himself thought about various matters. By *extending*, we mean the attempt to launch off from Willard's views and arguments into a dimension of study

Theology of Dallas Willard: Discovering Protoevangelical Faith (Eugene, OR: Wipf and Stock, 2013). See also Michael Stewart Robb, "The Kingdom among Us: Jesus, the Kingdom of God, and the Gospel according to Dallas Willard," PhD diss., University of Aberdeen, 2016.

that was largely unexplored by him. In extending, we are trying to go farther with Willard's thought than he himself went. By *enacting*, we mean the attempt to act out Willard's views and the implications of his arguments in some specific domain of life. In enactment, we are trying to apply Willard's thinking within a practical context.

These chapters aim to show what can be done when Willard's work is taken seriously, with the hope that increased scholarly attention will bring about further academic discussion. Indeed, our hope is that these chapters will stimulate your own thinking and that you too might decide to engage, extend, or enact Willard's ideas in your own context—not for the sake of another publication, blog, or talk, but for the sake of increased understanding and clearer articulation of the need and nature of spiritual formation in Christ Jesus.

And if Willard was right, increased understanding and clearer articulation of the need and nature of spiritual formation in Christ is desperately needed today. For instance, Willard writes:

> For serious churchgoing Christians, the hindrance to true spiritual growth is not unwillingness. While they are far from perfect, no one who knows such people can fail to appreciate their willingness and goodness of heart. For my part, at least, I could no longer deny the facts. I finally decided their problem was a theological deficiency, a lack of teaching, understanding, and practical direction. And the problem, I also decided, was one that the usual forms of ministry and teaching obviously do not remedy.[3]

If that diagnosis of the problem of spiritual immaturity among Christ-followers is even half right, there is a serious need for Christian scholars to look at how the ideas and paradigms within their respective fields and areas of ministry might be partly responsible for the deficient understanding of spiritual growth that plagues the church today and what can be done to remedy that.

[3] Dallas Willard, *The Spirit of the Disciplines: Understanding How God Changes Lives* (New York: HarperCollins, 1988), 18.

Of course, Willard's diagnosis of the problem is itself a matter for debate. It bears pointing out in that respect that several recent studies of spiritual growth among Christians appear to support Willard's thesis.[4] Indeed, Willard believed that spiritual and moral development was empirically observable and that there was, therefore, an experimental means to determine how and why growth does or does not occur.[5] Such psychological and sociological measurement of spiritual formation is one emerging field of study that would greatly benefit from interaction with Willard.[6]

We offer, then, the work that follows with the desire that this book helps to stimulate Christian scholarly engagement with Willard's writings on spiritual formation; not for the sake of scholarship alone, but for the sake of increased holiness in the lives of God's people. May we all learn, as Willard did, to struggle with the energizing presence of Christ as in the pains of childbirth until Christ is formed in you!

—Steven L. Porter, Gary W. Moon, and J. P. Moreland

[4] See, for instance, Greg L. Hawkins and Cally Parkinson, *Move: What 1,000 Churches Reveal about Spiritual Growth* (Grand Rapids, MI: Zondervan, 2011) and *The State of Discipleship: A Barna Report Produced in Partnership with The Navigators* (Ventura, CA: The Barna Group, 2015).

[5] Dallas Willard, "Measuring Spiritual Formation," in *Renewing the Christian Mind*, edited by Gary Black Jr., (New York: HarperOne), 83–91. See also Willard's fourth concern in J. P. Moreland, "Reflections on a Day with My Professor and Friend," in Gary Moon, *Eternal Living: Reflections on Dallas Willard's Teaching on Faith and Formation* (Downers Grove, IL: InterVarsity Press, 2015), 127–28.

[6] Thankfully there are some serious attempts to measure change and virtue formation that are being pursued, though again, often without much interaction with Willard. Some of this valuable work is being funded by the John Templeton Foundation. See https://www.templeton.org/funding-areas/character-virtue-development.

1

AN OVERVIEW OF WILLARD'S PRIMARY WRITINGS

The Willardian Corpus

STEVEN L. PORTER

Talbot School of Theology and Rosemead School of Psychology, Biola University

Abstract: Dallas Willard's initial five monographs devoted to Christian spirituality constitute a unified body of work that together present a comprehensive account of the nature and means of spiritual formation in Christ. This chapter approaches Willard's corpus chronologically for the purpose of culling the central components of Willard's understanding of spiritual formation. This is not meant to be a review or summary of Willard's writings, but rather an analytic study of Willard's work and is an implicit call for further second-order, scholarly reflection on the Willardian corpus.

The Importance of the Willardian Corpus

Within the last two or three centuries, Protestant theology has suffered from what one author termed an eclipse of holiness.[1] This eclipse does not refer to the disappearance of sanctity within the actual lives of Christ-followers, but instead the disappearance of substantive theological engagement with

[1] J. I. Packer uses the term "holiness in eclipse" in his *Keep in Step with the Spirit* (Grand Rapids, MI: Baker, 1984; repr., 2005), 82–84. For a more complete argument, see Richard Lovelace, "The Sanctification Gap," *Theology Today* 29, no. 4 (1973): 363–69, and Robert E. Weber, *The Divine Embrace: Recovering the Passionate Spiritual Life* (Grand Rapids, MI: Baker, 2006), 31–121.

the topic of sanctification/Christian spirituality.[2] J. I. Packer states the point this way:

> [I]n the twentieth century, most of the best evangelical brains have been put to work in other fields. The result is that much of our best modern theology (there are exceptions) is superficial about holiness, while modern treatments of holiness often lack the biblical insight, theological depth, and human understanding that are needed in order to do the subject justice. The most distinguished evangelical theologians have not always been the most ardent exponents of holiness, and the most ardent evangelical exponents of holiness have not always been the most reliable or judicious theologians.[3]

Packer provided this analysis in 1984. In that same year, Dallas Willard initiated what would become a twenty-five-year research project that yielded five books—roughly 1,500 pages—focused on the topic of Christian holiness. These five monographs are the following:

1984. *In Search of Guidance: Developing a Conversational Relationship with God*[4]

1988. *The Spirit of the Disciplines: Understanding How God Changes Lives*[5]

1998. *The Divine Conspiracy: Rediscovering Our Hidden Life in God*[6]

---

[2] The sanctification gap meaningfully overlaps with, but is not identical to, the neglect of pneumatology within Protestant theology. On the neglect and recovery of pneumatology, see Veli-Matti Kärkkäinen, *Pneumatology: The Holy Spirit in Ecumenical, International, and Contextual Perspective* (Grand Rapids, MI: Baker, 2002), 11–13; Daniel L. Migliore, *Faith Seeking Understanding: An Introduction to Christian Theology* (Grand Rapids, MI: Eerdmans, 1991/2004), 224–26; and Daniel B. Wallace and M. James Sawyer, *Who's Afraid of the Holy Spirit?: An Investigation into the Ministry of the Spirit of God Today* (Dallas: Biblical Studies Press, 2005).

[3] Packer, *Keep in Step with the Spirit*, 84.

[4] Dallas Willard, *In Search of Guidance: Developing a Conversational Relationship with God* (Ventura, CA: Regal Books, 1984). A second edition of this book was published by HarperSanFrancisco in 1993. A third edition was published as *Hearing God: Developing a Conversational Relationship with God* (Downers Grove, IL: InterVarsity Press, 1999).

[5] Dallas Willard, *The Spirit of the Disciplines: Understanding How God Changes Lives* (New York: HarperCollins, 1988).

[6] Dallas Willard, *The Divine Conspiracy: Rediscovering Our Hidden Life in God* (New York: HarperCollins, 1998).

2002. *Renovation of the Heart: Putting on the Character of Christ*[7]

2009. *Knowing Christ Today: Why We Can Trust Spiritual Knowledge*[8]

The above monographs are what will be referred to here as the Willardian corpus.[9] In what follows it will be contended that this body of work—this pentalogy—presents a unified and comprehensive account of spiritual growth in Christ and that this body of work has gone some way toward remedying the eclipse of holiness. That is, the concepts that are developed across the span of these five books hang together and provide a thorough accounting of the nature and means of Christian formation with, as Packer puts it, "the biblical insight, theological depth, and human understanding that are needed in order to do the subject justice."[10] This is an important thesis to demonstrate because, for one, it helps pave the way for other biblical, theological, historical, psychological, and philosophical scholars to seriously approach Willard's work as a significant contribution to the theology of Christian spirituality.

The Lack of Scholarly Engagement with the Willardian Corpus

Paving the way for other scholars to seriously approach Willard's work is important precisely because there is some concern that Willard's corpus has not received the scholarly attention it warrants. For while Willard's books are widely read and discussed, there is at present little scholarly interaction with Willard's corpus.

---

[7] Dallas Willard, *Renovation of the Heart: Putting on the Character of Christ* (Colorado Springs: NavPress, 2002).

[8] Dallas Willard, *Knowing Christ Today: Why We Can Trust Spiritual Knowledge* (New York: HarperCollins, 2009).

[9] Willard's *The Great Omission: Reclaiming Jesus's Essential Teachings on Discipleship* (New York: HarperCollins, 2006) will be omitted in this discussion from the Willardian corpus. This is because *The Great Omission*, while important and valuable in its own right, is a collection of occasional papers/essays, the content of which largely (though not entirely) overlaps with what is covered more fully in the five monographs listed above. Willard's four posthumous publications—*The Divine Conspiracy Continued*, *The Allure of Gentleness*, *Living in Christ's Presence*, and *Renewing the Christian Mind*—will also be omitted. For one, these publications had not appeared when this chapter was first written. Second, while there are significant developments and applications of Willard's thought in these posthumous publications, there is an important sense in which Willard's original pentalogy can be thought of as the coherent basis for these later works.

[10] Packer, *Keep in Step with the Spirit*, 84.

For instance, a recent search of "Willard, Dallas" in the main theological research database—the ATLA Religion Database—generates 115 records. But of those 115 records, the vast majority refer to book reviews of Willard's published monographs, short essays about Willard in popular magazines, and Willard's own publications. Besides earlier versions of the chapters in this book, only three of the records are articles published in scholarly journals that substantively engage Willard's work.[11] In other words, secondary scholarly literature (excluding book reviews) on Willard's spiritual formation material is almost non-existent.[12]

This lack of scholarly engagement is troubling because the thinkers, theories, and ideas that tend to leave a lasting mark on theological education within the university, seminary, and the local church are those thinkers, theories, and ideas that get scholarly attention. Scholarly engagement, both positive and critical, generates greater awareness, interest, and (hopefully) deeper comprehension of a particular thinker and his or her points of view. In turn, this can lead to a thinker and/or concept becoming well entrenched in the theological scene. The concern is this: as long as Willard's corpus is not substantively engaged by Christian academics and is left as collateral reading in theological education, the influence of Willard's account of the spiritual life will not be as great as it otherwise would be.[13]

The question arises as to why the Willardian corpus has not received substantial scholarly interaction. There are several things to consider. First, undoubtedly the vast majority of published theological writing does not garner a sizeable academic audience, let alone significant scholarly interaction. Even without much secondary literature, in terms of readership and influence, Willard's corpus is doing far better than most recently

---

[11] The three articles that appeared in the ATLA Religion database search are: Richard Reisen, "'Jesus the Logician': A (Very) Modest Proposal," *Christian Scholar's Review* 34, no. 3 (Spring 2005): 341–51; Michael W. Mangis, "Spiritual Formation and Christian Psychology: A Response and Application of Willard's Perspective," *Journal of Psychology and Theology* 28, no. 4 (2000): 259–62; and Greg Jesson, "The Husserlian Roots of Dallas Willard's Philosophical and Religious Works: Knowledge of the Temporal and Eternal," *Philosophia Christi* 16, no. 1 (2014): 7–36.

[12] Again, earlier versions of the chapters in this book and other articles that were a part of a special issue on Willard and formation in the *Journal of Spiritual Formation & Soul Care* offer a partial corrective to this situation.

[13] Alternatively, there is something to be said for thinkers and ideas that dodge the scholarly maelstrom. In the best of cases, academic engagement enriches a discussion, but there is also the tendency for it to distort and deaden a discussion. I still believe Willard's corpus would be better served by increased attention, but I am assuming the best of academia.

published monographs in Christian spirituality. Second, there is no way to judge what sort of scholarly attention will come to Willard's corpus in the future. Third, Willard did not write in the style of contemporary theology, his books were not published by typical theology publishers, he was not regularly found at theology conferences (e.g., ETS, AAR, etc.), and he was not a theologian in terms of his terminal degree, primary area of scholarly expertise, or regular course offerings. All of this kept him off the radar of academic theologians. Fourth, Willard's biblical/theological/historical argumentation is often underdeveloped. For example, Willard will frequently cite one or more biblical passages in support of a particular point, but it is rare that he will delve into an extended discussion of his interpretation and application of these passages in dialogue with current biblical scholarship. The same is often true of Willard's appeal to church history or philosophy as a means of supporting his contention. This leaves the biblical scholar, church historian, and philosopher unsure of precisely how to engage Willard.

The later point is potentially the most serious hurdle to an increase in Willardian scholarship. But the point must not be overstated. In the vast majority of cases, Willard's argumentation is quite developed and explicit. And even in those cases where the arguments are nascent, there remains a way to reconstruct Willard's positions in order to defend and/or critique them. Several of the chapters in this book offer examples of this approach to Willard's corpus.

A Unified and Comprehensive Theory

Whatever the precise reason for the apparent lack of engagement with the Willardian corpus, in the remainder of this chapter it is urged that the corpus presents the Christian scholarly community with a body of work on spiritual formation that has theological heft. Against any misinformed notion that Willard's five books are a loose collection of disconnected musings on the spiritual life, the argument here is that the Willardian corpus offers a unified and comprehensive theory of spiritual formation in Christ, developed out of a robust theological methodology, and is a fertile source for scholarly engagement. So, in many ways, what follows is an interpretation of Willard's views on spiritual formation using his corpus as the primary source material. The main purpose of this interpretation is to demonstrate that a unified and comprehensive view of spiritual growth emerges from Willard's writings. Whether this interpretation of Willard is right—both in the sense of being faithful to Willard and in the sense of being a correct account of the reality of spiritual formation in Christ—is the type of question that future scholarly interaction on the Willardian corpus should decide.

As with any author's body of work, there are various ways that the Willardian corpus can be approached. A chronological approach is pursued in this chapter. That is, the development of Willard's view of spiritual formation is traced through each of his five books in their order of publication. This approach emphasizes the unity of the corpus by showing the logical flow and interconnectedness of Willard's view through the five monographs. The downside of a chronological approach is that it does not offer a systematic, organizing framework for Willard's position other than the one that arises from the chronology. Having said that, there is most certainly a subjective selectivity in what is being extracted and when it is extracted from each of Willard's books. The selectivity is guided by what this author takes to be the main components of each book, as well as how these components contribute to Willard's overall theory of spiritual formation.

Hearing God

While *Hearing God* (also known as *In Search of Guidance*) covers a vast range of relevant themes, five major components of Willard's overall theory of spiritual formation surface from this book. Most of these components are developed more thoroughly in later monographs, but the temptation to extensively refer to later monographs in the initial development of these components will be mostly resisted. This is for two reasons. First, a truly chronological approach that attempts to show the development of Willard's view across the corpus must take care not to bring too much of the later specifications back into earlier statements. And second, the attempt to exhaustively consider all that the Willardian corpus contributes to each of these components would turn out to be a much longer and quite different project—more akin to an encyclopedic index of Willard's writings.

Component #1: An Adequate Understanding of Spiritual Formation Is Needed to Effectively Care for One's Spiritual Life

A major unifying theme of the Willardian corpus is Willard's diagnosis of the current problem when it comes to Christian maturation. It is important to note that Willard's corpus as a whole is in response to what Willard consistently sees as a deficit in the Christian community's *understanding* of spiritual growth in Christ. While Willard's diagnosis unfolds and deepens as the corpus develops, the essential problem is clearly put forth in *Hearing God*: "Those who operate on the wrong information are likely never to know the reality of God's presence in the decisions which shape their lives and will miss the constant divine companionship for which their souls were made" (10; cf. 16, 26, 29).[14] Later in the book Willard writes, "what we do or do not understand, in any area of our lives, determines what we can or cannot believe and therefore governs our practice and action with an iron hand" (193).[15]

Willard's judgment that a lack of understanding as well as positive *mis*understanding is the central problem may come off as a commonplace description of what ails the Christian community. But it is important to see that Willard has a view of 'understanding' that makes it an essential and fundamental element in any practical endeavor. For Willard, the problem is *not* biblical illiteracy, nor deficient relationships among believers, nor doctrinal error, nor lack of sustained effort in Christian living, nor even the failure to utilize spiritual disciplines. For Willard, the crisis among us is the failure to adequately understand and therefore effectually enter into a transformational relationship with God. Perhaps in a way that only becomes clear in Willard's final book—*Knowing Christ Today*—understanding (or knowledge) is essential to successfully interact with any reality. Since God calls human persons into responsible participation in

---

[14] All parenthetical page notations in this section of the chapter refer to *Hearing God* unless otherwise noted.

[15] In *The Spirit of the Disciplines*, Willard puts the point as follows: "I believe our present difficulty is one of misunderstanding how our experiences and actions enable us to receive the grace of God" (x); "I finally decided their problem was a theological deficiency, a lack in teaching, understanding, and practical direction" (18). In *Renovation of the Heart*, Willard writes, "Because we are active participants in the process [of spiritual formation] and what we do or do not do makes a huge difference, our efforts must be based on understanding. The degree of success in such efforts will essentially depend upon the degree to which this general pattern is understood and intentionally conformed to" (83).

their growth, having knowledge regarding what it is that one is participating with is indispensable.

It is also noteworthy that Willard's diagnosis of the problem of Christian immaturity among Christ followers is consistently related to the problems confronting human existence on a national, international, and global scale. Willard insists time and again that the lack of understanding of the Christian community leads to a spiritual mediocrity, which in turn does nothing to help the dire condition of humanity in general, and that the corresponding corrective begins with the spiritual transformation of the inner life of the Christ-follower (cf. 146). In a period of time in which there is an increasing awareness of the need for social justice and cultural engagement, Willard's emphasis on the connection between the inner life and the outer/active life is timely.[16]

Component #2: The Nature of Spiritual Formation in Christ Determines the Method by Which It Is to Be Known

While Willard's theological method is exemplified throughout his writings and is discussed further in the remainder of his corpus, it is important that it be laid bare at the start. Put simply, Scripture is a unique and privileged source of knowledge, for Willard, that is supported and augmented in substantial ways by church history (both the history of biblical interpretation and historical exemplars of Christian devotion), personal experience (his own and his appeal to others), and philosophical analysis. Willard writes, "The Bible . . . is inerrant in its original form and infallible in all of its forms for the purpose of guiding us into a life-saving relationship with God in his kingdom. It is infallible in this way precisely because God never leaves it alone . . . [The Bible] reliably fixes the boundaries of everything [God] will ever say to humankind" (141, 142).[17] For Willard, "God never leaves" Scripture alone in the sense that the Spirit of God illumines the biblical text in a manner that is transformational (142–143).

Willard's clear stress on Scripture and the Spirit's role in Scripture is seamlessly integrated with his emphasis on relating one's own experience to the words of Scripture and looking for the lives of others (both

---

[16] For extended discussion on this theme, see *Renovation of the Heart*, 217–32, and *Knowing Christ Today*, 193–211.

[17] See his "assumptions about the Bible" in *The Divine Conspiracy*, xvi–xvii.

contemporary and historical others) to help clarify both the meaning of the text and one's own experience of God's truth (cf. 36). For instance, early in *Hearing God* Willard discusses his own experiences with hearing God's voice (16) as well as the writings of "great Christians of the past such as John Calvin and William Law," which gave him "further insight into what was happening in my experiences and why it was happening" (17; cf. 23). Another example of Willard's integrative method comes in his discussion of the spiritual force of words. Willard discuss three biblical passages that he takes to support his point (John 6:63; Heb. 6:6; John 15:7) and continues with references to Plato (pagan philosopher, c. 347 BC), Augustine (early church theologian, d. 430 AD), and William Penn (Quaker political theorist, d. 1718) that further confirm and elaborate on the biblical exposition (120–121; cf. 167, 176, 183–184).

Of course, Willard is in good company with his utilization of Scripture, experience, tradition/history, and reason.[18] And yet, it is rare to see a theological writer who navigates biblical texts (most often direct quotes), experiential appeals and testimonies, and relevant statements from historical sources in the integrated manner that Willard does. The pervasive influence of his philosophical insights often go unnoticed in that the very way Willard approaches and initiates discussions already presuppose a thoughtful analysis of the topic in question.[19]

This focus on Willard's theological method is by no means perfunctory. In the case of Christian spirituality, having a theological method that takes both Scripture and Christian experience seriously is essential to developing a psychologically realistic view of spiritual growth.[20]

---

[18] For a discussion of such a methodology, see Steve L. Porter, "The Wesleyan Quadrilateral as a Theory of Integration," *Journal of Psychology and Theology* 32, no. 3 (2004): 190–99.

[19] Willard's philosophical orientation is rooted in the phenomenological tradition, particularly the views of Edmund Husserl. A core feature of this tradition is the notion that reality can be grasped through intuitive insight and that the most effective way to enable others to come to one's point of view is to assist them in coming to see the truth for themselves. See Willard's *Logic and the Objectivity of Knowledge: A Study in Husserl's Philosophy* (Athens, OH: Ohio University Press, 1984), and his "How Concepts Relate the Mind to Its Object: The God's Eye Point of View Vindicated," *Philosophia Christi* 1, no. 2 (1999): 5–20.

[20] See John Coe, "Spiritual Theology: Bridging the Sanctification Gap for the Sake of the Church," *Journal of Spiritual Formation and Soul Care* 2, no. 1 (2009): 4–43. See also Philip Sheldrake, *Spirituality and Theology: Christian Living and the Doctrine of God* (Maryknoll, NY: Orbis, 1998), 33–95.

Component #3: Relationship with God Is an Experiential Reality

The third major component of Willard's unified view of spiritual formation is the central focus on and detailed specification of the experiential nature of relationship with God. Willard's analysis of the divine-human relationship is the core element of his understanding of Christian growth. For Willard, this relationship is grounded in the ontology of the person in the sense that the human person was designed/structured by God to exist within a certain kind of relatedness to the Trinity as well as other persons. In *Hearing God,* this divine relationship is most often countenanced as a conversational relationship, but Willard also uses the following descriptors: "intimate friendship" (10), "close personal relationship" (10), "constant divine companionship" (10), "richly interactive relationship" (10), "hand-in-hand, conversational walk with God" (11), "God's indwelling his people through personal presence and fellowship" (18), "personal communion" (22), "loving fellowship with the King" (31), "a direct and fully self-conscious personal relationship" (46), and so on. Willard clearly sees the divine-human relationship as involving more than conversation: " . . . in the progress of God's redemptive work *communication* advances into *communion* and communion into *union.* When the progression is complete we can truly say, 'It is no longer I who live, but it is Christ who lives in me' (Gal 2:20)" (155).

This relationship with God is experiential in at least two senses for Willard. First, the relationship is experiential in the sense that one can be *consciously aware* of the communication, communion, and union. And second, the relationship is experiential in that it has a *personal impact* on the person's emotional, cognitive, volitional, and embodied existence. God, Willard writes, "is able to penetrate and intertwine himself within the fibers of the human self in such a way that those who are enveloped in his loving companionship will never be alone" (43).

Willard distinguishes four ways in which God can be experienced. The first is a "blind faith" that God is with the believer when there is "no awareness of his being here with us at all and no evidence of his action in or around us" (46). Willard sees this as a limited though still important form of God's presence. Second, there is an "indeterminate but often very powerful sense, feeling or impression of God's presence" (47). This is the conscious awareness referred to above. Third is the experience of God through the occurrence of events that cannot be plausibly attributed to merely natural causes—that is, God is present to a person or group through what he accomplishes through that person or group (49–50). The fourth kind of experience of God is the conversational relationship in which God's thoughts and intentions are consciously communicated to believers (51–57). This way of experiencing God proves to be the most significant, given both the human need for God and how God desires to work in human lives. This point is further elaborated in the next component.

Component #4: The Word of God Carries with It God's Experiential Presence

The fourth major element of Willard's overall theory is his analysis of how the word of God is at the core of this life-giving, experiential relationship. In a manner that illustrates Willard's philosophical acumen, Willard discusses how a word conveys a person's meanings—"the thought, feeling or action *that person* associates with it" (119). Meaning "hooks into the hidden levers of mind and reality and gives [words] their immense power" (119). This power is a *spiritual* power in that it connects spirit ("unbodily, personal force") with spirit (120–121).

Since words are meaningless without personal intention, God is always present with his word. These expressions/communications from God can be external to the human mind (e.g., natural phenomena, the words of other human beings, the incarnate Christ, or the Bible) or internal to the human mind (i.e., communications from God in one's own thoughts, intentions and feelings) (121). Since words (thoughts/intentions) have power to govern reality—"to direct action and events"—when they are spoken by "authorized individuals" (129–130), so too, God's word, when it is received, governs the reality of the human system. On the basis of this understanding, Willard maintains that the proper use of the Bible is central to human transformation (160).

Willard's analysis on this point is invaluable in that it makes sense of how the word of God is both personal and transformational as a corrective to views of the Christian life that depersonalize the Bible and thereby denude it of its power to transform. All that can be done with a depersonalized and denuded Bible is to hold right views of what it says or approach it superstitiously, and neither approach will actually nurture an interactive relationship with God (cf. John 5:39–40). On this Willard writes, "It is better in one year to have ten good verses transferred *into the substance of our lives* than to have every word of the Bible flash before our eyes. Remember that 'the letter kills, but the Spirit gives life' (2 Cor. 3:6). We read to open ourselves to the Spirit" (163; cf. 171).

Component #5: God's Experiential Presence (or Word) Is Inherently Transformational

Bringing together Willard's understanding of the experiential nature of the divine-human relationship (component #3) and the transforming power of God's word (component #4), the last feature drawn from *Hearing God* is what might be called Willard's relational theory of human transformation. Since human persons were created in the very fibers of their being to exist in communication/communion/union with God, when God's word (meaning) and Spirit (presence) are received by a person, this enlivens the previously dead dimensions of the human heart. So for Willard,

> The gospel . . . opens the door of the mind and enters the heart. From there it is able to progressively transform the whole personality. Thus "the sower sows the word" of the kingdom (Mark 4:14). When this takes root in the heart and mind, a new life enters our personality and increasingly becomes *our* life as we learn to "be guided by the Spirit" (Gal 5:25) and "sow to the Spirit" (Gal 6:8)." (150)

It is the meaningfulness (the truth) of the divine presence in the person's life that brings about change. Truth alone does not change, nor does the human will bring about change by effort alone. Rather, "God causes the growth" through the penetration of his divine life into the structures of the human personality that were made to receive and draw life from him.

Willard makes clear that "impurities," "distractions," "false ideas," "attitudes," "fears," and "lusts" stand in the way of God's cleansing/life-giving word (153). But again, the change-agent is the person of God through Christ by the Spirit:

> The *literal* truth is that Christ through his word removes the old routines in the heart and mind—the old routines of thought, feeling, action, imagination, conceptualization, belief,

> inference—and in their place he puts something else: *his* thoughts, *his* attitudes, *his* beliefs, *his* ways of seeing and interpreting things, *his words*. He washes out our minds, and in the place of confusion and falsehood—or hatred, suspicion and fear, to speak of emotions—he brings clarity, truth, love, confidence and hopefulness. (154, italics original)

Seeing relationship with God as the transforming principle/person leaves open the question of human responsibility in Christian growth. And yet, it also makes clear that whatever role human agency plays, such efforts do not *cause* transformation. Nonetheless, *Hearing God* initiates a discussion of human responsibility: "Once the new life begins to enter our soul, however, we have the responsibility and opportunity of ever more fully focusing our whole being on it and wholly orienting ourselves toward it. This is *our* part, and God will not do it for us" (158). While *Hearing God* introduces Willard's take on "our part," Willard's understanding of this crucial dimension of Christian formation comes to fruition in *The Spirit of the Disciplines.*[21]

The Spirit of the Disciplines

A major thesis of this chapter is that there is a cohesiveness to the Willardian corpus. Moving from *Hearing God* to *The Spirit of the Disciplines* is the first major test of that cohesiveness. The question becomes: in what manner does *The Spirit of the Disciplines* coherently build upon *Hearing God*? Willard himself signals a continuity between the two monographs in his introduction to *The Divine Conspiracy*, a book which he sees as completing a "trilogy on the spiritual life":

> In the first, *In Search of Guidance* [i.e., *Hearing God*], I attempted to make real and clear the intimate quality of life with [Jesus] as a "conversational relationship with God." But that relationship is not something that automatically happens, and we do not

[21] One element of *Hearing God* that was not developed in this overview is Willard's practical theology of, believe it or not, *hearing God*. Since this overview is meant to paint with broad strokes Willard's theology of formation, a summary of Willard's view of how one goes about hearing God was omitted. But Willard's guidance on hearing God's voice is certainly the central feature of the book, and in many ways what has been laid out in the five components is the theoretical husk to this practical kernel.

> receive it by passive infusion. So the second book, *The Spirit of the Disciplines*, explains how disciples or students of Jesus can effectively interact with the grace and spirit of God to access fully the provisions and character intended for us in the gift of eternal life.[22]

The kind of transformational interaction with God that Willard envisions and explicates to some degree in *Hearing God* is only possible through the intentional efforts of the already reborn individual. The main components of *The Spirit of the Disciplines* center around developing an understanding of salvation and the spiritual life that makes sense of both the role and the effectiveness of spiritual disciplines.

Before moving on to these elements, it is important to more clearly expose the fifth component developed from *Hearing God*—relational transformation—within *The Spirit of the Disciplines.* In *The Spirit of the Disciplines,* Willard has been at times misunderstood as suggesting that disciplines alone transform human persons—perhaps in the sort of way that Aristotle might have envisioned certain practices bringing about virtue formation.[23] But Willard clearly reiterates in *The Spirit of the Disciplines* his view from *Hearing God,* in which he maintains that it is the enlivening presence of God that brings about transformation due to the human capacity and anthropological need for such a relationship and that the disciplines are at their core means to align one's self, in loving union, with God. For instance, in the preface of *The Spirit of the Disciplines* Willard writes:

> My central claim is that we *can* become like Christ by doing one thing—by following him in the overall style of life he chose for himself . . . We can, through faith and grace, become like Christ by practicing the types of activities he engaged in, by arranging our whole lives around the activities he himself practiced in order to remain constantly at home in the fellowship of his Father. (*The Spirit of the Disciplines*, ix)

---

[22] Willard, *The Divine Conspiracy*, xvii.

[23] For some discussion of what might be termed Aristotelian virtue formation, see M. F. Burnyeat, "Aristotle on Learning to Be Good," in *Essays on Aristotle's Ethics,* edited by Amélie Oksenberg Rorty (Berkeley: University of California Press, 1980): 74–88.

Note that the disciplines are activities aimed at remaining in *constant fellowship* with God the Father. Fasting, prayer, meditation on Scripture, and the like are not transformative in and of themselves, but only as they attach the disciple to the transforming resources of the Godhead. Disciplines are "an avenue to life filled and possessed of God" (18). In this way, the five components presented in *Hearing God* are really foundational to *The Spirit of the Disciplines*, although it is not as if *The Spirit of the Disciplines* essentially depends on *Hearing God*. One could read *The Spirit of the Disciplines* without reading *Hearing God* and still grasp Willard's position on these matters, but the reading of *The Spirit of the Disciplines* is nonetheless well-served by a comprehension of the main components of *Hearing God*. And it is in this sense that there is a unity between the two books, as well as a logical progression from the main themes of *Hearing God* to the major components *The Spirit of the Disciplines*. This leads to the three main components of *The Spirit of the Disciplines* that build upon the earlier components extracted from *Hearing God*.

Component #6: As Embodied Persons in Relationship with a Loving God, Informed Human Participation Is Essential for Spiritual Growth

The first of these (sixth component overall) is Willard's understanding of the role of the intentional efforts of the Christ-follower in spiritual growth. This issue has been a major area of doctrinal dispute in church history.[24] Within Protestant theology, the discussion centers around the sense in which human effort is required, and yet growth occurs by faith and grace alone.[25] A tension arises as to *why* human effort is needed, as well as *what kind* of human effort is needed given *sola gratia* and *sola fide*.[26] This discussion often gets conflated with a related discussion regarding the place of "works"—typically understood as overt good acts—in the Christian life. At times the human effort required for spiritual change is identified with the human effort involved in practicing good works, and spiritual change itself then becomes identified with doing good works. Once this occurs, there

---

[24] See Jaroslav Pelikan, *The Christian Tradition: A History of the Development of Doctrine*, vol. 4 (Chicago: University of Chicago Press, 1984), 127–82.

[25] See, for instance, G. C. Berkeouwer's discussion of this tension in his *Studies in Dogmatics: Faith and Sanctification* (Grand Rapids, MI: Eerdmans, 1952), 17–46.

[26] As an illustration of this, see John Webster's treatment of the issue in his *Holiness* (Grand Rapids, MI: Eerdmans, 2003), 79–92.

really is no *transformation*, only mere human effort to do good, perhaps out of a sense of obligation to Christ or out of autonomous obedience to a set of biblical commands (Paul's "confidence in the flesh"; Phil. 3:4). The vital question remains: what sort of effort is required to be conformed to the image of Christ in a manner that is consistent with God's sanctifying grace?

Willard could not be clearer in *The Spirit of the Disciplines* that human agency is essential for growth: "the harmonization of our total self with God will not be done *for* us. *We* must act" (68; cf. 93). "Now that new life is graciously visited upon me, my part in the redemptive process is to [submit myself to God]. God will not do it for me any more than he did it for Moses or Elijah, for his son Jesus or his apostle Paul. And if I do not submit my actions through the disciplines that fit my personality, I will not enter into the powerful, virtuous new life in a psychologically real way" (120). Of course, the requirement for persons to be active in spiritual growth does not negate the necessity of God's grace: "We are saved by grace, of course, and by it alone, and not because we deserve it . . . But grace does *not* mean that sufficient strength and insight will be automatically 'infused' into our being in the moment of need" (4). Instead, God calls his children to exercise themselves in learning to live under his care and provision. It is all by grace because human effort does not merit God's transforming work, nor is God's transforming work accomplished by human effort alone.

Willard's view on why human effort is necessary will become more apparent upon treating *The Divine Conspiracy*, but in *The Spirit of the Disciplines* Willard does maintain that human cooperation in spiritual formation is essential to the nature of a personal relationship that operates on the basis of love and not coercion. It is on the basis of being in the image of God, according to Willard, that God invites persons to co-labor with him in their sanctification.[27]

[27] Willard certainly has in mind, though does not explicitly say so in *The Spirit of the Disciplines*, that humans have libertarian agency as opposed to a compatiblist view (see his discussion on top of page 53). Nevertheless, it would be an interesting exercise to consider how Willard's explanation of the necessity of human involvement in spiritual formation could be applied to a compatiblist understanding of human agency. For more on Willard's view of free will, see his "Spiritual Formation and the Warfare between the Flesh and the Human Spirit," *Journal of Spiritual Formation and Soul Care* 1, no. 1 (2008): 79–87, as well as a response to this article, Dan Speak, "Willard, Warfare, and Will," *Journal of Spiritual Formation and Soul Care* 1, no. 2 (2008): 207–16.

And yet, to insist on human agency in spiritual formation due to issues of freedom and the nature of personal relationship does not explain in what way human agency can make a difference in formation. Is human involvement required only because human nature and the divine-human relationship necessitate it, or is human involvement also required due to the nature of spiritual growth itself? Willard thinks it is a both/and. For Willard, not just any exercise of the human will is called for, but an informed exercise of the human will. There are certain activities which are well-suited or fitting for growth given the nature of God's transformation of the human self. What sort of efforts are required?

Willard is quite unique in his understanding of human responsibility in formation. The responsibility humans have is primarily grounded in the human body:

> It is precisely this appropriate recognition of the body and of its implications for theology that is missing in currently dominant views of Christian salvation or deliverance. The human body *is* the focal point of human existence. Jesus had one. We have one. Without the body in its proper place, the pieces of the puzzle of new life in Christ do not realistically fit together, and the idea of *really* following him and becoming like him remains a practical impossibility, (*The Spirit of Disciplines*, 29–30)

> Although we call the disciplines "spiritual"—and although they must never be undertaken apart from a constant, inward interaction with God and his gracious Kingdom—they never fail to require specific acts and dispositions of our body as we engage in them. We are finite, limited to our bodies. So the disciplines cannot be carried out except as our body and its parts are surrendered in precise ways and definite actions to God. (*The Spirit of Disciplines*, 40; cf. 29–31)

The crucial point for Willard is that God has given persons some direct control over their bodies in a way that they do not have direct control over anything else.[28] A person may not have direct control over their thoughts

[28] For more on the body, see *The Divine Conspiracy*, 353–54, and *Renovation of the Heart*, 159–78.

or direct control over their attitudes or even direct control over certain ingrained behaviors, but typically a person does possess some measure of direct control, and therefore responsibility, over the parts of their body. Persons may not be able to stop sinning by direct effort alone (willpower) and certainly persons do not have the direct control to stop sinning *out of love for God*. Only God's transforming presence can bring about the character traits—the fruit of the Spirit—that will lead to righteousness motivated out of love.

So how do persons engage the transforming presence of God—what is the role of the human agent? Willard's response is that often the only thing that persons can do is to place their bodies in the conditions in which God regularly chooses to work. Willard writes, "The human body is the primary field of independent power and freedom given by God to people. Put simply—no body, no power. People have a body for one reason—that we might have at our disposal the resources that would allow us to be persons in fellowship and cooperation with a personal God" (*The Spirit of Disciplines*, 92). God has deposited a "measure of independent power" in the human body (*The Spirit of Disciplines*, 53, 54), and it is up to the individual person to place their body in submission to God. That is the "our part" of spiritual formation.[29]

This responsibility is magnified once it is realized that humans have an astonishing "power to *use* what is beyond ourselves" (61) to accomplish in their bodies what are otherwise impossible feats. For instance, persons join their bodies with various tools and raw materials to make musical instruments, bulldozers, computers and so on, and then join their bodies with these mechanisms to do things that could not be done by the human body operating alone. But joining one's body with mechanisms that extend the powers of the body takes bodily training. Willard regularly appeals to the baseball player or the pianist each of whom train their bodies to effectively interact with powers outside themselves to accomplish what would otherwise be impossible (e.g., hitting a fast ball or playing Rachmaninoff). There is no more direct control over hitting a fastball or playing Rachmaninoff than there is putting another's needs before one's own. But there is a bodily

[29] Again, it is important to see that Willard's view of human effort in spiritual formation makes it very difficult to applaud one's self regarding "our part" in sanctification. All we have done is place our body in the right places; God has done all the rest.

preparation that is under one's direct control that with sufficient practice will lead to one's body being able to join itself with a power outside of itself (the bat or the piano or the Spirit of God) to accomplish what could not be accomplished by direct effort.

No doubt the ultimate resource beyond one's self is the infinite God. Persons were "designed by God, in the very constitution of their human personalities, to carry out his rule by meshing the relatively little power resident in their own bodies with the power inherent in the infinite Rule or Kingdom of God" (54). Such a meshing requires training of the body because the body is oftentimes one's only hope. One's thoughts, attitudes, desires, dispositions, and so on may be set on the kingdom of self, but if there is at least some thought of and desire for the kingdom of God, one has the opportunity to begin placing their body in postures of prayer, worship, meditation on Scripture, Christian fellowship, solitude, and so on. All of these practices are at their core bodily in nature (*The Spirit of Disciplines,* 56–62). This naturally leads to Willard's understanding of the disciplines themselves (component #8), but prior to that is a brief summary of Willard's view of sin.

Component #7: Sin is Primarily a Disconnection from the Life-giving Resources of God

The seventh overall component of Willard's view as it is developed in *The Spirit of the Disciplines* is Willard's harmartiology. Willard discusses the nature and effects of sin in *Hearing God,* and this is more fully developed in *Renovation of the Heart* (esp. 45–61), but in the logical flow of the Willardian corpus it is important to take stock of sin at this juncture. Within *The Spirit of Disciplines,* Willard presents sin as the disconnection of human life from the life of God, which results in a "pervasive distortion and disruption of human existence from the top down" (63). "The evil that we do in our present condition is a reflection of a weakness caused by spiritual starvation" (*The Spirit of Disciplines,* 63).

Willard consistently pictures the divine-human relationship in terms of nourishment/sustenance. This positions sin as a severance from the life-giving divine substance (i.e., "spiritual starvation") and subsequently the attempt to live on "bread alone." As Willard puts it elsewhere, "We are our own god, and our god doesn't amount to much" (*Renovation,* 56). As embodied selves, humans become habituated in "automatic tendencies" to live life on their own, apart from the empowering, interactive relationship with God (72; cf. 54, 85, 89–91). The body, or flesh, is not inherently evil but becomes bent away from dependence on God and "serves as primary host for sin" (90). Willard continues, "*In this condition* the flesh opposes the spirit, does that which is evil, and must be crucified to restrain it (Gal. 5:16, 19f)" (90).

Component #8: Bodily Disciplines Place the Regenerate Person into Contact with the Life-Giving Resources of God

With this understanding of sin and the role of human effort, the third component of *The Spirit of Disciplines*—Willard's theology of the disciplines—fits well:

> The disciplines are activities of mind and body purposefully undertaken, to bring our personality and total being into effective cooperation with the divine order. They enable us more and more to live in a power that is, strictly speaking, beyond us, deriving from the spiritual realm itself, as we "yield ourselves to God, as those that are alive from the dead, and our members as instruments of righteousness unto God." (68)

One helpful biblical example from Willard is Jesus' recommendation to Peter, James, and John to "Watch and pray, that you may not enter into temptation" (Matt. 26:41). The text continues that "the spirit indeed is willing, but the flesh is weak." Willard writes:

> The plain meaning of this advice to his sleepy and worried friends was that by engaging in a certain type of action—keeping of vigil combined with prayer—they would be able to attain a level of spiritual responsiveness and power in their lives that would be impossible without it. In this simple but profound episode we find the whole nature and principle of the kind of activity that is a spiritual discipline. Such an activity implants in us, in the embodied personality that is the carrier of our abilities (and disabilities!) a readiness and an ability to interact with God and our surroundings in a way not directly under our control. (*The Spirit of Disciplines*, 151)

Willard understands disciplines to be bodily exercises over which persons have some direct control that place them into contact with God in ways that "cannot always be realized by direct and untrained effort" (*The Spirit of Disciplines*, 151–152). Peter, James, and John were not able to train their bodies to draw strength from God, and so, even though they desired to remain faithful, their lack of faith soon prevailed when they were tempted to abandon and/or deny Christ. The discipline of keeping watch in prayer would have bought about "habitual reliance upon God," which makes "sin dispensable, even uninteresting and revolting . . . Our desires and delights are changed because our actions and attitude are based upon the reality of God's Kingdom" (*The Spirit of Disciplines,* 118).[30]

Willard is clear that the disciplines themselves do *not* change believers. Rather, the disciplines make the follower of Jesus more available to the gracious operation of God by his Spirit and it is that personal, gracious presence of God and his kingdom that is transformational. Willard writes, "the disciplines *have no value in themselves.* The aim and substance of spiritual life is not fasting, prayer, hymn singing, frugal living, and so forth. Rather, it is the effective and full enjoyment of active love of God and humankind in all the daily rounds of normal existence where we are placed" (138).

Even when a person acts against their sinful inclinations to do what is right, that performance of a righteous act is *not* to be identified with transformation nor is it what Willard calls "pure discipline" (*The Spirit of Disciplines*, 120). For instance, Willard urges that believers should submit their bodies to righteous deeds by choosing to bless those that curse them, even when they would rather curse back or use their legs to walk the extra mile with someone they would rather kick (*The Spirit of Disciplines*, 119). But the performance of righteous deeds, according to Willard, is simply another way to offer up one's self to God's transforming presence. Willard writes:

> I submit my body to righteousness when I do my good deeds without letting them be known, though my whole frame cries

[30] It is important to note that Willard believes that the disciplines are not only explicitly discussed in the Scriptures but are implicitly referred to and assumed in various biblical texts. See his discussion, for instance, of Pauline psychology, pgs. 95–129. This is another place where some attention of biblical scholars would be welcome.

> out to strut and crow. And when I do, I offer up my body as the place of God's action. I prepare myself for God's action in me . . . Our eyes and our life are fixed upon God who is our life and who sets us free from bondage to all that is less than himself, including the bondage to righteous deeds. (*The Spirit of Disciplines*, 119)

Willard is clear that the disciplined effort to do the good act becomes a means of further dependence on God's strengthening presence. Doing the good act without the thoughts, feelings, and dispositions that naturally give rise to such an act is not the "easy yoke" to which Christ calls his followers. So when Christ-followers do such acts without the inner goodness that naturally gives rise to them, they do them as indirect efforts to find "gracious strength beyond ourselves" (*The Spirit of Disciplines*, 118). The *performance* of the righteous act is itself a means of drawing near to God. Nonetheless, the "pure disciplines" are those activities undertaken (e.g., solitude, meditation on Scripture, prayer) to prepare one's self to do the good act out of a good character which has been formed by the grace of God.

While there is certainly more to be drawn out from *The Spirit of the Disciplines*, these three components joined with the earlier five constitute the core of the evolving picture of Christian formation that emerges from the Willardian corpus. In many ways the central themes of the three remaining monographs reinforce the view already developed and attempt to clear away *mis*understandings regarding God, Jesus, salvation, and eventually, knowledge itself.

The Divine Conspiracy

Moving from book to book in the chronology of the corpus gives ample opportunity to revisit and further expand on components already explored. Perhaps *The Divine Conspiracy* is the most fertile in this regard. For instance, component #1 from *Hearing God* explored Willard's diagnosis of the problem when it comes to spiritual formation. Both *Hearing God* and *The Spirit of the Disciplines* insist on the problem being a lack of understanding among well-meaning Christ-followers. In *The Divine Conspiracy*, Willard goes even further, explaining some of the historical and sociological forces that place persons in this situation:

> It is the failure to understand Jesus and his words as reality and vital information about life that explains why, today, we do not routinely teach those who profess allegiance to him how to do what he said was best . . . It is a matter of how we *cannot but* think and act, given the context of our mental and spiritual formation. So any significant change can come only by breaking the stranglehold of the ideas and concepts that automatically shunt aside Jesus, "the Prince of Life," when questions of concrete mastery of our lives arise." (*The Divine Conspiracy*, xiv–xv)

Rehearsing Willard's diagnosis of the problem is particularly important to understand the central themes of *The Divine Conspiracy* for in many ways the goal of the book is to break "the stranglehold of the ideas and the concepts that automatically shunt aside Jesus" (xv). As Willard explains in his introduction to *The Divine Conspiracy*, the disciplined life in relationship with God that was made available through Jesus and is still found in him is seen by many as a "costly option," rather than as "the very heart of the gospel" (xvii). *The Divine Conspiracy* uncovers misconceptions that prevent persons from seeing life with God as attractive and available as well as offering a theological framework within which such a view can be grounded.

Component #9: The Good News Is That God's Reign Is Available to Anyone Who Relies on Jesus

The first misconception that Willard addresses is the way in which many Christians view the good news (*euangelion*) of Jesus Christ. For Willard, and many other biblical scholars, the gospel that Jesus and his early followers taught was the gospel of the kingdom of God and *not* merely the good news of forgiveness of sins.[31] Willard's analysis of the kingdom breaks through (or perhaps better, skillfully dodges) many of the common debates that surround the timing and nature of the kingdom of God in order to provide an account of the kingdom that illuminates the accessibility of God's kingdom as well as the personal impact of God's kingdom.

Willard understands a person's kingdom to be the "range of [their] effective will" (21). It is what a person, whether human or divine, has

[31] See, for example, G. E. Ladd, *The Gospel of the Kingdom: Scriptural Studies in the Kingdom of God* (Grand Rapids, MI: Eerdmans, 1959).

control over. God has allowed human persons to have "dominion in a limited sphere" (21) and yet has made them to exercise their dominion under his loving rule and drawing off his resources (22). "God equipped us for this task [i.e., stewarding the earth] by framing our nature to function in a conscious, personal relationship of interactive responsibility *with* him. We are meant to exercise our 'rule' only in union with God, as he acts with us. He intended to be our constant companion or co-worker in the creative enterprise of life on earth" (22). As discussed above (component #7), Willard maintains that human persons "fell away from our intended divine context" and consequently the divinely given task to rule the earth with him has been distorted (23). The hope of redemption then—the good news—is that through reliance on Jesus Christ human persons can once again align their kingdom with the present availability of the rule of God:

> From the very beginning of his work, those who relied on him had, at his touch, entered the rule, or governance, of God and were receiving its gracious sufficiency. Jesus was not just acting for God but also *with* God—a little like the way, in a crude metaphor, I act *with* my power steering, or it with me, when I turn the wheel of my car. And this "governance" is projected onward through those who receive him. When we receive God's gift of life by relying on Christ, we find that God comes to act with us as we rely on him in our actions. (20, italics original)

This view of the gospel—the gospel of the kingdom—does not disconnect Christian conversion and justification from sanctification and discipleship. Entrance into the rule of God through confidence in Jesus is what happens at conversion and is precisely what persons grow up into through the sanctifying process of the Spirit. Willard writes, "[Jesus'] basic message, 'Rethink your life in the light of the fact that the kingdom of heavens is now open to all' (Matt. 4:17), presents the resources needed to live human life as we all automatically sense it should be and naturally leads one to become his student, or apprentice in kingdom living" (274).

But if the gospel of the kingdom seamlessly propels one forward into a life of interactive discipleship to Jesus, the "gospels of sin management" make such notions of discipleship pointless and seemingly avoidable (41). For Christians on the conservative "right," salvation is often reduced to getting one's sins forgiven as a means to enter heaven upon death. For Christians on the liberal "left," salvation is often reduced to a commitment to eradicate social evils (41–55). Either way, according to the essence of these "gospels," there is no need or call to look to Jesus here and now as the master teacher of life under the loving reign of his heavenly Father. Without the gospel of the kingdom, the Christian convert is initiated into a social situation (either conservative, liberal, or something in between) that is ill-equipped to adequately address the questions and problems of practical human existence in a manner that makes Jesus and his Father integral.

Component #10: Jesus Is the Master of Living Life under God's Reign and He Wants to Teach His Students How to Live under That Reign in Their Actual Lives

Once the gospel of the kingdom begins to overrun more narrow visions of the gospel, an account of what is involved in discipleship to Jesus is required. A key to understanding Willard's view of discipleship is contained in the following: "Jesus' good news about the kingdom can be an effective guide for our lives only if we share his view of the world in which we live" (61). A crucial part of entering into training under Jesus is to develop the mindset that he had:

> To his eyes this is a God-bathed and God-permeated world. It is a world filled with a glorious reality, where every component is within the range of God's direct knowledge and control—though he obviously permits some of it, for good reasons, to be for a while otherwise than as he wishes. It is a world that is inconceivably beautiful and good because of God and because God is always in it. It is a world in which God is continually at play and over which he constantly rejoices. Until our thoughts of God have found every visible thing and event glorious in his presence, the word of Jesus has not yet fully seized us. (61–62)

Willard conveys that Jesus regarded God as a joyous Father who is vitally available in the surrounding atmosphere and in whose power and goodness there is no fear or ultimate harm (61–95). Jesus taught that the kingdom of God was freely available to anyone who puts their trust in him (97–127) and that deepening reliance on Jesus transforms the inner resources of the human heart such that outward expressions of love flow naturally (129–185).

Persons can accept Jesus' understanding of these things precisely because "he is the best and smartest man who ever lived in this world . . . He always has the best information on everything and certainly also on the things that matter most in human life" (90, 94).

So a crucial dimension of discipleship for Willard is that Jesus' view of things (his word) must come to richly dwell in his students. "In order to develop as his disciple one must progressively come to believe what he knew to be so" (319). This is not, though, simply a download of information. Essential to learning to view the world the way Jesus does is to come to understand and experience that disciples are to live with him:

> The assumption of Jesus' program for his people on earth was that they would live their lives as his students and co-laborers. They would find him so admirable in every respect—wise, beautiful, powerful, and good—that they would constantly seek to be in his presence and be guided, instructed, and helped by him in every aspect of their lives . . . In his presence our inner life will be transformed, and we will become the kind of people for whom his course of action is the natural (and supernatural) course of action. (273)

Christ's presence is mediated by the Holy Spirit—the strengthener—and God's preferred way of relating to persons is through communication. This makes Scripture and prayer central to discipleship as well as solitude and silence as "an appropriate context for listening and speaking to God" (277). Discipleship for Willard is both a learning *from* Jesus and a learning *with* Jesus that is ultimately focused on aligning one's actual life with the kingdom of God, which brings about the transformation of human character.

Willard has much to offer regarding entering into a discipleship relationship to Jesus (281–310). For one, discipleship is not an option for the Christian—one is either intending to live their life as Jesus would or they are not. Second, discipleship must be intentionally entered into—a person must decide to make Jesus the master teacher in everything that they do. And then, disciples simply try to do what Jesus asks them to do within the concrete details of their daily existence, coming to believe more and more that he is right there with them, empowering their efforts through his constant companionship. Jesus knew how to live in the kingdom of God and apply that kingdom for the good of others, and that is what disciples of Jesus learn how to do in their lives (282–283).

In his theology of discipleship, Willard emphasizes that Christ-following is not primarily about external conformity to biblical commands nor profession of correct doctrine (320). Rather, Willard lays out two objectives: (1) "bring apprentices to the point where they dearly love and constantly delight in that 'heavenly Father' made real to earth in Jesus and are quite certain that there is no 'catch,' no limit, to the goodness of his intentions or to his power to carry them out" (321); and (2) "remove our automatic responses against the kingdom of God, to free the apprentices of domination, of 'enslavement' (John 8:34; Rom. 6:6), to their old habitual patterns of thought, feeling, and action" (322). Willard writes, "When the mind is filled with this great and beautiful God, the 'natural' response, once all 'inward' hindrances are removed, will be to do 'everything I have told you to do'" (321). This is the curriculum of the student of Jesus and can be reliably entered into with Jesus involving many of the earlier mentioned components (e.g., the role of the body and spiritual disciplines—components #6 and #8).

Component #11: Students of Jesus Will Rule the Universe with Him for Eternity

Another crucial component for Willard's view is his articulation of the future state of disciples of Jesus. "We will not sit around looking at one another or at God for eternity but will join the eternal Logos, 'reign with him,' in the endlessly ongoing creative work of God" (378). We are being trained to reign. The practical implication of this is that the progress disciples make here and now is somehow transferred to the eternal state. Willard suggests that one's character is carried over and continued in the eternal state as well as the corresponding ability (or lack thereof) of humans to faithfully serve God in his eternal kingdom (378). So, what is at stake in spiritual formation is not simply for this present order, but also for the order to come. Willard writes, "Perhaps it would be a good exercise for each of us to ask ourselves: Really, how many cities could I now govern under God? If, for example, Baltimore or Liverpool were turned over to me, with power to do that I want with it, how would things turn out? An honest answer to this question might do much to prepare us for our eternal future in this universe" (398).

Of course, students of Jesus do not need to worry about their level of preparedness. There is no need for concern because the ultimate meaning of their future is secured:

> The purpose of God with human history is nothing less than to bring out of it . . . an eternal community of those who were once thought to be just "ordinary human beings." Because of God's purposes for it, this community will, in its way, pervade the entire created realm and share in government of it. God's precreation intention to have that community as a special dwelling place or home will be realized. He will be its prime sustainer and glorious inhabitant. (385–386)

In many ways, this component brings to completion Willard's view of spiritual formation. And yet, there are two monographs left within the Willardian corpus. These remaining books serve to flesh out several more detailed components of the Willardian account.

Renovation of the Heart

Turning to *Renovation of the Heart* (hereafter *Renovation*), Willard presents his most comprehensive overview of spiritual formation.[32] Each of the eleven components culled so far show up in *Renovation* to one degree or another. But there is at least one development in *Renovation* that advances Willard's overall view of formation. This is Willard's theological anthropology.

Component #12: Understanding Formation in Christ Involves Understanding How to Bring the Various Dimensions of the Human Self under God's Reign

Willard's theology of human nature is present throughout his corpus, but *Renovation* offers the clearest and most detailed presentation. Willard's specificity on the nature of the person is another characteristic of his view that stands in contrast to other treatments of sanctification/Christian spirituality, which often leave the theology of the person nebulous. In many accounts, anthropological terms such as "soul," "mind," "flesh," "image

---

[32] See Klaus Issler's helpful review of *Renovation* in *Christian Education Journal* 3, no. 1 (2002): 158–64.

of God," "spirit," "will," "heart," "character," and so on are used without settled definitions or distinctions, let alone an account of how the different aspects are interrelated in the transformation process. Is the object of God's transforming work the human body, soul, mind, will, heart, spirit, or all of the above? And if the latter, what does transformation in Christ look like, given the interrelatedness of these various dimensions of the person? Willard's theological anthropology is aimed at answering these types of questions.

Accordingly, Willard sees the delineation of human nature as central to understanding spiritual formation in Christ. Jesus' revolution of the human person "proceeds by changing people from the inside through ongoing personal relationship to God in Christ and to one another. It is one that changes their ideas, beliefs, feelings, and habits of choice, as well as their bodily tendencies and social relations. It penetrates to the deepest layers of their soul" (*Renovation*, 15). In order to fully comprehend the dynamics of God's transforming work, it is important to get clarity on these distinct aspects of the human self and how God is involved in them.

For Willard, the fundamental dimension of the person has three aspects: the heart, spirit, and will. The "will" refers to the core dimension's "power to initiate, to create, to bring about what did not exist before" (29). This is the unforced 'yes' or 'no' that decides the eventual character of the human person (33; cf. 141–157). The "spirit" refers to the core dimension's "fundamental nature as distinct and independent from physical reality" (29). The human spirit, like all spirit, is "unbodily, personal power" (34). And "heart" refers to the core dimension's "center or core [position] to which every other component of the self owes its proper functioning" (29). This is due to the fact that the will (heart or spirit) possesses "the power to select what we think on and how intently we will focus on it" (144). The heart/will/spirit, therefore, governs every other aspect of the human self and is the primary dimension of the person that must be properly aligned with God's rule (34).

But while the will (heart or spirit) is meant to govern the mind, it is also largely at the mercy of the mind. The mind is the realm of the person that includes thought and feeling. "To choose, one must always have some object or concept before the mind and some feeling for or against it" (34). Through thought (ideas, images, and information) the human mind becomes consciously aware of what one takes to be real, true, and good. Through feeling (sensations, desires, and emotions) the human mind is either attracted or repulsed by the ideas, images, and information that come before the mind in thought—"feelings move us" (121). Thought and feeling in the mind are always working in concert (32–33; cf. 95–139). As mentioned above, the will has some power over what is thought and felt, but once particular thoughts and feelings are fostered in the mind, the will eventually succumbs to their directionality.

The will and the mind are intimately connected to the human body. The body is the human "power pack" in which there is strength to live out human existence in a physical, social context (35; cf. 159–177). Habituated choices (or character) become ingrained in the body "where they then occur more or less 'automatically,' without our having to think about what we are doing" (35; cf. 142). This is why the body becomes crucial for spiritual formation—both the need to *re*form the body away from its ungodly habits as well as the body's role in forming the will and mind.

Next Willard discusses the social context of the human. It is significant in a time where many are calling for a relational ontology of the person that Willard himself emphasizes the necessity of "rootedness in others" for human persons (36).[33] "We only live as we should when we are in a right relation to God and to other human beings" (36). And yet, the necessity of relationality for the human self on Willard's view is interrelated with more fundamental structures and capacities of the person.

The human soul, for Willard, is that aspect of the person that "*correlates*, *integrates*, and *enlivens* everything going on in the various dimensions of the self" (199). Since each of the previous dimensions of the person is intermingled and interdependent, the soul is that which unifies the person. The soul holds the self together and brings "strength, direction, and harmony to every other element of our life . . . When we speak of the human soul, then, we are speaking of the *deepest level of life and power* in the human being" (204, 205, italics original).

Willard's delineation of human nature not only offers a heuristic through which to grasp Christ's transforming work, but coupled with

---

[33] For example, the call for a relational ontology, see F. Leron Schults, *Reforming Theological Anthropology: After the Philosophical Turn to Relationality* (Grand Rapids, MI: Eerdmans, 2003).

components #1–11, it brings a level of specificity to Willard's overall view of transformation. For instance, understanding the role of the heart/spirit/will as the chief operating center of the person further clarifies Willard's emphasis on bodily discipline (presented most fully in *The Spirit of the Disciplines*—component #8 above). The will's inner 'yes' or 'no' can be used to redirect the body to certain disciplines and experiences in which God is received more deeply into the will, mind, body, and soul. And yet, the human will won't function in this way unless it is first reborn by the Word and Spirit of Christ (41). Then, the regenerated mind must have before it thoughts and feelings about God and his kingdom (a vision) that offer the reborn will sufficient motivation (intention) and an object of choice (means). The human social context is essential in this process in terms of encouragement, comfort, edification, and so on. But the ultimate relational rootedness is in the person of God, as the will by means of the body directs the whole person (the soul) into growing communion and union with God. And, once again, it is through this divine relationship that the various dimensions of the person are reordered and conformed to the image of Christ. As Willard writes, "[Sanctification] is a consciously chosen and sustained relationship of interaction between the Lord and his apprentice, in which the apprentice is able to do, and routinely does, what he or she knows to be right before God because all aspects of his or her person have been substantially transformed" (226).

Knowing Christ Today

The last monograph of the Willardian corpus covers an array of issues (epistemology, moral theory, apologetics, religious pluralism, etc.).[34] But the element of the book that offers an essential piece to Willard's overall view of spiritual formation is Willard's realism regarding knowledge of the spiritual life.

---

[34] See my précis of *Knowing Christ Today* in *Journal of Spiritual Formation and Soul Care* 2, no. 2 (2009): 245–47. See also the symposium discussion that follows the précis in which John Ortberg, J. P. Moreland, Aaron Preston, and Kelly Kapic respond to *Knowing Christ Today* and Willard's replies to their respective responses (247–85).

Component #13: Knowledge of the Reality of Christ and His Kind of Life Is Available

This final component of Willard's theory of spiritual formation in Christ—his theory of knowledge—is foundational to his entire project. No doubt Willard's commitment to epistemological realism was well-developed far before he began to write on Christian spirituality.[35] There is equally no doubt that Willard's understanding of how the human mind can grasp reality as-it-is-in-itself fueled and guided his persistent and careful attentiveness to the nature and dynamics of spiritual formation. This is to say, there is a reason why a professional philosopher has produced one of the most detailed treatments of Christian spirituality in church history. The reason is not simply that Willard is a well-trained philosopher per se, but that his philosophical work led him to a view of knowledge that, once understood, yields an appropriate confidence about coming to know things as they are through sustained attention. Willard has developed a unified and comprehensive account of spiritual formation precisely because his mind was seeking to know things as they are. Things-as-they-are are unified wholes, so to describe such a thing is to describe the parts and properties of that thing, including the relations between those parts and properties and how they function together as a whole. Once again, while this view grounds Willard's entire project, it is in some ways fitting to have at the conclusion of this analysis. For it is through such an account of knowledge that others can come to see for themselves how what Willard has presented is true.

Willard maintains that knowledge is "essential to faith and to our relationship with God in the spiritual life" (*Knowing Christ Today*, 10). He defines faith as a "commitment to action, often beyond our natural abilities, *based upon knowledge of God and God's ways*" (20, italics original). On Willard's view, persons have knowledge of something when they are representing the thing, as it actually is on an appropriate basis of thought and experience (15). Willard discusses how knowledge secures access to reality while "Acting on false or ungrounded beliefs . . . leads to destructive encounters with reality" (39). At the level of worldview, knowledge of what

[35] Willard's dissertation and early philosophical publications largely defend a Husserlian realism regarding the mind-world relationship. For instance, see Willard's *Logic and the Objectivity of Knowledge*.

is real, who is well-off, who is a good person, and how one becomes a good person governs one's attitudes and actions. So to know Christ's answers to these questions on an appropriate basis of thought and experience orients the whole of one's life to how things actually are. According to Jesus, God and his kingdom are the ultimate reality, anyone who is living under his kingdom rule is well-off, the good person is the one filled with love for God and neighbor, and the way to become this kind of person is to "*place your confidence in Jesus Christ* and *become his student or apprentice in kingdom living*" (53, italics original). But how does one come to possess knowledge of Jesus' understanding of these things? Willard holds that three sources of knowledge—authority, reason, and experience—supplement each other in providing the appropriate basis on which to know Jesus' answers and to come to experience Jesus himself.

The problem remains that many Christians do not *know* these realities and only profess belief in them, which leaves them with only willpower or feelings as the means to sustain their spiritual lives. So here, as before, understanding is the basis of care. Willard attempts to show forth the requisite understanding of human knowledge in order to help persons come to have spiritual knowledge.

Conclusion

The main intent of this chapter was to present the Willardian corpus as a unified and comprehensive account of spiritual formation in Christ. Willard's five initial monographs on the spiritual life are not a collection of assorted musings, nor do they simply restate or reorganize what has been said previously. Each volume offers distinct elements of Willard's overall theory and takes the attentive reader into nuanced treatments of the anticipated parts of a theology of sanctification (e.g., human nature, sin, salvation, etc.). In addition to this, Willard offers an in-depth analysis of various elements of Christian spirituality that are often overlooked or given superficial attention (e.g., the role of the body in formation). No doubt some will find some important element missing from the thirteen components culled from Willard's corpus. Others will disagree with the interpretation of Willard presented in this chapter or with Willard's analysis itself. Still others will desire to take one these points or some other concept that Willard addresses further and develop it theologically, historically, psychologically, and so on.

Whatever the case, the suggestion here is that the Willardian corpus stands as a major contribution to the church's reflection on what it is to follow Jesus Christ and be conformed to his image. It is a unified and comprehensive theory that warrants the attention of the Christian scholarly community. As Protestant theology recovers from the eclipse of holiness mentioned at the start of this chapter, it behooves the Christian scholar to carefully reflect on what can be learned from the Willardian corpus.

ENGAGING WILLARD

2

BODY AND SOUL

Tweaking Dallas Willard's Understanding of the Human Person

J. P. MORELAND

Talbot School of Theology, Biola University

Abstract: While my own philosophical views are largely in keeping with my mentor, Dallas Willard, nevertheless, I find his conception of the human person puzzling, hard to specify precisely, and prima facie contradictory in a few places. Dallas's central goal in formulating his anthropology was to develop a model that shed light on, allowed for deeper insight into, and fostered interest in spiritual formation, especially the role of the body in spiritual maturation. I share this goal, and agree with most of his model. But in what follows, I will make more precise what his views were, try to clear up what, prima facie, seem to be contradictions in his theory, and, finally, recommend an alternative that captures the central concerns Dallas had for his own position. Thus, I will lay out a few general points of Dallas's ontology (points with which I agree), provide a description of his philosophical/theological anthropology, along with two problems that seem to be present, and offer a slightly adjusted alternative to his position that accomplishes his main goal (regarding spiritual formation) in a way with which I believe he would be satisfied.

I had the privilege of doing my PhD under Dallas—he was my dissertation supervisor—and, subsequently, along with my wife, Hope, of being close friends of Dallas and Jane from 1985 until the time of his departure. When church history looks back on this time period, the movements in philosophy and spiritual formation he generated will, no doubt, place him among a very small handful of influential names for the kingdom.

My own philosophical views are largely in keeping with his. But I find his views of the human person puzzling, hard to specify precisely, and prima facie contradictory in a few places. This is an odd situation in which to be, since Dallas was a deep philosophical genius and a standout wordsmith in his manner of presentation. I tell my students that at places where I disagree with Thomas Aquinas, I must be wrong so do not trust my teaching. I feel the same way about Dallas's teaching. Yet I cannot escape the sense that my observations are correct.

Dallas had two goals in formulating his anthropology. First, he wanted to get at the truth of the matter. Consequently, he used reason and Scripture very carefully in developing his views to increase the odds that his position was a set of justified true assertions. Second, he wanted his model to shed light on, allow for deeper insight into, and foster interest in spiritual formation, especially the role of the body in spiritual maturation. I share these goals and, in fact, I actually agree with most of his model. But in what follows, I will make more precise what his views were I shall try to clear up what, based on first impressions, seem to be contradictions in his theory; and, finally, recommend an alteration that captures the central concerns Dallas had for his own model. So, in what follows, I will, first, lay out a few general points of Dallas's ontology (points with which I agree); then offer a description of his philosophical/theological anthropology, along with two problems that seem to be present in his system; and, finally, offer a slightly adjusted alternative to his that accomplishes his second goal (regarding spiritual formation) in a way with which I believe he would be satisfied.

Contours of Willard's Ontology Relevant to His Anthropology

Dallas was smart enough to know that you do not sit down and develop an ontology out of nothing without relying on the sages of the past. Now Dallas was definitely a fan of Plato, but in my view, two streams of thought influenced his ontology the most: the works of Edmund Husserl and the metaphysics of Aristotle and the late Medieval Aristotelians, including

Thomas Aquinas.[1] What follows is a list of basic categories of reality that Dallas accepted and used to formulate his understanding of a human person.

Substance

In the *Categories*, Aristotle clarified two different senses of "substance": primary substance (e.g., Socrates, a particular dog) and secondary substance (humanness, doghood). Dallas follows Aristotle in this distinction and, accordingly, he used "substance" in two different ways.[2] First, a substance is an individual thing that has properties and dispositions (powers or capacities to do certain things, e.g., the capacity to think about American history when one is asleep and not actualizing that capacity) according to the kind of thing it is (for example, dogs have certain capacities, humans have others) that endures through time and change, and receives and exercises causal influence on other things.[3] The paradigm case of a substance in this sense is a living thing (e.g., a human person).

Second, substance can refer to a thing's essence, a range of actual and potential properties such that the thing could not exist if it lost one of these properties. Essential properties are difference from accidental properties. Examples of the former are being human for Socrates and being even for the number two. Examples of the latter are weighing 150 pounds for Socrates or being Simon's favorite number for the number two. Something can lose accidental properties and still exist; not so with essential properties.

Properties

A property (attribute, quality) is a universal (a characteristic that can be non-spatially in, exemplified, possessed by many things at the same time). Thus, redness or humanity can be had by more than one thing simultaneously. Grasping a thing's properties is crucial to understanding the important features of the thing in question. For instance, understanding the properties of an electron is essential for developing an informed view of

---

[1] Willard was, of course, an expert on and admirer of Husserl, and in The *Spirit of the Disciplines: Understanding How God Changes Lives* (San Francisco: Harper & Row, 1988), 82, he explicitly makes reference to phenomenological writers and their influence. In the same book, on pg. 88, he also mentions the importance of Aristotelian thought for his own views.

[2] In Elane O'Rourke's otherwise excellent work, *A Dallas Willard Dictionary* (Soul Training Publications, CreateSpace, 2013), the entry "Substance" is quite confused.

[3] Dallas Willard, *The Great Omission: Reclaiming Jesus's Essential Teachings on Discipleship* (New York: HarperCollins, 2006), *138*.

what an electron is and how it works. Similarly, for Dallas, understanding the properties of the soul and of the body were essential for developing an informed view of spiritual formation. Also, properties are abstract objects (they are not in space and time). Finally, Dallas accepted constituent realism regarding properties (and relations). According to constituent realism, properties (and relations) are universals that, when exemplified (and they need not be to exist), become constituents of the ordinary particulars that have them. Thus, if the mind exemplifies a mental property, say, the property of being a thought of London, then that property enters into the very being of the mind as a metaphysical constituent.[4]

Relations

Dallas also held that relations (being larger than, being sweeter than, being brighter than) were universals and abstract objects. He divided relations into internal and external. If something, A (say the color yellow) stands in an internal relation (brighter than) to B (say the color purple), then anything that did not stand in that relation to B could not be A. So if any color was not brighter than purple, it could not be the color yellow. If a thing X stands in an internal relation to another thing Y, then part of what makes X the very thing it is, is that it stands in that relation to Y. X could not exist if it did not stand in that relation to Y. External relations are those that are not internal, that is, if A (a ball) stands in the external relation "on-top-of" to B (a table), then A (the ball) could cease to stand in that relation to B (by, say, falling on the floor and, thus, being in the lower-than relation to B, the table) and still exist.

As we will see later, for Dallas and for me, the body stands in an internal relation to the soul such that the soul could exist without the body but not vice versa. A "body without a soul" is not a body; it's a corpse. Further, Dallas and I both take the mind, the spirit, the emotions and the will to stand in internal relations to the soul. Among other things, this implies that in order to understand how the soul grows and functions, one must understand the items (the mind and so forth) that are internally related to the soul.

---

[4] See Dallas Willard, "How Concepts Relate the Mind to Its Objects: The 'God's Eye View Vindicated,'" *Philosophia Christi* 1, no 2 (1999): 5–20.

Parts

One way Dallas used the term "part" was what philosophers call a separable part. In this sense a part belongs to some whole (the door is a part of the house; the engine is a part of the car), and it could exist if taken out of that whole (the door could be removed from the house and it would still be the same door). Some Christians claim that a human person is made of different parts—the soul, the spirit, the body, and so on. While I cannot argue it here, Dallas (and I) rejected this idea and, instead, found the notion of a faculty or mode to be more relevant to understanding the human person than the idea of a part.

Faculties

The human person has literally thousands of capacities within its structure, most of which that person is not currently actualizing or using. But the human person is not just a collection of isolated, discrete, randomly related capacities. Rather, the various capacities within the human person fall into natural groupings called *faculties* of the human person. In order to get hold of this, think for a moment about this list of capacities: the ability to see red, see orange, hear a dog bark, hear a tune, think about math, think about God, desire lunch, desire a family. The ability to see red is more closely related to the ability to see orange than it is to the ability to think about math. We express this insight by saying that the abilities to see red or orange are properties of the same faculty—the faculty of sight. The ability to think about math is a capacity within the thinking faculty (viz., the mind). In general, a faculty is a mode of the human person that contains a natural family of related capacities. A mode, such as the mind, is internally related to the soul (a.k.a. the self or the I). The mind cannot exist on its own if removed from the soul of which it is a mode. Because modes are so intimately related to the things that have them, understanding a thing's modes is of great help in understanding the thing itself. Understanding the modes/faculties of the soul—the mind, the spirit, the emotions, the will, and so on—and how they interact with each other and with the body will allow us to develop a model of the human person that yields insights about how a human person is formed in various ways.

In sum, these metaphysical notions formed the core of Dallas's ontology, and they were constantly in his mind as he regularly used them to work on specific issues in philosophy (e.g., what is an atom, what is time, what is a human person).[5]

Dallas's View of the Human Person

It is clear that Dallas was a substance dualist in the sense that the person or self is a spiritual or personal substance not identical to his body.[6] However, although Dallas does say in one place, "You are a nonphysical reality with a physical body,"[7] nevertheless, he was not a Cartesian dualist. Cartesian dualism is the view that we are minds that happen to be "housed" in a purely physical body, and we and that body can cause things to happen to each other (e.g., a knife cut causes pain in my mind; a negative thought causes my heart to race). Dallas expresses agreement with phenomenological and existentialist writings in "denying that the body is 'just physical,' just some more or less *mechanical* device incidentally associated with a purely spiritual mind or self" (*The Spirit of the Disciplines*, 82).[8] Speaking of the (Platonic and Cartesian) dichotomy between the non-physical part (the soul, spirit, self) and the purely physical part (the body) of the person, Elane O'Rourke flatly states, "Dallas did not accept this dichotomy . . . This means that we are not essentially spirits or souls who happen to be lodged *in* bodies."[9]

Dallas is a bit unclear as to what he thinks we are, sometimes calling us humans, sometimes persons, and sometimes human persons. The reason this is important is because some thinkers believed one could be a human without being a person, and in this view, in the intermediate state

---

[5] To my knowledge, there is no single place that Dallas spelled out his general ontology in summary fashion. But if the reader is interested in seeing where Dallas stated and used these philosophical notions, then go to www.dwillard.org and look at his philosophical articles, especially the ones involving Husserl. See also Willard, *Logic and the Objectivity of Knowledge* (Athens: Ohio University Press, 1984).

[6] See Dallas Willard, "Intentionality and the Substance of the Self," Philosophia Christi 13, no. 1 (2011): 7–19.

[7] Dallas Willard, *Living in Christ's Presence: Final Words on Heaven and the Kingdom of God* (Downers Grove, IL: InterVarsity Press, 2014), 117.

[8] Short titles and parenthetical references are used throughout for the Willardian corpus. See *Hearing God: Developing a Conversational Relationship with God*, 3rd ed. (Downers Grove, IL: InterVarsity Press, 1999); *The Spirit of the Disciplines: Understanding How God Changes Lives* (New York: HarperCollins, 1988); *The Divine Conspiracy: Rediscovering Our Hidden Life in God* (New York: HarperCollins, 1997); *Renovation of the Heart: Putting on the Character of Christ* (Colorado Springs: NavPress, 2002); *Knowing Christ Today: Why We Can Trust Spiritual Knowledge* (New York: HarperCollins, 2009).

[9] O'Rourke, *A Dallas Willard Dictionary*, 29.

immediately following death, one was a person and not a human. And Thomas Aquinas believed that when, say, Peter died, he did not survive into the afterlife; rather, his soul did. But his soul was capable of sustaining Peter's identity such that when his soul was reunited with his resurrection body, he was a human person again.[10]

Now it may be that Willard agreed with Aquinas on this point and, accordingly, even in the intermediate state, there was a need for a spiritual body. But I think the corpus of Dallas's work would favor calling us human persons (hereafter, just persons). The person is the fundamental unit of analysis in that the person is a substance and the other dimensions/modes are seated in or dependent upon the person (*Renovation*, 30–39). As we will see later, if Dallas did agree with Aquinas, then it is very hard to see how it is I myself who survives death. Why? Well, on this view, when I die, I do not literally survive death; my soul does. Nor does my body survive death. Rather, a new spiritual body is provided. If I am neither the soul or the body, it is hard to see how it could literally be I that survives death. It is hard to see how some aspect of me—the soul—could fill the job of grounding my identity in the intermediate state. More on this later.

In addition, Dallas clarifies five features (dimensions, aspects, elements) of the person: soul, social context, body, mind (thoughts and feelings), spirit (heart or will) (*Renovation*, chapter 2). These five constitute the essence of human nature.[11] The terms "features," "dimensions," or "aspects" are not very precise, but fortunately, Dallas clarifies things when he claims that these five are inseparable from every human life (*Renovation*, 30). From this statement and knowledge of his general ontology, it is safe to say that these five are faculties of the person understood as inseparable parts or modes internally related to the person, and to understand them we need to grasp their properties. Thus, for example, a body that is not a mode of a person is not a body; it is a corpse. And when the human person is living, the body is actually a faculty of the soul, a set of powers and capacities in the soul for developing and structuring the body. I will touch more on this below when I clarify my own view of the human person.

---

[10] Cf. Christopher Brown, *Aquinas and the Ship of Theseus* (New York: Continuum, 2005).

[11] Gary Black Jr., *The Theology of Dallas Willard* (Eugene, OR: Pickwick Publications, 2013), 100.

While all five of these modes of a person are crucial, there are two of them that, in my view, require special mention: the body and the soul.

Dallas's treatment of the nature of the body and its role in spiritual formation may well have been his most important contribution to reflections on sanctification. When *The Spirit of the Disciplines* burst on the scene in 1988, it forever changed how many of us view spiritual growth. For Dallas, the body is an aspect of the image of God in us, and it is a power pack, a source of independent power by way of which we can interact with the world and make a difference in it (*The Spirit of the Disciplines*, 52–53). Human personal relations cannot be separated from the body (*Renovation*, 35).

At times, Dallas's words about the body can sound shocking or even at first glance heretical. For example, in *Spirit of the Disciples* he states, "In an important sense to be explained, a person *is* his or her body" (*The Spirit of the Disciplines*, 76). Again, "The union of spirituality with the fullness of human life finds its deepest ground in the identification of the person with his or her body" (*The Spirit of the Disciplines*, 82). Finally, "*Human personality is not separable in our consciousness from the human body. And that fact is expressed by asserting the IDENTITY of the person as his or her body*" (*The Spirit of the Disciplines*, 84, italics original).

Below, I will provide reasons for not taking these statements as literal assertions of the identity of a human person and his or her body. For present purposes, it seems best to understand Dallas as saying that the body is not a mere container in which we live (as would be held by a Cartesian dualist). No, we are far more intimately related to the body than that and, according to Dallas, it is not an exaggeration to say that the spiritual formation of the body is crucial to our growth as disciples. To explain how Dallas conceives of this, it may be wise to note a statement he makes in the midst of these identity assertions. He claims that phenomenological and existential writers of the recent past have argued that the body is not simply a "physical thing"; in fact, there is far more to a living body than matter (*The Spirit of the Disciplines*, 82).

For Dallas, different modes/regions of the body contained two things relevant to spiritual health. The first are meanings and sensations that occupy specific modes of the body.[12] For example, upon meeting someone of whom you are jealous, there might arise a sensation of a certain sort in your stomach or shoulders. This sensation would have a specific texture and location, and it may be associated with the meaning, "I am such a looser. Why can't I be like him?" Brute physical matter—the kind that can be completely described in the language of physics, chemistry, neuroscience and biology—is not capable of having sensations and meanings in it. It is only if there is more to the body than its physicality that it can have sensations and meanings. From personal conversations with Dallas and from his general metaphysical views, the following is beyond reasonable doubt for Dallas: it is because the body is informed and diffused by the immaterial, substantial person that the body can have these things.

Second, Dallas noted that various modes of the body contain grooves, ingrained habits formed through repeated practice of some sort to constitute character. Thus, spiritual growth requires the repeated practice of various disciplines in order to replace the old groove with a new one in keeping with the nature of the kingdom. In this way, the body is literally formed in a new way by obtaining a new character consisting of habits stored as grooves in various regions of the body.[13]

Finally, we turn to Dallas's teaching on the soul. In my opinion, this area of his anthropology is the most puzzling. The best thing to say at this point is that for Dallas, the soul is a mode or inseparable part of the person, taken as an unanalyzable primitive entity, just like the other four modes, except that the soul is the deepest aspect of the person. Moreover, it is a non-physical mode that *resides in* the person (and in this sense, the person is the seat of the soul), yet the soul, while an aspect of the person, functions to bring together and unify into one life the activities of all the other dimensions. In this way, the soul is the source and coordinating principle of the

---

[12] The first person to develop an entire approach to therapy based on this insight was Eugene T. Gendlin, *Focusing* (New York: Bantam Books, 1987).

[13] Steve Porter has pointed out that elsewhere (see *Hearing God*) Dallas says our old routines of feeling, thought, belief, and so forth are stored in the heart/mind. In my view, in *Hearing God*, Dallas was not attempting to provide a full explanation for how these things are stored in the heart and mind. He simply wanted to state the fact that they are and that Christ can and does replace them. But in *The Spirit of the Disciplines*, Dallas does give a fuller picture of how these mental states are stored, namely, as dispositions of, say, the mind, and the dispositions to think certain ways are groves in the brain that are or ground these mental dispositions.

person's life. Dallas writes, "Because the soul encompasses and 'organizes' the whole person, it is frequently taken to *be* the person. We naturally treat persons as 'souls.' But of course, the soul is not the person. It is, rather, the deepest part of the self in terms of overall operations; and like the body, it has the capacity to operate (and does, largely, operate) without conscious supervision" (*Renovation*, 37). Dallas's favorite illustration of the soul was to liken it to a computer that quietly runs a business or manufacturing operation and only comes to our attention when it malfunctions. Without the soul, the other modes of the person would fragment and go their own way.[14]

Two Possible Difficulties in Dallas's Philosophical/Theological Anthropology

Dallas said so much about these matters that it would take an entire book to do him justice. Still, I think this précis of his thought is accurate and adequate for my purposes. If there are places where I have misunderstood Dallas's thought, I would love to have that pointed out to me. I now turn to two possible difficulties in his philosophical/theological anthropology.

A Person's Relationship to His Body

As I said above, Dallas made the claim that we are to be identified with our bodies (*The Spirit of the Disciplines*, 76, 82, 84.) But this cannot be what he meant because he identified four other modes, alongside the body, that constitute the human self. I think this alleged problem is capable of a fairly easy resolution. When Dallas said this, he means the following: (1) The human body is more than physical, so in a real sense, I am more closely related to my body than in the container model, that is the body is purely a physical container into which my soul has been inserted (*The Spirit of the Disciplines*, 82).[15] (2) My body is essential to my identity (*Renovation*, 161). In fact, it is a part of the image of God in me (*The Spirit of the Disciplines*,

---

[14] The information in this paragraph is repeated by Dallas in a number of places: *Renovation of the Heart*, 37–38; 199–216; "The Texture an Substance of the Human Soul" (presented paper Biola Philosophy Group, Biola University, November 22, 1994); "Grey Matter and the Soul," in *Renewing the Christian Mind: Essays, Interviews, and Talks*, edited by Gary Black Jr. (New York: HarperOne, 2016), 158–60; "Spiritual Disciplines, Spiritual Formation, and the Restoration of the Soul," *Journal of Psychology and Theology* 26, no. 1 (1998): 101–09; O'Rourke, *A Dallas Willard Dictionary*, 243–46; Black, *The Theology of Dallas Willard*, 107.

[15] Willard makes a similar case in "Grey Matter and the Soul," in *Renewing the Christian Mind*, 158–60.

52–53). (3) Human personal relations cannot be separated from my body, and human personality is not separable in our consciousness from the human body (*Renovation*, 35; *The Spirit of the Disciplines*, 84).

To sum up, Dallas is emphasizing the closeness we have to our (more than physical) bodies and how crucial the body is to our development. But the way he puts all this raises a difficulty: If we take these statements at face value, then it means that there is no disembodied intermediate state at death. If we continue to survive between death and final resurrection, we will need to be given a temporary body, which implies that, contrary to Dallas's teaching, my current body is not, in fact, essential to me, and I can continue to engage in personal relationships without my current body.

Moreover, there are reasons to believe that Dallas did believe in a disembodied intermediate state between death and final resurrection.[16] For one thing, Dallas explicitly says, "When we pass through the stage normally called 'death,' we will not lose anything but the limitations and powers that specifically correspond to our present mastery over our body, and to our availability and vulnerability to and through it. We will no longer be able to act and be acted upon by means of it" (*The Divine Conspiracy*, 394.) Later, he says, "Our experience will be much clearer, richer, and deeper, of course, because it will be unstrained by the limitations now imposed upon us by our dependence upon our body" (*The Divine Conspiracy*, 395).[17]

For another thing, Dallas was a believer in the general truthfulness of many, if not most, near death experiences (*The Divine Conspiracy*, 397). In fact, he regularly taught a course on life after death at USC, and one

[16] Though, as Gary Black has told me, sometimes Dallas talked about the possibility of having a sort of ethereal, glowing body that was made out of light; now, some near death experiencers report something like this, but such a body is so different than the one we have now that it becomes hard to see how our current body, with its particular makeup to serve as a dimension, along with all the other dimensions making up human personhood, is as essential to the tasks Dallas assigns it, since these tasks can be accomplished with a radically different body—one, in fact, that is more like light than a more substantial body.

[17] To be sure, on page 396 of the same book, Dallas does interpret 2 Corinthians 5:1–8 as saying that when we die and our "earthly tent is torn down," we are not thereby deprived of a body because "we will be clothed with a dwelling place of the heavenly sort" (a new body) and, thus, will not be "left naked" (disembodied). Since Dallas was such a careful scholar, I am not clear as to exactly what he is saying here. Why? Because most commentators who take this text in an ontological way as does Dallas, claim that Paul is expressing his desire to be around at the second coming of Christ so his new body will be given to him immediately and he will not have to go through a period of disembodiment, a possibility that Paul clearly affirms in this text (cf. vs. 3, 4). The real possibility of disembodiment in this text seems clear, and surely Dallas recognized that the text taught this.

of his regular texts—one he told me he agreed with—was Jeffrey Long's *Evidence of the Afterlife* (New York: HarperOne, 2010). As Long points out, while some near death experiences report receiving some sort of heavenly body, the majority claim that during the experience they existed without any body; this is true for almost every near death experiencer while they are still in the room with their dead corpse, watching what is going on. However, if one exists after death in a disembodied state, and if the body is part of the image of God, then the disembodied human person will not exemplify the full image of God during that time, and this result seems troubling. Disembodied existence also shows that human personal relationships do, indeed, take place without a body and consciousness and human personality can function quite nicely with no body at all.

But maybe there is a further way out here. It may be that Dallas is speaking in these sources like a pastor and not like a philosopher. Now it seems to be rare for Dallas to divide these, but in these sources, he may have been less than precise in some of his word usage in order to communicate. So, when he says that my body is essential to my identity and part of the image of God in me, perhaps he meant to say that, while embodied, my body is crucial to my identity, and that while I can be in the image of God without my body, nevertheless, the body is an important part of that image. I do not know what else to say, so I leave it to the reader to ponder the issues I have surfaced.[18] But if there are ways to clarify alleged problematic aspects of Dallas's view of the body, I think that two difficulties with his teaching on the soul will be much harder to dismiss.

The Person and His Soul

It is clear that Dallas taught that the soul was a mode of the person just like the other four in his diagram in *Renovation of the Heart*, though it was for

[18] Steve Porter suggests that, perhaps, Dallas was distinguishing minimal personhood, which continues to exist apart from the body, and full-fledged personhood, which requires a body. So we are still minimally persons in a disembodied state, but we are not full-fledged or fully operational persons. As Porter rightly points out, there is a long tradition that there is something lacking/unnatural about the disembodied state. That may be what Dallas is after. And he is highlighting it because of the tendency Christians have to denigrate the role of the body. This may be right, but it is a stretch that I do not think matches Dallas's language. He knew very well what it means to say something (the body) is essential to something else (the person, the image of God): a thing cannot exist without those things that are essential to its existence. So I suspect that Dallas did not intend this gloss on his statements.

him a special mode. The soul is the deepest "aspect" of the person, seated in that person, and the integrator and unifier of the different components of the person.

On the other hand, Dallas clearly states in some places that the soul is an individual substance in its own right. As O'Rourke points out, for Dallas, unlike the other aspects of the person, the soul "has independent life and substance: souls can exist without the body, mind, will, or interaction."[19] Elsewhere, Dallas says, "The soul is, as professor Moreland indicates, a substance, in the sense that it is an individual entity that has properties and dispositions natural to it, endures through time and change, and receives and exercises causal influence on other things, most notably *the person* of which it is the most fundamental part."[20]

Dallas is approvingly citing an article I wrote in the same issue of *The Journal of Psychology and Theology*, in which I explicitly define the classic definition of a substance (one Dallas accepted), claim that the soul is such a substance, and identify the person with the soul.[21] From Aristotle to the present, there is a fundamental axiom for those, including Dallas, who accept this classic understanding of substance: No substance contains another substance within its being. As Aristotle put it, "No substance is composed of substances."[22] From this, it follows that substances cannot have separable parts because such are substances. When Dallas says here that the soul is a part of the human person, he cannot mean here "inseparable part" or "mode," as he does elsewhere, because he has already called the soul a substance in this citation and not a mode. By the way, the reason that a substance cannot have another substance as a constituent is that such entities that *do* have substances as separable parts are not themselves substances. Rather, they are merely structured collections of parts like a car or house. Such entities do not have the unity required of a real substance (e.g., if a structured collection of parts gains or loses a part, it is literally a different thing). If the soul is a substance, the unity of the person is lost

---

[19] O'Rourke, *A Dallas Willard Dictionary*, 243.

[20] Willard, "Spiritual Disciplines, Spiritual Formation, and the Restoration of the Soul," 101.

[21] J. P. Moreland, "Restoring the Substance to the Soul of Psychology," *Journal of Psychology and Theology* 26 (March 1998): 29–43 .

[22] Aristotle, *Metaphysics* VII.16, 1041a4–5. Cf. *Metaphysics* VII.13, 1039a7–8. See also Robert Pasnau, *Metaphysical Themes: 1274–1671* (Oxford: Clarendon, 2011), 607–10; Brown, *Aquinas and the Ship of Theseus*, 53–57, 72–73, 87–90.

because one substance (the person) contains another substance (the soul) as a substantial, separable part. Instead, the person becomes a mere structured collection of parts.

There is a second difficulty with the soul in Dallas's teaching: in the Aristotelian tradition, the integrative, unifying role of the soul is given to the particular essence (e.g., Socrates' human personhood) of the living organism, not to some mode among other modes within the living thing. Thus, the human person is the same thing as the soul, and the various faculties—mind, volition, emotion, body, and so on—are seated in and unified by the particular essence that makes up the soul's nature. If this is true, there is no unifying work left for a mode of the substance (the human person) to perform. Rather, the soul is identical to the person and the soul/person is identical to a particular example of the essence of "human personhood." Further, the mind, will, body, and so forth are modes internally related to the human person (a.k.a. the soul, self, or I).

It is interesting to note that Dallas seemed to identify the underlying unifier of an individual substance with its (particular) essence. In an advanced class I took with Dallas at USC in the fall of 1982 entitled "The Metaphysics of Substance," Dallas gave out an (unpublished) handout he had written for the class entitled "Nominalism and the Theory of Substance." In it, he says that the substance (here he means "essence") of a thing stands under the individual substance constituted by that essence. He then goes on to say, "It is better to follow Aristotle in taking the substance (ousia) of a thing to be that *within* it which governs its career of existing, and thus supports or stands under it. The substance [note: essence] in this sense was taken by Aristotle to be its *species*, a special sub-set of its properties which provides the framework for all of the other properties which it may, must, or cannot have."[23]

A Thomistic-like Tweaking of Dallas's Anthropology

I hope these issues will become clearer as I try to develop an alternative model of the human person that is very similar to Dallas's and that accomplishes the things of concern to him as he developed his own model. There seem to be three such concerns: (1) The human person is an immaterial

[23] Willard, "Nominalism and the Theory of Substance," unpublished handout.

substance with a deep unity beyond that of an ordered aggregate or mere collection of atoms and molecules. (2) The various modes of the human person (mind, will, etc.) can become fragmented and, yet, they were meant to function in a deep unity and this can be achieved through various practices. (3) The body is not just a physical container for the human person; no, it is more than just physical such that meanings, feelings, and habituated dispositions reside in it and it is deeply integrated with the human person. I turn, now, to my own model to see if I can capture these concerns.

The Soul

The human soul (hereafter simply "soul") is a simple (containing no separable parts), spatially unextended substance that contains the capacities for consciousness and for animating, enlivening, and developing its body. The essence of the soul is constituted by certain properties, namely, those that make up human personhood. Thus, being a human is a sufficient condition for being a person. The faculties of the soul (e.g., the mind, will, spirit, emotions, powers to produce and enliven a body) are inseparable parts or modes of the soul containing a group of naturally resembling powers/capacities. The essence of the soul (e.g., human personhood for Joe, Sally, you, and me) grounds membership in a thing's natural kind, and it should be understood in terms of Aristotelian essentialism. Thus, it is because Joe has the essence "human personhood" that he is classified in the class of human persons instead of, say, penguins.

The late Medieval Aristotelians (1225–1671) drew a distinction between a thick particular (the entire concrete organism including the body; the thin particular plus accidental properties and the thin particular (the essence/form—e.g., human personhood, the relationship of something having that essence, and the thing that has that essence to make it a particular example of human personhood, for example, Socrates' human personhood as opposed to Plato's).[24] In this and my view, the human person is identical to his soul (the thin particular) and his soul contains three metaphysical constituents—a human essence, exemplification, and something that makes that universal essence a particular example of it, something that turns

[24] Pasnau, *Metaphysical Themes*, 99–114.

human personhood into Socrates' own human personhood.[25] The particular example of the essence in a particular soul is the ground, developer, unifier, and coordinator of the various modes that are seated as faculties (natural groupings of potentialities/dispositions) within it.

The Body and the Body/Soul Relationship

In this section I will offer an analysis of Aristotelian-style dualism that provides an understanding of the body and the body/soul relationship. I shall call the view Metaphysical Aristotelianism (MA), and while it does not reflect the views of Thomas Aquinas in all its details, it is close enough to be viewed as a Thomistic-like Dualism.

According to MA, living organisms are not mere structured collections of separable parts. Rather, the consensus during this period was that the living organism is a thin particular (viz., a particular soul), an essence exemplified by something that makes it a particular example of that essence, that stands under (sub-stands), supports, and grounds the accidental features of the organism, including its body.[26] The thin particular is identical to the organism's soul; it is not composed of separable parts, but it is metaphysically complex (containing a complex essence with various faculties or modes, exemplified by something that makes it a particular example of that essence). Further, the soul is fully present throughout the organism's body in that it is fully present at each part of the body. In this way, according to some models of omnipresence, spatially speaking, the soul is to the body as God is to space in general. Since the soul is entirely present in more than one place at the same time, namely, at each location of the body, that is why you don't lose, say, 10% of your soul when your arm is cut off, or you don't become less than half a human person when 55% of the brain is removed in surgery.

There were four central metaphysical roles played by the thin particular: (1) It grounded the special sort of deep, unity of living things at an individual point in time, especially in comparison to mere structured combinations of separable parts. (2) It grounded a living thing's ability

---

[25] J. P. Moreland, "Theories of Individuation: A Reconsideration of Bare Particulars," *Pacific Philosophical Quarterly* 79, no. 3 (1998): 251–63. Dallas was a huge advocate of bare particulars as a crucial part of his ontology.

[26] Pasnau, *Metaphysical Themes*, 99–134.

to be a continuant, sustaining strict, absolute identity through certain changes (including part replacement in the organism's body). (3) It provided the ontological ground for placing the organism in its natural kind (e.g., grounding Socrates' membership in the natural kind "human person) and unifying that kind (the reason Socrates and Plato are members of the kind human person and Fido the dog is not is that the former have but the latter lacks human personhood). (4) It unified and developed over time in a law-like way the various modes of the substantial soul.

Another feature of MA is the central importance of the body for the functioning of the thin particular's (soul's) powers in the normal course of things and the actualization of its various capacities. Speaking of the human soul, Des Chene observes, "The human soul is not merely joined with the body in fact. It is the *kind* of soul which, though capable of separate existence . . . nevertheless by its nature presupposes union with a body, and moreover with a particular kind of body, a body with organs, in order to exercise all its powers—even reason . . ."[27] Elsewhere, Des Chene notes, "Even the intellect requires, so long as the soul is joined with a body, a certain disposition of the brain."[28]

Thus, the search for specific neurological causal/functional/dependency conditions associated with the actualization of the soul's capacities for consciousness is not only consistent with, but is entailed by MA. Such a search would not provide information about the intrinsic nature of the capacity or the property it actualizes (e.g., pain) nor about the possessor of that capacity (the soul, not the brain). But it would provide information about the bodily conditions required for its actualization. This form of dualism is quite at home with the existence of contemporary neurological findings.

As Pasnau notes, a further feature of MA is the view that the soul "plays a straightforwardly causal role, explaining both the behavior and the physical structure of an animal's body."[29] In this sense, the soul is not only the formal/essential cause of the body, but it also becomes (1) an internal efficient first-moving cause of the development and structure of the body

---

[27] Dennis Des Chene, *Life's Form: Late Aristotelian Conceptions of the Soul* (Ithaca, NY: Cornell University Press, 2000), 71.

[28] Des Chene, *Life's Form*, 96.

[29] Pasnau, *Metaphysical Themes*, 558; cf. 549, 560–65.

and (2) the teleological guide for that development and structure (thus, function determines form).

Here, the soul is a substance with an essence or inner nature that contains, as a primitive unity, a complicated, structural arrangement of capacities/dispositions for developing a body (and, of course, the other faculties or modes). Taken collectively, this entire ordered structure is unextended, fully present throughout the body, and constitutes the soul's principle of activity that governs the precise, ordered sequence of changes that the substance will (normally) go through in the process of growth and development. The various physical/chemical parts and processes (including DNA) are tools—instrumental causes—employed by higher-order biological activities in order to sustain the various functions grounded in the soul.

Thus, the soul is the first efficient cause of the body's development as well as the final cause of its functions and structure, which are internally related to the soul's essence.[30] The functional demands of the soul's essence determine the character of the tools, but they, in turn, constrain and direct the various chemical processes that take place in the body as a whole. In this way, MA implies that the organism as a whole (the soul) is ontologically prior to its bodily parts. This understanding of the soul's essence, along with the soul's presence in and to the body, makes such an essence very similar to the notion of information as it is used in biology today.

Moreover, an organism's parts are actually modes or inseparable parts that stand in internal relations to other parts and to the soul's individuated essence (Socrates' very own human personhood); they are literally functional entities constituted by their role in the organism as a whole. The body is developed and grows in a goal directed way by means of a series of law-like developmental events, rooted in the internal essence of the soul. The first-efficient cause of the characteristics of an organism's body is its soul (which contains a blueprint or information in its individuated essence); the various body parts, including DNA and genes, are important instrumental causes the soul uses to produce the traits that arise. This sort

[30] Cf. Tom Kaiser, "Is DNA the Soul?" (presented paper, West Coast Meeting of the Society for Aristotelian and Thomistic Studies, June 14, 2014). The paper is posted at https://thomasaquinas.edu/pdfs/aquinas-review/2015.pdf.

of view, along with the holism with which it is associated, is also gaining ascendency in biology.[31]

In summary, according to the classic Aristotelian view of substance expressed in MA: (1) the organism as a whole (the soul) is ontologically prior to its inseparable parts/modes; (2) the parts of the organism's body stand in internal relations to other parts and to the soul's essence and they are literally functional entities/modes (the heart functions literally to pump blood); (3) the operational functions of the body are rooted in the internal structure of the soul, and in this way, the internal structure or essence is the blueprint, the information that is responsible for the body's structure and functions; (4) the body is developed and grows in a goal directed way as a series of developmental events that occur in a law-like way rooted in the internal essence of the human soul; (5) the first efficient cause of the characteristics of the human body is the soul, and various body parts, including DNA and genes, are important instrumental causes the soul uses to produce the traits that arise; (6) the body is a mode of the soul (the soul could exist without the body but not conversely; a body without a soul is a corpse), and as such it is an ensouled physical structure; thus, there are two aspects to the body—a soulish, immaterial and a physical aspect.

I now turn to two final reflections. First, I want to explain how conscious states (e.g., thoughts, memories, sensations) are and are not in the body. To begin with, it is important to say that here, as usual, the methods and findings of neuroscience are unable to address the question and, in general, are largely irrelevant to the central questions that constitute philosophy of mind.[32] To see this, consider the discovery that if one's mirror neurons are damaged, then one cannot feel empathy for another. How are we to explain this? Three empirically equivalent solutions come to mind: (1) strict physicalism (a feeling of empathy is identical to the firings of mirror

---

[31] See Brian Goodwin, *How the Leopard Changed Its Spots* (New York: Simon & Schuster, 1994); Michael Denton, Govindasamy Kumaramanickavel, and Michael Legge, "Cells as Irreducible Wholes: The Failure of Mechanism and the Possibility of an Organicist Revival," *Biology & Philosophy* 28, no. 1 (2013): 31–52.

[32] J. P. Moreland, "A Christian Perspective on the Impact of Modern Science on Philosophy of Mind," *Perspectives on Science and Christian Faith* 55, no. 1 (March 2003): 2–12. It is important to note that Willard thought the same thing. See Dallas Willard, "Reductionism: A Response to Professor Ellis," accessed November 27, 2017, http://www.dwillard.org/articles/artview.asp?artID=117. Dallas also makes clear in this article that he has no penchant for non-reductive physicalism.

neurons); (2) mere property dualism (a feeling of empathy is an irreducible state of consciousness in the brain whose obtaining depends on the firing of mirror neurons); and (3) substance dualism (a feeling of empathy is an irreducible state of consciousness in the soul whose obtaining depends, while embodied, on the firing of mirror neurons). No empirical datum can pick out which of these three is correct, nor does an appeal to epistemic simplicity help. Epistemic simplicity is a tie-breaker, and the substance dualist will insist that the arguments and evidence for substance dualism are better than those for the other two options mentioned above.

Now consider a music CD (it would be more technically accurate to employ vinyl records, but for communication purposes, I will stick with a CD). Strictly speaking, there is no music in the CD; there are only grooves. But if the CD is not damaged, when placed in the right retrieval system, the grooves trigger musical sounds. According to my Thomistic-like view, the body is an ensouled physical structure. The soul is fully present at each point of the body, and its essence informs the body and gives it its nature as *living human* body. Thus, for a current human body to be a body, it must have a soulish and a physical dimension to it.

Now certain grooves associated with memories, thoughts, sensations, and so forth are formed and stored in the physical dimension of the body. (Since the physical aspect of the body is brute matter and a complex aggregate according to physical theory, it cannot literally store conscious states. Brute matter is just the wrong type of thing to possess consciousness. Moreover, whatever the physical aspect of the body stores is spatially extended, but most, if not all, mental states are unextended.) But when these are triggered, whether spontaneously by getting hit in the knee or by the mind searching to bring back a memory, the conscious state will obtain in the soulish aspect of the body. Since the soulish aspect of the body is just the soul being holenmerically present to and in the body, it is the soul that exemplifies conscious properties, not the physical body.

Thus, MA explains and entails the things in Dallas's model that were important to him:

(1) The human person is an immaterial substance, namely, the thin particular or soul. The unifying, developing, coordinating entity is the essence of the soul.

(2) It contains and organizes/coordinates its various faculties/modes (e.g., mind, emotions), and the body is a mode of the soul like the other faculties. So, in my view, there is a unifying factor to the aspects of the human person; it is the essence of the soul, not the soul per se.

(3) The body is not just physical. The physical aspect of the body contains habitually formed grooves that must be replaced through bodily practices that shape the body's grooves more in accordance with the nature of the kingdom. The soulish aspect of the body contains meanings, sensations, and other conscious states since the soul is fully present at the place of, say, the sensation, and the body qua soul contains the conscious state.

Dallas's model of the human person is rich and deep. And it has many practical implications for life in the kingdom. I have tried to clarify certain features of his model that seemed to need such clarification, to surface and provide answers while staying within his model to some problems in need of solution. But certain difficulties regarding his view of the nature and role of the soul seem problematic, at least to me, so I have offered a slightly different model that, I hope, is in the spirit of Dallas's views and that accomplishes the goals he thought to be important.[33]

[33] I want to thank Steve Porter, Greg Jesson, and Jason Fikes for a number of very insightful, valuable comments they made on earlier drafts of this chapter.

3

NEITHER BECAUSE NOR IN SPITE OF

A Critical Reflection on Willard's Read of the Beatitudes

GREGG TEN ELSHOF

Biola University

Abstract: In *The Divine Conspiracy*, Dallas Willard offers a much-needed corrective to a prevailing understanding of the Beatitudes according to which they are virtues or conditions for blessing in God's kingdom. Unfortunately, Willard weds this corrective to an implausible read of the more positive sounding beatitudes (e.g., purity of heart and peacemaking), according to which they are vices or unattractive conditions *in spite of which* one can be blessed. In what follows, I hope to rescue the main thrust of Willard's gloss on the beatitudes from his interpretation of these particular traits.

In his foreword to Dallas Willard's masterpiece, *The Divine Conspiracy*, Richard Foster calls Willard's treatment of the beatitudes a stunning and soul-satisfying banquet that upsets many of our common notions of this famous passage. He goes on to say that the entire book is well worth the discussion of these few verses alone (*The Divine Conspiracy*, x).[1] Countless readers, no doubt, have been brought for the first time into a reading of the

[1] Short titles and parenthetical references are used throughout for the Willardian corpus. See *Hearing God: Developing a Conversational Relationship with God*, 3rd ed. (Downers Grove, IL: InterVarsity Press, 1999); *The Spirit of the Disciplines: Understanding How God Changes Lives* (New York: HarperCollins, 1988); *The Divine Conspiracy: Rediscovering Our Hidden Life in God* (New York: HarperCollins, 1997); *Renovation of the Heart: Putting on the Character*

beatitudes that they can make sense of and that has relevance for their lives thanks to Willard's contribution. Unfortunately, though, Willard's gloss on the beatitudes seems to force an unsatisfying interpretation of what it means to be "pure of heart," "merciful," or "a peacemaker," and some have rejected his account of the beatitudes because of what it seems to imply about these traits. It is the purpose of these reflections to suggest that the main thrust of Willard's gloss on the beatitudes can be rescued from his interpretation of these traits.

Because of . . .

As a foil for the presentation of his own view, Willard introduces a widespread understanding of the beatitudes, according to which they are instructions for how to be blessed. According to this teaching, each of the beatitudes gives us a condition that is especially pleasing to God, good for human beings, or conducive to full participation in God's kingdom. They are virtues or excellences in the economy of God's Way. To live appropriately in response to the beatitudes, then, is to be set upon a course of life that would make these conditions a reality in one's own experience. It is to be on the path toward becoming increasingly poor in spirit, mournful, peacemaking, pure of heart, and so on. According to this interpretation of the beatitudes, one is blessed precisely *because of* and to the extent that one has taken on the traits and conditions listed. If you want the fullness of blessing available in God's economy, you must become (either by grace or by effort or by some combination of both) poor in spirit, persecuted, merciful, pure of heart, and so on.

Willard argues at length against this widespread understanding of the beatitudes. At the center of his critique is the claim that it presents us with a profoundly counter-intuitive and unattractive picture of the good life. It is true that a few of the beatitudes look like virtues or ideals (e.g., "peacemaker" and "pure of heart"). But beyond endorsing these virtues, the view in question suggests that the Christian ideal is to become poor, sad, weak, mild, and persecuted—hardly the kind of person we naturally envision reigning with and for Christ over his created order for all of eternity. If

of Christ (Colorado Springs: NavPress, 2002); *Knowing Christ Today: Why We Can Trust Spiritual Knowledge* (New York: HarperCollins, 2009).

the news of the kingdom is that you can find your way into a life characterized by hunger, poverty, sadness, weakness, persecution, and spiritual bankruptcy, then most people will need considerable reprogramming to receive the news as "gospel" good news.

In order to make this a plausible description of the ideal Christian, these conditions *must* be interpreted in such a way as to make them laudable or otherwise attractive. "Poor in spirit," for example, will be given to mean "humble" or "aware of one's own spiritual bankruptcy." But this, complains Willard, is simply not what the text says. Jesus was a fan of humility. He had language to discuss humility and often employed it. He does not here. In the beatitudes, he speaks instead of spiritual bankruptcy and simple poverty (financial poverty) themselves. Likewise, if the condition he wished to describe were one of *recognizing* one's own poverty or spiritual poverty, he would have said so. But he does not. He simply pronounces blessing on those without spiritual and financial resources—without any hint of reference to awareness of the poverty. Similarly implausible interpretations are required, argues Willard, in order to make the whole list of beatitudes into laudable traits that can service as conditions for blessing in God's kingdom or as ideals for the Christian life.

It is worth noting here that the critique stands whether the beatitudes are taken to be conditions for blessing *or* ideals. Some who deny that the beatitudes are conditions for blessing go on to affirm them as ideals or virtues of Christian living.[2] On this view, the characteristics listed in the beatitudes are not pre-requisites for entrance into God's kingdom. But since they are understood as virtues or ideals, they will still need to be interpreted in such a way as to make them plausible *as* virtues or laudable ideals. So, for example, "spiritual bankruptcy" becomes "awareness of spiritual bankruptcy" or "humility." But, again, Jesus simply does not make this point.

---

[2] See, e.g., Glen Stassen and David P. Gushee, *Kingdom Ethics* (Downers Grove, IL: InterVarsity Press, 2003), 37–40; Michael J. Wilkins, *The NIV Application Commentary: Matthew* (Grand Rapids, MI: Zondervan, 2004), esp. 217–19; Joel B. Green, Scot McKnight, and I. Howard Marshall, *Dictionary of Jesus and the Gospels* (Downers Grove, IL: InterVarsity Press, 1992), esp. 216.

In Spite of . . .

The beatitudes, says Willard, are not a list of instructions for receiving blessing. Nor do they give us a handy list of Christian virtues. Instead, Willard argues they are "explanations and illustrations, drawn from the immediate setting, of the present availability of the kingdom through personal relationship to Jesus" (*The Divine Conspiracy*, 106). According to Willard, Jesus is drawing on the prophetic expectation of fortune-reversal associated with the coming of God's kingdom. He uses his audience (filled with the religious, social, physical, and financial zeros of his day) to illustrate and emphasize the first-shall-be-last consequences of the Messianic reign. He overturns a prevailing understanding about who could be a recipient of blessing when God's kingdom finally broke into human history through Messiah.

Jesus' audience had been conditioned to think that folks like the Pharisees (the rich, the powerful, the privileged, and those seemingly full of spirituality and righteousness) were well positioned to receive the blessings of the kingdom but that they, themselves, were not. That they had made their way *off* of God's list of folks to be blessed was evidenced (for them) by their religious and spiritual poverty, their sickness, their social exclusion, and their persecution. They would have thought themselves more likely recipients of the judgments associated with the coming of Messiah than the blessings. They were starving to be righteous since it was precisely their unrighteousness (or that of their fathers) that excluded them from society, from privilege, from physical health and well-being, and from financial success. To these, according to Willard, Jesus came and made the shocking announcement that full participation in the kingdom of God was presently available *to everybody* (now imagine him pointing at the audience)—even *y'all!*

Spiritual bankruptcy, then, is not a condition *because of which* one is positioned well to receive the kingdom. It is a condition *in spite of which* one is positioned well to receive the kingdom. Jesus is not inviting his audience to pursue, idealize, or even recognize poverty—spiritual or otherwise. (Is there really any doubt that these folks were aware of their spiritual and financial poverty? Did anyone ever call on them to produce or supply "goods" of either sort?) Jesus is giving them the incredibly good news that their bankruptcy is not a condition that disqualifies them from blessing.

Contrary to their expectations, they were perfectly well positioned to walk right into the blessings of God's presently available kingdom—this despite the fact that their condition was nothing like that of the Pharisees whom they assumed to be uniquely positioned (or, at least, best positioned) for blessing.

But there is trouble for Willard's view, too. It makes good sense to say to someone that they can receive God's blessing *despite* their poverty, spiritual bankruptcy, persecution, and tragic circumstances, because they might plausibly have taken these conditions as evidence that God had no intention of blessing them. But what about being pure of heart? What of the peacemaker? Can Jesus plausibly be construed as announcing that you can receive God's blessing today *even though—despite the fact that*—you are pure of heart? This is plausible, it seems, only if there was a widespread assumption that being pure of heart disqualified you from the blessings of God's kingdom. But who would have thought a thing like that? Similar troubles arise, it seems, for the other more positive-sounding beatitudes (e.g., merciful, peacemaker).

Saving this view thus may require an understanding of these more positive-sounding beatitudes that renders plausible the suggestion that they would have been thought of as possibly disqualifying one from the good life or from God's blessing. Cognizant of this seeming requirement, Willard provides such an understanding. To be pure of heart, according to Willard, is to be a perfectionist—someone who is a pain to himself and everyone else around because nothing is ever good enough. But blessing is available to these miserable people *despite their purity of heart* (i.e., despite the perfectionism that renders them otherwise miserable). The peacemaker is the one who somehow always finds herself in the miserable middle position—hated by both sides. Blessing is available to her *despite* this miserable condition. The merciful person is the person who, in the world's economy, is constantly taken advantage of. But the good news is that God's blessing is available to this person despite the worldly disadvantage of having been merciful.

But on its face, it is just not very plausible that Jesus meant to teach about perfectionism with his talk of purity of heart. At least, this is no more plausible than the suggestion that Jesus meant to teach about humility with his talk of spiritual poverty. And while it is likely that Jesus' audience considered poverty and tragic circumstance to be evidence of exclusion from God's blessing[3], it is unlikely that they thought of peacemaking, mercy, and purity of heart in these terms.

Two Failed Unifying Themes

So far, two very different ideas emerge about what is happening in the beatitudes. With the first view, we get a collection of conditions for blessing or ideals for the Christian life. In this view, living appropriately in response to the beatitudes is a matter of having one's life come into conformity (either by grace or by effort or both) with the description we find in the text. To live appropriately in response to the beatitudes is to be increasingly poor, poor in spirit, mourning, peace-making, pure of heart, and so on. But this requires making ideals of hunger, poverty, spiritual bankruptcy, and sadness, or adjusting our understanding of these terms so that the conditions they denote fit our existing ideals.

On Willard's view, we get a collection of illustrations intended to demonstrate the availability of God's blessing to *everyone*—even those thought of as least likely to receive it. Since the illustrations are intended to correct widespread assumptions about who could and who could not receive God's blessing, they each take a condition thought of as a disqualifier of blessing and pronounce the availability of blessing on folks in that condition. To live appropriately in response to the beatitudes is to be ready to pronounce the availability of God's kingdom to exactly *everyone*—even those folks who are often thought of as least well positioned to receive it (a terrorist cell leader, perhaps, or a single mother who works nights at the strip club). But this requires the plausibility of purity of heart, mercy, and peace-making as potential disqualifiers from God's blessing or adjusting our understanding of these terms so that the conditions they denote might plausibly be thought of as disqualifiers.

The beatitudes seem to resist smooth unification under either of these descriptions. They seem not to be conditions *because of which* blessing becomes available to us. But neither do they seem to be conditions *in spite of which* blessing is available. How then should the beatitudes be unified?

[3] See, for example, John 9:1–2.

Neither Because of Nor in Spite of . . .

In what follows, I wish to affirm Willard's general suggestion about what Jesus is doing in the beatitudes. Jesus is announcing that " . . . no one is beyond beatitude, because the rule of God from the heavens is available to all. Everyone can reach it and it can reach everyone" (*The Divine Conspiracy*, 122). Moreover, I wish to affirm his suggestion that the specific conditions Jesus lists were intended to overturn prevailing assumptions about who could receive God's blessing (folks like the Pharisees) and who could not (folks like Jesus' audience). It would not have done much good to give instructions about how to move forward into life in God's kingdom to an audience who thought themselves excluded from the very possibility of such a thing. They would never have bothered to do what he said. The first order of business was to convince his audience that the good news about God's kingdom was, indeed, good news *for everybody—including them!* This is the goal of the beatitudes.

What I wish to leave behind from Willard's interpretation is the suggestion that Jesus accomplishes this goal by giving his audience a list of conditions *in spite of which* blessing could be theirs. But if this is not a list of conditions *in spite of which* blessing could be received, what is it? What unifies this list of conditions/traits if not that? In what follows, I offer two unifying themes: the "anti-Pharisee theme" and the "spectrum theme." Neither of these themes depends on the other for its plausibility. They are, in that sense, independent. One could reasonably accept either while rejecting the other. But they are not exclusive. Both, I think, accurately represent the unity of the beatitudes.

The Anti-Pharisee Theme

What Jesus most needs to get across to his audience at the front end of this talk is that the life he is about to describe—a life of blessing in God's kingdom—is really and truly available to them. What they *think* is that when the Messiah comes and the kingdom really breaks into human history, they (the poor, the excluded, the spiritually impoverished, the sick, the demon-possessed) are not at all well positioned to receive the blessing. If asked to point to a model of readiness for blessing in God's kingdom, they would have pointed to the Pharisees. So what Jesus needs to do is to make it as clear as possible that someone can look not at all like a Pharisee and be perfectly positioned to walk into the kingdom.

Think about the beatitudes in connection with how Jesus' audience (the sick, poor, spiritually impoverished, demon-possessed, and socially excluded) would have perceived the Pharisees. Jesus says, "Blessed are the poor in spirit." If we are members of this audience, that does not sound like a Pharisee. That sounds a lot like *us*! The Pharisees were the ones with the spiritual goods! "Blessed are those who mourn." Once again, the Pharisees lived lives of honor and privilege. These hungry, sick, and excluded folk were doing the lion's share of the mourning. "Blessed are the meek." I doubt these folks experienced the Pharisees as a very meek group. There is good reason to think they were often harsh and unfeeling in their enforcement of the law. "Blessed are those who hunger and thirst for righteousness." Jesus' audience did not think of the Pharisees as starving or desperate to be righteous. When it came to righteousness, they were full of it. It was the audience who craved to be righteous. Righteousness, for this audience, would mean re-entry into society, health, and well-being. "Blessed are the merciful." This audience did not experience the Pharisees as a merciful bunch. "Blessed are the pure of heart." What socially excluded group does not question the purity of the ruling class? This audience surely suspected that the Pharisees were mixed in their motives. "Blessed are the Peacemakers." The New Testament does not give us the Pharisees as a particularly peace-making group. They were regularly stirring up controversy and generating strife. "Blessed are those who are persecuted for righteousness." The Pharisees were not persecuted for their righteousness. In fact, they were in a position of power and privilege because of it.

What all of these conditions have in common is that they are *not* true of the Pharisees (or would not have been thought true of the Pharisees by Jesus' audience). This is not a list of virtues or ideals. But neither is it a list of unfortunate characteristics that might be thought of as disqualifying one from blessing in God's kingdom—traits *in spite of which* one can be blessed. Some of the beatitudes give us unfortunate characteristics. Others give us virtues. What all of these things have in common, though, is that they would not have been thought true of the Pharisees or the other members of the ruling religious class. Jesus is saying, as forcefully as he can, "You don't have to look anything like *them*. In fact, you can look an awful lot like *y'all*!"

Spectrum Theme

I had a class not long ago with a basketball player (David) who sat in the back corner of the room and a paraplegic (Chris) who sat up near the front. I told the class to get out their calendars because I had an important announcement to make and that they would probably want to make significant adjustments to their schedules in light of it. I then announced to them that an NBA scout would be on campus all next week for the purpose of recruiting players. They did not believe me. But I asked them to humor me and pretend to believe me. They did. But only David seemed to be doing anything at all with his calendar—drawing lines through every appointment and making notes to himself to phone friends and cancel commitments. Nobody else made any adjustments *at all* to their calendars. And we all know why. It is not that they thought the life of an NBA player would be unattractive. Many would have loved that life. But the announcement was clearly not of any relevance for them. They knew themselves to be excluded at the very outset from the opportunity I was presenting.

Next I pointed to a tall young woman in the front row. "Hannah," I said, "they're looking for a strong woman to fill the forward position." Confusion. Did he say "NBA" or "WNBA"? Suddenly Hannah was paying more attention to her calendar and David was putting his away. Next I pointed to Chris and said that they were looking for folks *just like him* to play point guard. Chris? In a wheelchair? Finally, I pointed at David and said that they really needed an outside shooter and that he should think about showing up for the tryouts.

I asked my class what they were experiencing. Confusion! They thought they knew what a good candidate for the NBA looked like. But when they tried to take me seriously and tried to imagine that what I said was true, they found themselves completely clueless about what the NBA was doing—what it would look like after this next scouting season. Were I only to have pointed to Hannah, they would have understood me to be talking about the WNBA. Were I only to have pointed to Chris, they might have thought I was talking about a wheelchair league. Were I only to have pointed to David, it would have simply confirmed their limited view of who could play in the NBA. But as it stands, they found themselves wondering if, maybe, the NBA were being restructured so that *everyone* could play. This would be good news indeed (so long as they were not also massively restructuring the pay scale)! Suddenly *everyone in the room* had reason to adjust their lives in the light of this news about the availability of NBA life. News that would have been dismissed as irrelevant to all but a very few was now causing alterations in the schedules of the most unlikely of people.

Jesus came with news that the kingdom life is available—that a life of unimaginable goodness, strength, and joy is ours for the taking and that we should re-organize our affairs in order to lay hold of it. But he knew that his news would be dismissed as irrelevant to all but a select few who were thought of as well positioned to be blessed by God. In the beatitudes, he cites a full spectrum of conditions in order to make clear to his audience that this is for *everyone*. Jesus drives home the suggestion that *everyone* can enter with a series of illustrations along a very wide spectrum that includes virtues *and* unfortunate conditions.

The Apostle Paul gives us a parallel teaching both in his letter to the Galatians (chapter 3) and in his letter to the Colossians (chapter 3). He informs his readers that in Christ there is no Greek or Jew, circumcised or uncircumcised, male or female, slave or free. Paul is saying that the life of Christ is available to *everyone*. It is obvious that Paul is not offering a list of conditions *because of which* one can be in Christ—though it is true that some of these characteristics are attractive and to be sought after (e.g., freedom as opposed to slavery). But neither is Paul offering a list of characteristics *despite which* one can be in Christ. Though some of the characteristics would have been thought of as potential disqualifiers from full participation in Christ (being a slave, being a woman, being uncircumcised, being a Scythian), others clearly would not have been (e.g., being a man, being a Jew, being free). Nobody would have thought that being free might somehow disqualify you from full participation in the life of Christ. Rather, Paul is presenting as wide a spectrum as possible in order to highlight the irrelevance of these distinctions to the life available in Christ Jesus. Christ is *all and in all*!

This is precisely the message of Jesus in the beatitudes. The life of blessing in God's kingdom is available to *everyone* and *everyone* should adjust his or her calendars accordingly. In order to emphasize the universal availability of this life, Jesus informs his listeners that they need not look like the Pharisees and he illustrates the availability of the kingdom by pointing to a wide spectrum of conditions. He is not saying that the kingdom is available *because of* the having of these characteristics—though it is true that some of these characteristics are attractive and to be sought after (e.g., peacemaking, mercy, and purity of heart). But neither is he saying that the kingdom is available *despite* the having of these characteristics—though some of them would have been thought of as potentially disqualifying one from blessing in God's kingdom (e.g., poverty, spiritual bankruptcy). Rather, Jesus is presenting a wide spectrum of conditions in order to highlight the irrelevance of these conditions to the availability of God's kingdom life now.

Willard has it right, then, in his understanding of how we ought to live in response to the beatitudes. We ought to stand ready to invite absolutely anyone at all into the life of Christ. The distinctions we might take to be relevant to a consideration of one's suitability to take up discipleship to Jesus simply are not relevant—gay or straight, tattooed or not, piercings or not, married or single, Protestant, Catholic, Orthodox, atheist, or terrorist. None of these conditions disqualifies a would-be disciple of Jesus from surrendering his or her life today and walking into the fullness of life in God's great economy. This is the good news of the gospel. The good hermeneutical news is that we do not have to think of peacemaking and purity of heart as unattractive qualities in spite of which we can be blessed in order to understand Jesus to be preaching this gospel good news in the beatitudes.[4]

---

[4] Many thanks to Tom Crisp, Dallas Willard, and two anonymous referees for their thoughtful interactions with an earlier draft of this chapter.

4

REDEEMING MORAL FORMATION

The Unity of Spiritual and Moral Formation in Willardian Thought

AARON PRESTON

Valparaiso University

Abstract: This chapter offers an interpretation of Dallas Willard's views on the relation of morality to spirituality by way of a critique of a recent article by John Coe—or perhaps a critique of Coe by way of an interpretation of Willard. Coe has argued that a certain erroneous view of the relationship between moral and spiritual formation poses a serious threat to the latter by encouraging believers to hide spiritual and moral failures behind their moral successes. In this he is correct, but his own approach to the matter poses an equally serious threat by obscuring the fact that moral formation is integral to spiritual formation. In order to address the matter successfully, we need an adequate view of the *positive* relationship between moral and spiritual formation. Such a view is implicit in the work of Dallas Willard. My aim is to make this view explicit.

1. Coe on Moral and Spiritual Formation

In the inaugural issue of the *Journal of Spiritual Formation and Soul Care*, John Coe argued that many Christians are hampered in their quest for spiritual growth by what he calls "the moral temptation," the temptation to substitute *moral* formation for *spiritual* formation.[1] Coe has put his finger on a genuine problem. In fact, I think it amounts to nothing more or less than that familiar adversary of grace, *legalism* (a term he also uses to describe the problem). However, I think that his approach to it is flawed in two ways. First, using the label "moral formation" for legalism threatens to mislead. Genuine moral formation is not legalistic, and is an important dimension of spiritual formation, for Christians and non-Christians alike. But Coe's presentation of spiritual and moral formation as *opposed* may cause readers to miss both the important *fact that*, and the important *ways in which*, the two are united—a result ultimately as detrimental to spiritual formation as the legalism Coe sets out to address. Second, insofar as Coe has put his finger on a genuine problem (i.e., legalism), I fear the remedy he proposes can have only limited success; for it generates conditions favorable to the very problem of legalism that it is meant to solve. In this chapter I will be able to address only the first of these flaws, leaving the second for future work.

Before making my case against Coe, I want to acknowledge that the distance between us *may* not be as great as the foregoing comments may suggest; for there is some evidence that his critique of "moral formation" applies to something that is "moral" only in a carefully qualified, and in fact an *ironic*, sense. In the opening pages of his article, Coe identifies "the moral temptation" as follows:

> The moral temptation is the attempt to deal with our spiritual failure, guilt and shame by means of spiritual efforts, by attempting to perfect one's self in the power of the self. It is the attempt of the well-intentioned believer to use spiritual formation, spiritual disciplines, ministry, service, obedience—being good in general—as a way to *relieve the burden of spiritual failure, lack of love and the guilt and shame that results. It is the temptation to try to relieve a burden that Christ alone can relieve.*[2]

So it seems that by "moral formation" Coe means to indicate a *misuse* of what ordinarily would count as spiritual/religious or moral activities. And

---

[1] John Coe, "Resisting the Temptation of Moral Formation: Opening to *Spiritual* Formation in the Cross and the Spirit," *Journal of Spiritual Formation and Soul Care* 1, no. 1 (2008): 54–78.

[2] Coe, "Resisting the Temptation," 55–56.

it is a misuse, I submit, precisely because it involves the mistaken idea (and attitude) that good deeds "make up for" misdeeds, whether before God or anyone else. It is a simple fact of personal relationships *in specie* (whether the persons are divine, human, or otherwise) that misdeeds can never be "made up for" by counterbalancing them with good deeds. They can only be repented of, apologized for, and forgiven. To think otherwise is to assume that acceptance, affection, and so on—the qualities of desirable personal relationships—can be "bought." Such an assumption can be seen only as a manifestation of ignorance, foolishness, or arrogance, and this renders the associated activities—the attempts to "buy" the relationship—neither genuinely spiritual, nor genuinely moral.

Thus, hot on the heels of this last statement, Coe rightly offers the following terminological proviso:

> Throughout this paper, . . . I will be using the term[s] "moralism" and "moral" in a certain pejorative manner in order to make a point. What I mean by *moralism* [or moral formation] is any attempt on the part of the believer or unbeliever to deal with guilt and shame before God and others or to try to grow oneself by being good *in the power of the self, to live the moral life in autonomy from the transformative power of the Spirit.*[3]

Furthermore, he acknowledges that

> the Christian has the possibility of being the most "moral" in the fullest and best sense of the term. That is, it is possible for the believer to be good and grow in virtue not as a way to deal with failure, guilt and shame in the Christian life but to do so in freedom, on the basis of the cross and in the Spirit.[4]

These two statements seem to imply that "moral formation" in Coe's special sense is a narrowly restricted phenomenon that leaves room for a *genuine* type of moral formation that is at least *not opposed* to spiritual formation. (Whether it would be *integral* to spiritual formation is a further matter, and Coe's paper gives no clear indication what his view on this might be.)

---

[3] Coe, "Resisting the Temptation," 56. Italics original.
[4] Coe, "Resisting the Temptation," 56.

Thus, perhaps the first of my criticisms is misguided: perhaps I am wrong to worry that his attack on "moral formation" threatens to mislead by obscuring the unity of spiritual and moral formation.

Perhaps. But I still worry. For there are also indications that Coe intends "moral formation" in his special sense to include *everything normally recognized as morality*, at least by those who have thought seriously about it. First among these indications are his claims about the persistence of morality in our fallen world. Coe comes to this issue because he anticipates that readers will see a paradox in his claim that humans are tempted to be *moral* rather than *immoral*. But it is difficult to see why anyone would find this claim paradoxical, given that Coe is using "moral" (etc.) to name something other than genuine morality, something that is, in fact, a subtle form of moral failure. Thus, the "paradox" here is merely verbal, not substantive, and it should be easily avoided with a bit of terminological clarification such as Coe's proviso. But instead of sending us back to his proviso to clear up the confusion, Coe begins to explain why we might be tempted to engage in *morality as normally understood*:

> [M]ost humans throughout history have learned that a life of rampant immorality does not work in the long run [and for this reason they] have tended to congregate in social communities with some wisdom or moral codes for the sake of human flourishing.[5]

Although they understand the exact shape and texture of "flourishing" differently, no major ethical thinker has ever departed entirely from the idea that being good is worth the effort because of its relationship to human flourishing. Plato, Aristotle, Augustine (at his best), Aquinas, and Butler all fit this model, as do the Epicureans, the Stoics, Hobbes, and the classical Utilitarians. Even Kant, famous (or infamous) for defending a morality of "duty for duty's sake," grounds his views in our nature as rational beings, and in what it means for such beings to attain their highest end (to flourish).[6] So, by focusing on the connection between morality and flourishing as an explanation for humanity's persisting interest in morality, Coe seems to

[5] Coe, "Resisting the Temptation," 60.

[6] Immanuel Kant, *Grounding for the Metaphysics of Morals*, 3rd ed., translated by James W. Ellington (Indianapolis: Hackett, 1993), 9.

be focusing on human morality *as such*, and not some narrower phenomenon. This is immediately confirmed when, at the end of the last passage cited, Coe identifies the universal human practice of organizing social life by means of moral codes or moral wisdom so as to facilitate flourishing as "a kind of encouraged moralism."[7] I take it that "moralism" here is to be understood in the pejorative sense stipulated in Coe's proviso. If so, he is here identifying human morality *as such* with moralism in that pejorative sense.

This is also indicated by his assertion—for which he offers no argument—that humans are attracted to morality not only on account of its connection with human flourishing, but also, and even more so, by its usefulness in hiding from God:

> [M]ore importantly [than the point about flourishing] . . . the reason why human beings have been tempted to be moral and why they have rejected a thoroughgoing immorality is that this is the most effective human strategy to hide from God.[8]

That the connection between morality and human flourishing should be secondary to its usefulness in hiding from God as an explanation for morality's persistence in our fallen world is contrary to the stated interests and motivations of every major ethical thinker in both Western and Eastern traditions, all of whom see morality as an attempt to live in cooperation with nature, and thereby with its Divine author, insofar as they recognize one. Coe tacitly acknowledges this when he says that "natural morality . . . is at least partly in harmony with the way we are created," but quickly qualifies his remark by saying that "even here, it [natural morality] is a violation of natural law insofar as we were created to do good works 'in God.'"[9] As a violation of the natural law, Coe goes so far as to identify natural morality as a form of sin:

> Sin is both a violation of (a) one's relationship with God, which is the essence of sin and with (b) how God intended for humans to live in accordance to his commands and the way he created

[7] Coe, "Resisting the Temptation," 60.
[8] Coe, "Resisting the Temptation," 60.
[9] Coe, "Resisting the Temptation," 62.

> their natures (natural law). The good works of the unbeliever are still sin, in fact they reflect the *essence* of sin, insofar as they are not done "in relationship to God" but in autonomy, pride and the absence of faith. . . .[10]

Now in one sense it is trivially true that morality is genuinely moral only when it stands in its proper relationship to God: insofar as goodness is part of God's essence, and insofar as morality is a matter of people and their acts being good, those people and acts must indeed stand in an appropriate relationship—perhaps resemblance or exemplification—to God (or his essence). But I think Coe sees the requisite relationship very differently, not as a merely ontological relationship, but as an existential relationship of faith in God as revealed historically in Jesus. For Coe seems to think that any attempt to be good apart from an *explicit recognition* of one's moral *corruption* as revealed in (Coe's understanding of) the cross of Christ, and one's moral *inability* apart from the regenerative and sanctifying work of the Holy Spirit, necessarily counts as an attempt to ignore or deny one's moral failures and to cover them up with good works.

This comes out most clearly in Coe's proposed solution to the problem of moralism in Christians, which is to focus on the doctrines of justification and double imputation as understood by the Reformers. "We must learn," says Coe, "to be open to the full justification by God and the unbelievable truth that I am not only fully pardoned but also fully acceptable to God on the basis of Christ's merited righteousness that has been imputed to me and not on the basis of what I have done."[11]

This is what Coe is getting at when he identifies being moral "in the fullest and best sense of the term" as a matter of being good and growing in virtue "on the basis of the Cross and in the Spirit."[12] One can be moral "in the fullest and best sense," and in what now appears to be the only genuine sense—since otherwise one's good works count as sin rather than morality—when we accept, with the Spirit's help, that "transformation is the result of the Spirit of God opening our hearts more deeply to Christ's work on the cross and the judicial or forensic realities of justification in

[10] Coe, "Resisting the Temptation," 62.
[11] Coe, "Resisting the Temptation," 75; cf. 73–77.
[12] Coe, "Resisting the Temptation," 56.

love,"[13] and not the result of our own efforts. "Our actions work in synergy and participation with the Spirit," says Coe, "but *He is the agent of change.*"[14]

Now, if conceptualizing and grounding one's moral efforts in this way is alone capable of transforming "moralism" into genuine morality for Christians, it seems that it will also be the only way to transform "the good works of the unbeliever" from sin into genuine morality. This is why Coe thinks that, apart from an *explicit recognition* of the above theological "facts," all moral efforts count as attempts at self-justification in relation to God, and why, in turn, he says that:

> what the secular moralists of all the ages have attempted to do from the Egyptian and the Babylonian sages, to Plato and Aristotle, to the Stoics, to Kant and Mill [is] to use morality as a defense against seeing their need for a savior.[15]

And:

> From the ancient sages to Aristotle to the modern moralist, the project of morality and the claim that "I am good, I am moral" has been the most used defense as a way to hide from God and the need for a Savior.[16]

Thus, Coe identifies *morality as normally understood*, by thoughtful Christians and non-Christians alike, with "moralism" in his pejorative sense.

2. Willard on Moral and Spiritual Formation

We find a different perspective on these matters in the writings of Dallas Willard, one we can begin to see by bringing together some of his statements on "secular moralists," especially Plato, with some of his statements about spiritual and moral formation.

In "A New Age of Ancient Christian Spirituality,"[17] Willard makes a surprising remark. "When I began to study Philosophy," he says, "I saw from

---

[13] Coe, "Resisting the Temptation," 76.
[14] Coe, "Resisting the Temptation," 75.
[15] Coe, "Resisting the Temptation," 56.
[16] Coe, "Resisting the Temptation," 60.
[17] Dallas Willard, "A New Age of Ancient Christian Spirituality," in *Renewing the Christian Mind: Essays, Interviews, and Talks*, edited by Gary Black Jr. (New York: HarperOne, 2016), 146–53.

the very beginning that Plato's *Republic* is essentially a book on spiritual formation." But how can this be, since the *Republic* is normally regarded as a work of moral philosophy? Part of the answer lies in Willard's understanding of spiritual formation. In what is to my knowledge Willard's most complete statement on the nature of spiritual formation,[18] he distinguishes "three different meanings" of the term "or moments" of the phenomenon.[19] The first (hereafter, "spiritual formation$_1$") has to do with training in "special spiritual activities," spiritual disciplines, relevant to a vocation in ministry or to the spiritual life in general. The third (hereafter, "spiritual formation$_3$") is "a shaping by the spirit or by the spiritual realm, and by the Holy Spirit and other spiritual agencies involved in the kingdom of God, especially the Word of God." In between these falls the second meaning or moment (hereafter, "spiritual formation$_2$"), which is the one most directly relevant to our present interest:

> spiritual formation may be thought of as the shaping of the inner life, the spirit, or the spiritual side of the human being. The formation of the heart or will (which I believe is best taken as the "spirit") of the individual, along with the emotions and intellect, is therefore the primary focus, regardless of what overt practices may or may not be involved. Here, what is formed is explicitly the spiritual dimension of the self. We speak of *spiritual* formation in this case precisely because that which is formed (the subject matter shaped) is the spiritual aspect of personality. (*Renovation*, 19–20)[20]

---

[18] Dallas Willard, "Spiritual Formation in Christ: A Perspective on What It Is and How It Might Be Done," in *The Great Omission: Reclaiming Jesus's Essential Teachings on Discipleship* (San Francisco: HarperCollins, 2006), 68–79.

[19] "Moments" is naturally taken to suggest *sequential stages of a process*; but Willard may be using "moment" in a sense borrowed from the philosophical sub-discipline of ontology, where it means something like "a dependent or inseparable part of a whole," a part that is distinguishable in thought but not separable in reality (e.g., shape and size are "moments" of any spatial object).

[20] Short titles and parenthetical references are used throughout for the Willardian corpus. See *Hearing God: Developing a Conversational Relationship with God*, 3rd ed. (Downers Grove, IL: InterVarsity Press, 1999); *The Spirit of the Disciplines: Understanding How God Changes Lives* (New York: HarperCollins, 1988); *The Divine Conspiracy: Rediscovering Our Hidden Life in God* (New York: HarperCollins, 1997); *Renovation of the Heart: Putting on the Character of Christ* (Colorado Springs: NavPress, 2002); *Knowing Christ Today: Why We Can Trust Spiritual Knowledge* (New York: HarperCollins, 2009).

And it is in this sense, I believe, that Willard sees Plato's *Republic* as a book about spiritual formation, for in this sense "spiritual formation" just is "moral formation."

To see that this is so, one has to know a bit about Plato's moral theory, so we must turn to Plato for the next page or two. In doing so, I will sometimes make remarks that assume some prior knowledge of Plato; but for the most part, and especially on those issues crucial to understanding how Platonic moral formation is the same as spiritual formation$_2$, I will assume no prior knowledge of Plato and give as complete an account as I can while maintaining brevity.

The central question of the *Republic*, is What is justice? The word "justice" as we use it today has obvious legal overtones. To an extent, this was also true of Plato's word for justice: *dikaiosune*—which also shows up frequently in the New Testament and the Greek translation of the Old Testament (the Septuagint) that was in use during Jesus' lifetime, where it is usually translated *righteousness*. On the basis of this connection to law, one might think that justice is simply a matter of acting in accordance with certain principles, rules, or laws. Such a view is defended by several of Socrates' interlocutors in Book I of the *Republic*, including Cephalus, Polemarchus, and (in his own way) Thrasymachus. We can call this the *act-focused* theory of justice. It says that *being* a just person depends on *doing* what is just (i.e., performing just *acts*), and it usually involves the notion that the relevant acts can be nailed-down "in advance" by a set of prescriptive principles, rules, or laws.

Plato rejects this view. Through the character of Socrates, he argues that a person cannot qualify as *just* simply by acting according to laws or rules, for it is possible that a rule, perfectly useful under normal circumstances, might, in unusual circumstances, lead one to act unjustly (as when one returns a borrowed weapon to a friend who has gone insane). Moreover, it is possible to obey rules outwardly while remaining unjust inwardly (this is one lesson of the "invisibility ring" story in Book II). Plato's alternative to act-focused justice is what we may call *character-focused* justice. For Plato, being a just person has to do primarily with the inner constitution or character of the person, and the ways in which this *disposes* a person to act (character is the root, action is the fruit). So, instead of starting with a notion of just actions and defining a just person in terms of them, Plato begins with a conception of a just person and defines just action in terms of him/her.

And what is his conception of a just person? It is the conception of a person whose soul is properly ordered: ordered according to its nature, and the nature of its parts, as indicated by their natural functions. As Plato sees it, every type of thing that exists, exists to serve some good purpose. There is some activity that things of a given kind alone can do, or can do better than any other kind of thing; for example, eyes alone can see, and pruning knives cut vines better than anything else. He calls such activities "functions." And in order for anything to perform its function well, it must possess attributes that enable it to do so; for example, a pruning knife must be *sharp* in order to cut vines. These attributes, over and above those that make something the kind of thing it is, that enable it to perform its natural function well, Plato calls *virtues*. When something possesses the virtues relevant to its function, it is good.

For Plato, this general model for thinking about goodness applies to the human soul both as a whole and at the level of its individual parts. Plato tells us in Book I of the *Republic* that, as a whole, the soul's function is living, and justice is the virtue that enables it to live well. But a more detailed account of justice in terms of the soul's parts is given in Book IV. By this point in the dialogue, Plato has argued that the soul has three main components: *logos* (reason), *thumos* (heart, spirit, or emotion), and *epithumia* (desire, appetite). Reason's function is ruling or directing, since it alone is suited by nature to grasp truth and reality. But in order to rule well, it needs the virtue of wisdom. The heart or spirit's function is to enforce the wise dictates of reason, and to do this well it needs the virtue of courage. The various desires have no common function, but each of the naturally occurring desires has a function unique to itself, intended for some good purpose. For instance, hunger drives us to eat even when, as babies, we do not know what eating is or why it is important. According to Plato, the desires lack not only a common function, but also a virtue of their own. Desires can get out of hand, and so need to be kept in check by the virtue of moderation or temperance; but this is not an attribute of any desire considered in itself. Rather, it is a matter of the way a person's desires stand in relation to wise reason and courageous spirit. If one's spirit is able to keep the desires within the boundaries established by wise reason, then the soul *as a whole* is moderate. Justice also, according to Plato, is a holistic virtue—that is, applicable to the soul as a whole, rather than any of its parts considered in isolation. We may gloss Plato's definition of justice (*dikaiosune*) by saying that it is a state of a complex whole—be it a soul or anything else—in which each part performs its own function, rather than trying to perform the function of another part. In other words, it is a state in which each part of a complex whole is as it ought to be, on account of which the whole is as it ought to be. So, the soul is just when the *logos* rules wisely and the *thumos* enforces its dictates courageously, and when the *epithumia* do whatever they are meant to do, but under the cooperative guidance and restraint of *logos* and *thumos*.

We are now in a position to see why spiritual formation is the same thing as Platonic moral formation. Recalling Willard's description of spiritual formation as "the shaping of the inner life, the spirit, or the spiritual side of the human being . . . the formation of the heart or will . . . of the individual, along with the emotions and intellect," we can now see that this is exactly the task of *moral* formation as Plato understands it (thus, henceforth the reader should keep in mind that "spiritual formation$_2$" and "moral formation" will sometimes be used interchangeably, to refer to this simultaneously *spiritual* and *moral* project of formation). This is why, in chapter 5 of *The Divine Conspiracy*, in a section subtitled "*Dikaiosune*," Willard can argue for the confluence of the biblical and Athenian (i.e., Socrates, Plato, and Aristotle) traditions. As noted above, *dikaiosune* is Plato's word for "justice," and the word in biblical Greek for "righteousness." Willard makes much of this connection, arguing that, with the selection of *dikaiosune* to translate the Hebrew *tsedawkaw* and *tsehdek* in the Septuagint, "the two greatest traditions of moral reflection in the ancient world are brought together in the term *dikaiosune*" (*The Divine Conspiracy*, 146). In both the Old and New Testaments, as in Plato, Willard claims, *dikaiosune* has to do with "the character of the inner life when it is as it should be," "what it is about a person that makes him or her really right or good," or "true inner goodness."

Thus here (and elsewhere, *Renovation*, 22–25) Willard presents Jesus' take on *dikaiosune* in terms of the same contrast between act-focused and character-focused views that we see in Plato. The righteousness that Jesus calls us to is a righteousness which surpasses that of the Scribes and the Pharisees (Matt. 5:20). But, whereas many have understood this as a demand for obedience to a higher and more stringent law, Willard's view is that it is a call beyond any act-focused approach to righteousness and to a character-focused view. All the "*you-have-heard-that . . . but-I-tell-you*'s" of the Sermon on the Mount are not, according to Willard, commands to perform particular kinds of acts, but illustrations of the kinds of things that come naturally to a person whose soul is just.

Thus, what is required to surpass the righteousness of the Scribes and the Pharisees is, first and foremost, simply to approach righteousness as a matter of the inner person rather than the outward act—not a very high bar at all, once you understand it. And in fact, it is not really about "setting a bar." When Jesus makes entrance into the kingdom of God conditional upon surpassing legalistic righteousness, he is merely stating a tautology: one cannot enter something except by its entrance, and since to enter the kingdom is to align oneself with God inwardly ("the kingdom of God is in the midst of you," Luke 17:21), one cannot enter it except through an inward approach to righteousness; so long as one retains the outward, act-focused approach to righteousness characteristic of legalism, one will *inevitably* miss the entrance to God's kingdom. Accordingly, Jesus' word in Matthew 5:20 is not so much "you'd better be less rotten than the Pharisees if you want God to accept you," but more "your whole approach to righteousness must be very different than theirs if you are really going to interact with God." And if this is what is meant there, then it is fair to say that, in seeing through the shallowness of act-focused *dikaiosune* (legalism) and recognizing that genuine *dikaiosune* is a matter of the inner person, Socrates, Plato, and Aristotle were "not far from the kingdom of God" (Mark 12:34).[21]

Of course, the *locus* of *dikaiosune* (inward rather than outward) is not the only thing that matters. The *qualitative character* of *dikaiosune* matters, too. For Jesus, *dikaiosune* is not blind, cold, and unrelenting, as purely legal justice is. Instead, the rightly ordered (just) soul is a loving soul. Thus, the qualitative character of Christian *dikaiosune* is *agape* love (as described in 1 Cor. 13, for instance). But this perspective is not wholly unique to Jesus. Willard says that

[21] See Charles Finney's sermon, "Not Far from the Kingdom of God," available here: http://www.gospeltruth.net/1849-51Penny_Pulpit/500909pp_not_far_frm_kngdm.htm. Finney argues that overcoming legalism and committing oneself to honesty are both ways in which one can be "not far from the Kingdom of God." Socrates, Plato, and Aristotle were clearly "not far" in these ways.

> a really good person, as Jesus teaches, is anyone who is pervaded with love. . . . *Agape* love, perhaps the greatest contribution of Christ to human civilization, wills the good of whatever it is directed upon. It does not wish to consume it. The teaching about love that still permeates Western civilization at its better moments understands that. The highest calling of moral beings is to love. Long before the coming of Christ, this was obscurely understood. Socrates remarked, according to Plato, that "the good do their neighbors good and the bad do them evil." (*Knowing Christ Today*, 53)

And in fact, Socrates' insight into the nature of true morality went further than this, for he agreed with Jesus (who of course had not yet come in the flesh) that *dikaiosune* demands love, or at least goodwill, be extended even to enemies (*Republic* I, 331d–335). On the other hand, it is true that this aspect of Socrates' thought tends to be overshadowed by his emphasis on rationality, an emphasis which, if anything, grows stronger as we move from Socrates to Plato and then to Aristotle. This difference in emphasis between Jesus and the philosophers is significant, but not so significant as to render philosophical *dikaiosune* fundamentally opposed to Christian *dikaiosune*, as that of the Pharisees was. It is not for nothing that Nietzsche called Christianity "Platonism for the masses."[22]

Readers of Willard will know his V-I-M framework for effective personal transformation: in order to change, a person must have a clear and compelling *vision* for change, form the *intention* to act on that vision, and have the appropriate *means* to act on it.[23] The twin emphases on the inward locus and loving quality of *dikaiosune* are elements of the guiding "vision" for morality and moral formation in both the Athenian philosophical tradition and the Christian tradition; but not only in these two traditions.[24] Willard observes:

---

[22] In the Preface to *Beyond Good and Evil.*

[23] See Dallas Willard, *Renovation of the Heart*, 77–93, or "Living A Transformed Life," in *Renewing the Christian Mind*, 11–54.

[24] And not only these two points, either. Willard observes that most cultures have had a sense of the eternal significance of this life's moral development, as shown by their usually having some conception of life after death (see *The Divine Conspiracy*, 375–400, esp. 397). He even presents Socrates as having achieved, via his insights into "the very nature of the human self," a grasp of "the importance of our eternal future," but minus any insight into "the purposes of God in human history and redemption that are unique to the Gospel of Jesus"

> What makes our lives go as they do? What could make them go as they ought? . . .Thoughtful people through the ages have tried to answer these questions, and *they have with one accord found . . . that what matters most for how life goes and ought to go is what we are on the "inside."* . . . This "within" is the arena of spiritual formation and, later, transformation. (*Renovation*, 16, italics added)

And:

> . . . the only hope of humanity lies in the fact that, as our spiritual dimension has been *formed*, so it also can be *transformed.* Now and throughout the ages *this has been acknowledged by everyone who has thought deeply about our condition—from Moses, Solomon, Socrates, and Spinoza, to Marx, Nietzsche, Freud, Oprah, and current feminists and environmentalists. . . .* Disagreements have only to do with *what* in our spirit needs to be changed and *how* that change can be brought about. (*Renovation*, 14, italics added)

So, there is significant overlap between Christianity and many other traditions of spiritual formation$_2$ in recognizing the inward nature of *dikaiosune*. And as to love, Willard says:

> It is not as if Christ alone knew or taught that love . . . is the center of what is right, obligatory, and good among human beings. It is indeed an "open secret"—something that everyone deep down knows, if they will but carefully consider it. [. . .] good and evil are by and large immediately sensed, and further reveal themselves to reflection and theoretical elaboration. This perception of good and evil is the fundamental intuition of the moral life, and it is given even to small children and unsophisticates at all levels, though they may be unable to articulate or defend it. (*Knowing Christ Today*, 86)

(*The Divine Conspiracy*, 387). I focus on the two points indicated because of their greater centrality to spiritual formation$_2$, especially when understood as moral formation for life in this world.

This is not to say, of course, that everyone does carefully consider what they know deep down, or even that those who do will know how to act on this fundamental moral intuition. Willard acknowledges that, despite having this knowledge deep down, "people are wary . . . of love, perhaps because they do not know how to meet . . . the demands of love in real life" (*Knowing Christ Today*, 86). Nonetheless, these two points of vision—that the locus of *dikaiosune* is the inner person and that its fundamental quality is love—are sufficient to point a person beyond pharisaic "*dikaiosune,*" with its focus on outward behavior and rigid rule-following. Given the widespread availability of these two insights in several of the major moral and religious traditions of humankind, it follows that there is the *possibility* within these traditions of surpassing the righteousness of the scribes and the Pharisees.

But what of *means*? In the Christian context, this is where Willard's theory of asceticism, the practice of spiritual disciplines—and so spiritual formation—comes into play. Thus we see that spiritual formation is a component of spiritual formation. It is training in the means by which effective spiritual formation is achieved. Willard's thought on the role of spiritual disciplines in Christian spiritual formation is so well known I will not bother to rehash it here in any detail.[25] Suffice it to say that Willard sees spiritual growth, like the acquisition of a skill, as something requiring training and practice, in the form of spiritual disciplines such as prayer, study, solitude, silence, and fasting. Willard presented this view to the Evangelical world in 1988, in his justly famous book *The Spirit of the Disciplines*. He presented essentially the same theory to a scholarly audience three years earlier, in a 1985 paper on "An Essential but Neglected Element in the Christian Theory of the *Moral* Life" (his subtitle, italics added). From this we may infer that Willard sees Christian spiritual and moral formation united in means, just as in vision, thus reinforcing the fact that Christian spiritual formation$_2$ is identical to Christian moral formation.

Moreover, as in the case of vision, Willard recognizes significant overlap in means between Christian and non-Christian traditions of spiritual formation:

---

[25] See Willard, *The Spirit of the Disciplines*, or almost any of Willard's papers referenced in these footnotes, most of which contain sections on the role of spiritual disciplines in spiritual formation.

> Thoughtful and religiously devout people of the classical and Hellenistic world, from the Ganges to the Tiber, knew that the mind and body of the human being had to be rigorously disciplined to achieve a decent individual and social existence . . . is . . . a wisdom gleaned from millennia of collective human experience. There is nothing especially religious about it, though every religion of historical significance is accepted and inculcated in one way or another. It has a special importance in religion, but it is also just good sense about human nature. (*The Spirit of the Disciplines*, 99)

Thus, Willard says, "whether or not we are religious, ascetic practices are relevant to the kinds of persons we become. Without them we can only drift, subject to whatever influences come our way. With them, on the other hand, we have the possibility of *some* significant control over our moral future."[26]

One might question whether it would occur to anyone outside of religious context to employ "ascetic practices" as means of moral formation. But Willard has a conception of asceticism broad enough to include practices with no overtly religious connections. In *The Spirit of the Disciplines*, Willard quotes R. L. Nettleship approvingly:

> If asceticism means the disciplined effort to attain an end which cannot be attained without giving up many things often considered desirable, the philosophical life (as Plato saw it) is ascetic; but if it means giving up for the sake of giving up, there is no asceticism in Plato. (*The Spirit of the Disciplines*, 136)

The quotation comes in the course of an argument that Judaism is an ascetic religion: if we are willing to accept Nettleship's definition of asceticism, Willard says, then Judaism is ascetic. But, ipso facto, so then is the philosophical life as Plato saw it. And not only Plato but, by Nettleship's criterion, Socrates, Aristotle, and many other philosophical and religious moralists from the East and West—even restrained "hedonists" like Epicurus and

---

[26] Dallas Willard, "Asceticism: An Essential but Neglected Element in the Christian Theory of the Moral Life," accessed November 29, 2017, http://www.dwillard.org/articles/artview.asp?artID=122. Italics added.

John Stuart Mill—would also qualify as having employed ascetic practices, or adopted an ascetic lifestyle. Thus Willard speaks of "[t]he deep wisdom of Jesus . . . that he who would save his life must lose it (Mark 8:35–36)" as being "fully congruent with all the great traditions of religion *and ethical* culture" (*The Spirit of the Disciplines*, 131).

Of course, most non-religious traditions of moral formation will not have as full a repertoire of ascetic practices as their religious counterparts. But that is beside the point: as with vision, overlap in the means of moral formation need not be complete in order to be substantial enough to yield meaningful results. And in fact, of the world's great traditions of moral formation, contemporary Western Christianity in its standard forms is arguably among the most deficient in its use of appropriate means (this is, of course, the situation that Willard's work on spiritual formation aims to correct). Even so, Willard thinks that Christianity has a decisive advantage as a tradition of moral formation, largely on account of unique elements in its vision of moral reality: namely, the nature and availability of God and his kingdom as exemplified in the totality of Jesus' earthly ministry, from incarnation to teaching to miracles and acts of kindness to his death and resurrection. These themes deserve more attention than I can give them here, and I hope to give them that attention in future work. For now, it will have to suffice to say that on Willard's view "it was not for nothing that Christian life and teaching supplanted" its competitors in the ancient world.[27]

So there are respects in which Christianity is not only unique but superior to other traditions of moral formation, and among these is the fact that the Christian vision gives us a more complete and accurate picture of what is happening in spiritual formation$_2$. This is why Willard says that his claim about disciplines giving us some significant control over our moral future, while true for all humans generally, "is especially true for the Christian, who can also count upon an assistance beyond him or her self—though not an assistance that *replaces* our own initiative toward moral realization through planned disciplinary exercises."[28] That is, the Christian can count on spiritual formation$_3$ entering the picture alongside spiritual

[27] Dallas Willard, "Idaho Springs Inquiries Concerning Spiritual Formation," in *The Great Omission: Reclaiming Jesus's Essential Teachings on Discipleship* (New York: HarperOne, 2006), 117. Italics added.

[28] Willard, "Asceticism"; italics added.

formation$_1$ as another part of spiritual formation$_2$. In fact, Willard in one place describes God's action toward and in humans as an additional *means* of spiritual formation$_2$, one distinguished from the use of disciplines by its not being directly under human control (*Renovation*, 90). Thus we can say that both spiritual formation$_1$ and $_3$ are means of Christian spiritual formation$_2$, Christian moral formation.

But to single out the Christian as one who can "count on" God's help in the form of spiritual formation$_3$ is not to say that God helps only Christians in their attempts at moral formation. Rather, it is that the Christian vision alone gives us reason to expect and anticipate such help. Only a person who knows their local bus system and schedule can "count on" there being a bus present at a certain place and time. Someone without that knowledge can certainly sit at a bus stop, blindly hoping one will come along sooner or later, but they can not "count on it" in the same way. Of course, the bus system itself functions the same either way: buses will arrive when and where they are supposed to whether those at the bus stop are waiting with assured expectation or desperate hope. Similarly, God's help may come to the Christian and the non-Christian alike, even though only the Christian vision enables (and warrants) "counting on it." So it still makes sense to consider whether the non-Christian might also have a share in spiritual formation$_3$ as she engages in spiritual formation$_2$ by means of spiritual formation$_1$.

And Willard's answer seems to be "yes." In chapter 6 of *Knowing Christ Today*, Willard elucidates his version of "Christian pluralism." Even "the weakest form of pluralism," he says, will concede that "no one religion captures and conveys *all* truths about God (or a spiritual 'beyond'), humankind, and their relationships." that "*many* religions . . . teach some essential religious truths" which "involve important aspects of truth and goodness and must be respected as such" (72). This much is clear from what we have already seen concerning the overlap of vision among Christian and some non-Christian traditions of spiritual formation$_2$. But here Willard goes even further. He is not, of course, willing to affirm "strong pluralism" by saying that all such traditions are equal. But he is willing to say that "people of 'other' religions or no religion at all *may* be 'right with God'" (*Knowing Christ Today*, 181) on account of the condition of their hearts, despite their misunderstandings about God. "If this is so in a given case, Willard says, "it will be because their lives are centered on that same love that is expressed in the person and teachings of Jesus and of his people at their best. It will be because God is love." Quoting 1 John 4:7–8 ("Everyone who loves has been born of God and knows God. . . ."), Willard affirms that "if you really do have the kind of *agape* love in question, God is living in you and you know God, whatever else may or may not be true of you" (*Knowing Christ Today*, 182). This is Willard's version of Christian pluralism.

It is crucial to note that "knowing God" here is not solely or primarily a cognitive thing, and in no way a matter of cognitively knowing and accepting anything about Jesus as a historical figure. It is a matter of integration with God in the deepest reaches of the self by accepting as *ultimately good and worth living for* the same thing(s) that God does. Thus it is fundamentally a *moral* agreement with God, albeit one that can exist independent of any explicit recognition of God *as such*. The overlap between Christian and non-Christian traditions of spiritual formation$_2$ is, I believe, part of what makes this possible for non-Christians. Another part is that "fundamental moral intuition" of which Willard speaks. But behind both of these, I believe Willard would acknowledge the action of God Himself. He says:

> [T]he fact that God is a being whose most basic nature is *agape* love for all human beings, *regardless* of their religion or culture, means that he cares for all human beings. That is merely the reverse side of biblical monotheism, properly understood, and the heart of the Abrahamic religions. Since he is the God of all, he cares for all. He does not sit in splendid isolation demanding that all worship and obey him. He reaches out to them, calls them to himself. His grace is an active principle in the universe. And the one we call "Jesus" is also the Cosmic Christ [i.e., the Word or *Logos* of God, cf. John 1], present throughout creation and history, inextricably "with" the God of all, throughout time and eternity. . . . [T]he Lord is active among human beings generally. He is their God, whether they know it or not. . . . [W]e may be sure that God loves all people and is involved with everyone, religious or nonreligious, though they may be unaware of it or reject it if they so choose. (*Knowing Christ Today*, 176–77)

What form might God's involvement with people take when it does not include disclosing himself as God, so that people may remain unaware of his involvement with them as *his involvement* with them? There are many possible answers, some of them readily acceptable to any Christian. For instance, one can say that God interacts with all humans through "secondary causes," like the laws and forces of nature—"He causes his sun to rise on the evil and the good, and sends rain on the righteous and the unrighteous" (Matt. 5:45). A more specific providence, in the form of ordering some of the particular facts and events of a person's life, would also qualify. But why not include ordinary moral experience as well? "The Cosmic Christ," Willard reminds us, "is a light that 'enlightens everyone' (John 1:9, ESV)" (*Knowing Christ Today*, 177). But what concrete form does this universal enlightenment take in human experience? I can think of no better candidate than Willard's "fundamental moral intuition." And insofar as some non-Christian traditions of moral formation are aimed at fanning this fundamental spark of divine illumination into a flame, why not take those traditions themselves as "secondary causes" through which God interacts with people "anonymously"? Willard suggests as much when he says:

> Much that is good is to be found in every great human tradition of spiritual formation, and the Christian will do well to respect what is good wherever it is found. "Every good thing bestowed and every perfect gift is from above, coming down from the Father of lights." (James 1:17)[29]

If we are willing to go this far with Willard, then we will acknowledge that non-Christians have the possibility of growth toward genuine *dikaiosune*, and of genuine though anonymous cooperation with God, through their moral experience and their traditions of moral formation. But these possibilities will not be realized without the relevant *intention*. Do some non-Christians engage in their traditions of moral formation, or respond to their own moral experience, with a genuine intention to be good? Or do all or even most non-Christians adopt the stance of "moralism" in Coe's

---

[29] Willard, *The Great Omission*, 117. Italics added. The translation here may be Willard's own; it closely resembles the New American Standard Bible. cf. *Knowing Christ Today*, 172–73.

pejorative sense, misusing morality as a way of hiding from their own moral failures, or even from God?

While it is fairly easy to document overlap in vision and means, proving *intent* is incredibly difficult. And it is not merely that intention is a matter of the invisible, spiritual side of the self. That makes it difficult enough. But, as Willard notes in *Renovation of the Heart*, the difficulty is exacerbated by the fact that, minus the successful carrying out of one's intentions, it can be difficult to tell whether one's—even one's own—inclinations are really intentions, or whether they are mere wishes or desires (88–89). Nonetheless, Willard seems willing to grant that all human beings desire to be good, and that some, Christian or not, form genuine intentions to be good insofar as they understand goodness. It is this genuine desire to be good—and not the desire to hide from God—Willard says, that explains the universal human interest in morality, and our persisting commitment to it in our fallen world: "The quest for spiritual formation . . . is in fact an age-old and worldwide one. It is rooted in the deep personal and even biological need for goodness that haunts humanity" (*Renovation*, 22). In *Knowing Christ Today*, Willard explains one aspect of this need for goodness in terms of the inevitability of possessing a worldview: "Our worldview is simply our overall orientation in life. You cannot 'opt out' of having a worldview. You can only try to have one that most accords with reality, including the whole realm of facts concerning what is *genuinely* good" (44). Accordingly, three of the four fundamental worldview questions that Willard identifies have to do with goodness: what is well-being or "blessedness," what does it mean to be a genuinely good person, and how does one become a genuinely good person (46–50)?[30] In order merely to act in the world, one must at least *assume* answers to such questions. Thus, "a worldview is . . . a *biological* necessity for human beings (43)."

But the biological necessity of having a worldview is not the only thing that drives us to search for answers to these worldview questions, especially in the case of the three that touch upon moral value, and most especially on the question that touches upon it most directly, the question of character. These are matters of desire. As Willard says, "people long to be good, to be worthy and not just to *be*—from tiny children to the elderly exiting the

[30] The fourth question is, What is real?

human scene" (*Knowing Christ Today*, 47). Moreover, "there is a lingering suspicion that you cannot have had a good life if you failed to be a good person, and that to be a good person is a large part of genuine success, or 'blessedness'" (*Knowing Christ Today*, 48). And from this genuine desire to be good and to live a good life emerges the human project of spiritual formation or moral formation. As Willard says elsewhere,

> Spiritual formation is indeed a human project. No society has ever existed without it. The human being is not an instinctual animal which naturally develops what is required for its existence. It must be taught, and primary to what is taught (and caught) are the inner conditions of life (thought, emotions, intentions, etc.) which make social existence possible *and enable the individual to hope for a life that is good.*[31]

This gets us very close to Coe's point that the universal human practice of organizing social life by means of moral codes or moral wisdom is done for the sake of human flourishing. But as Willard describes it, the moral motives are genuine, so this does not count as "a kind of encouraged moralism" in Coe's pejorative sense.[32] Not only are the motives genuine, but, says Willard, the human moral project involves a recognition of the severe challenges to becoming a good person, and that some of these challenges come from within the self:

> The problem that confronts us here [in thinking about spiritual formation $_2$] is not, we should note, one that is peculiar to Christians. It is a severe difficulty at the heart of humanity. It is the problem of not doing the good that you would sincerely say you intend to do, that you clearly wish you would do, and that you grieve over and regret not having done. *It is a fundamental problem for all who see life clearly and think deeply about it.*[33]

I think that Willard is right about this. Indeed, neither Plato nor Aristotle give any indication of trying to ignore or hide the problem of moral failure.

---

[31] Willard, *The Great Omission*, 116–17. Italics added.

[32] Coe, "Resisting the Temptation," 60.

[33] Dallas Willard, "Spiritual Formation and the Warfare between the Flesh and the Human Spirit," in the *Journal of Spiritual Formation and Soul Care* 1:1 (Spring 2008): 80. Italics added.

If anything, its reality is their preoccupation. They see it as the central human problem, and their moral theories are attempts not to cover it up, but to solve it—as Willard rightly sees. But neither of them presume that they have been or will be successful in doing so. To the contrary, in light of the well-known Socratic doctrine that virtue is knowledge, Socrates' famous profession of ignorance in the *Apology* can only be read as an admission of his own lack of moral perfection, and that admission should be taken as a sign of humility. Although there is certainly an ironic element to Socrates' profession of ignorance, his ultimate sincerity is borne out by the *aporetic* nature of Plato's early dialogues, which are usually thought to present the historical Socrates most accurately. And even in the *Republic* (which is a late, non-aporetic dialogue) Plato has Socrates explicitly disavow adequate knowledge of the good. This is why he is forced to discuss it by way of analogy (in the famous analogy of the sun) rather than giving a definition of it. And in his discussion of the philosopher-king as the missing link in achieving his vision of the good life in the good city (Books VII–VIII), Socrates predicts that, even if someone were to achieve an adequate knowledge of the good and so establish the city, success would not long endure precisely on account of human moral (*cum* intellectual) frailty (Book VIII, 546a ff). And in fact, Plato's pessimism about enduring moral success among humans combined with the suggestion, recurring throughout many of Plato's dialogues, that *virtue is a gift of the gods* has led one scholar to propose that this is Plato's actual view.[34]

Aristotle, for his part, is quite forthcoming about the extreme challenges facing anyone who aspires to moral perfection. In the *Nicomachean Ethics* he clearly writes with the presumption that the average person experiences an inner struggle to do what is right. For Aristotle, this is enough to disqualify a person from counting as truly virtuous, or good. The difference between the average, "morally decent" person and his immoral counterpart is only that the former successfully restrains the desires that tempt him to do wrong—an essential and morally significant achievement to be sure, but by no means the moral ideal. It is precisely because he takes the average,

[34] Michael N. Forster, "Socrates' Profession of Ignorance," *Oxford Studies in Ancient Philosophy*, 3, 2007. Reprinted in *The Philosopher's Annual*, vol. 27, here: http://www.philosophersannual.org. See also Josef Pieper's *Divine Madness: Plato's Case against Secular Humanism* (San Francisco: Ignatius, 1995).

morally decent person to be merely "continent" in this way that he counsels us to aim not at perfect virtue, "the golden mean," but at the extreme (the vice!) opposite to the one that tempts us. For instance, if we are tempted to indulge in too much pleasure (a vice of excess), we should aim to allow ourselves not the right amount (the virtuous mean), but what we know to be too little (a vice of defect). "We must drag ourselves off in the contrary direction," he says, "for if we pull away from error, as they do in straightening bent wood, we shall reach the intermediate condition" (*Nicomachean Ethics*, 1109b). In this, he counsels exactly the same kind of asceticism that Willard supports, and not as a way of covering moral failure, but as a way of trying to move beyond it by changing the texture of the inner person. Similar counsel is given in the Confucian tradition, where one major representative (Hsun Tzu) was so taken with the difficulty of making people good that he declared human nature to be intrinsically evil.[35]

It may well be the case—and in fact I am sure it is the case—that neither Plato nor Aristotle nor Confucius nor Hsun Tzu understood the human moral and spiritual predicament with full depth and accuracy. But to see this deficiency as an attempt to hide from God, or even from the truth about the human moral situation,[36] is hardly the view of a sympathetic interpreter of the human moral project, as Coe claims to be.[37] What is more, if Willard is right about the fundamental motives for the human moral project, then Coe's interpretation is not only unsympathetic, but false. If the universal drive to develop programs of spiritual formation$_2$ comes from a desire to be good coupled with the recognition of severe challenges to being good, then we can be sure that many people have not only desired but *intended* to be good; for this shows that they have sought

[35] See Hsun Tzu, *Basic Writings*, translated by Burton Watson (New York: Columbia University Press, 1996), 157ff.

[36] It is of course a historical impossibility that pre-Christian moralists like Plato and Aristotle could have used their interest in morality to deny their need for *a savior*, since the very idea of "a savior" in the relevant sense came only through the special revelation given progressively by God in the context of the evolving Judeo-Christian tradition. Plato and Aristotle had no access to this revelatory tradition, and even among those who did, the idea of "a savior" *as God intended it* was generally not well understood until after Christ's resurrection. (Arguably it is still not well understood, even among Christians. Much of Willard's work on the spiritual life is predicated on this assumption.) Lacking the idea, it simply would have been impossible for a person to use morality—or anything else—to avoid seeing their need for a savior. But they could still have tried to hide from or ignore God, of whom they had some concept, or from the moral truths that they were aware of.

[37] Coe, "Resisting the Temptation," 56.

out and discovered means by which to achieve that desire. Of course, those means would have to be implemented after they were discovered in order for the intention to continue *as an intention*. But the thing to note here is that *the seeking of means is itself the first and most fundamental of means.* It is the first *way in which* a sincere intention to be good manifests itself after one realizes that direct effort is not always adequate to the task. Thus, the mere fact that humanity has engaged in a quest for an adequate program of spiritual formation shows some level of intention to be good on the part of an appreciable percentage of human beings. Of course, it is an open question whether all such persons would have carried their intention through to the end if they had been fully exposed to the Christian vision and its corollary means, or whether, like the rich young ruler, they would have "gone away sad" (Mark 10:17–29). However, the same uncertainty obtains for most Christians as well. In neither case, I think, is this a reason to doubt the reality of people's intentions to be good at least *to a point*—and usually a point that surpasses the *dikaisoune* of the scribes and the Pharisees, and hence "moralism" in Coe's sense.

Moreover, the sincerity of this intention in some non-Christians is proved by the fact that it provided part of the psychological basis for conversion to Christianity once they were introduced to it. Willard explains that

> the question of how one becomes a good person was uppermost in the minds of classical and medieval moralists . . . they thoroughly understood that the well-being of the society depends upon the predominance of genuinely good people. That is one reason why the thinkers of the ancient world turned to Christ in the early centuries of the Christian era. They became convinced that he was the key to human transformation toward goodness. (*Knowing Christ Today*, 49–50)

Rather than using systems of morality in legalistic fashion to evade moral/spiritual reality, such persons were genuinely committed to those realities. As Willard supposes, they really wanted to be genuinely good, and had formed genuine intentions to become good by employing the best means available to them. Thus, rather than disposing them to reject Christ when he came—as did the Pharisees' legalistic approach to God's own revealed morality—their involvement with the moral systems of the Greek philosophical tradition actually disposed them to accept him. Like John the Baptist, the Greek philosophical tradition came before Christ "making straight the way of the Lord." And it was able to do so not merely because of its similarity to Christianity in terms of vision and means, but also because the moral intentions of many of its adherents were genuine. Only thus were they able to see in Christianity the fulfillment of *their own moral aspirations* as shaped by Greek philosophy.

3. Conclusion

So far we have seen that, on the Willardian view, moral formation and spiritual formation$_2$ are identical for the Christian, and that spiritual formation$_1$ and spiritual formation$_3$ are among its parts. We have also seen that, due to a partial but still significant overlap in vision and means, some non-Christian traditions aim to engage in fundamentally the same project as Christian spiritual formation$_2$, and stand a chance of partial but still significant success in that project. That is, non-Christians have the possibility of growth toward genuine *dikaiosune*, and of genuine though anonymous cooperation with God, through their moral experience and their traditions of moral formation. Christianity offers a unique advantage in moral formation on account of its unique vision of moral reality, but lacking this advantage does not preclude some degree of genuine success in spiritual formation$_2$. Finally, we have seen reason to think it false that *all* non-Christian moralists used morality to hide from God, or from the truth about the human moral condition.

Whether counterexamples to Coe's claim are rare or common—that is, whether "moralism" or genuine moral intentions have been *the norm* among non-Christians—is a different question, whose answer requires statistical information impossible to collect.

However, I find it implausible to suppose that the answer would be substantially one-sided. On the one hand, it would be foolish to deny that "moralism" is a significant human problem. The substitution of morality's outward forms for its inward reality, usually in order to cloak immorality, is common across cultures and through history. In fact, the great classicist Erik Havelock once observed that the *Republic*'s defense of inward *dikaiosune* was needed in Plato's day precisely because, at the time, "the Greek adolescent [was] continually conditioned to an attitude which at bottom is cynical" about morality, the attitude that "[i]t is more important to keep up appearances than to practice the reality."[38] One need only read the short stories of Lu Xun to see how the same corruption of morality occurred in the Confucian tradition.[39] And, of course, a similar pattern is visible in the history of Israel and the Church. But this pattern of corruption is matched by a pattern of renewal and return to true morality. Socrates and Plato are not the only ones to have recognized that the legalistic corruption of morality is not true morality, but a "twilight morality" in which "[d]ecorum and decent behavior are not obviously violated, but the inner principle of morality is."[40] That this is widely recognized is borne out by, among other things, the fact that Plato's views eventually triumphed over this cynicism in the cultural battle for "hearts and minds," and that his work has remained part of the "Western Canon" for more than two millennia. So, while Coe is correct to think that humans are regularly tempted to reduce morality to a matter of "outward show," he goes too far when he claims or implies that it is the norm for non-Christians to approach morality in this corrupt way. To the contrary, the recognition of such an approach *as a corruption of morality* is included in the moral wisdom of many non-Christian traditions. They therefore are sufficient to correct that mistake in the same way that Jesus takes "Moses and the Prophets" to be in the parable of the rich man and Lazarus (Luke 16:29–31).

By the same token, it is not quite right to say, as Coe does, that "the Christian life is not *fundamentally* about being moral in itself or about being a good Christian boy or girl," and that the mature Christian does "not want to be a good boy [or girl] any more," but rather wants only "to open more deeply to Christ's work on the Cross and the Work of the Spirit."[41] If Willard is right about the quest for spiritual formation being grounded in our desire for goodness, then the truth is that the Christian who desires to open more deeply to Christ, the Cross, and the Spirit will do so precisely because s/he desires to be genuinely good. For instance, it is only half true that, as Coe says, "*prayer is not a place to be good—it is a place to be*

[38] Erik Havelock *Preface to Plato* (Cambridge, MA: Harvard University Press, 1963), 12.

[39] "Diary of a Madman," "Kong Yiji," and "New Year's Sacrifice" are particularly potent on this score. See *Diary of a Madman and Other Stories*, translated by William A. Lyell (Honolulu: University of Hawaii Press, 1990).

[40] Havelock, *Preface to Plato*, 12.

[41] Coe, "Resisting the Temptation," 57.

honest." [italics original].[42] Prayer is indeed a place to be honest before God, but principally because it is *good* to be honest before God, both in itself and instrumentally, since progress toward greater goodness depends upon accepting that there are areas of one's life where improvement is possible and desirable. It is thus both a way of being good, and a way of becoming better; and this is *why* prayer (and not only prayer, of course) is a place to be honest. This shows that the desire to be good is partially constitutive of a right relationship to God. As such, it is neither more nor less fundamental to the Christian life than any other "required ingredient."

However, it may be an element in that relationship especially important to life in "this world." In an interview with *Cutting Edge* magazine, Willard makes the intriguing statement that "Scripture teaches personal, though not moral, development in the life to come."[43] This distinction between moral and personal development is not entirely clear to me from the context of the interview, and I have not found the details developed explicitly in any of Willard's other writings. What is clear from the context, however, is that he sees "moral development" as having to do with the ability to avoid outright rebellion against God, while "personal development" has to do with the ability to engage readily and easily in positive, creative tasks that God might assign to people in the life to come. It is also clear that, as Willard sees it, moral development is for "this age" alone. It is, to borrow a phrase from developmental psychopathology, the most significant "stage-salient task" for the lives we now live. If this is so, it makes it all the more crucial for us to understand the place of morality in Christianity, and the unity of moral and spiritual formation in Christian, and indeed human, life.

---

[42] Coe, "Resisting the Temptation," 63.

[43] Dallas Willard, "Rethinking Evangelism," *Cutting Edge* (Winter, 2001), accessed November 27, 2017, http://www.dwillard.org/articles/artview.asp?artID=53.

EXTENDING WILLARD

5

"LIVING WITH THE LORD ALWAYS BEFORE THEM"

Considerations of Spiritual Guidance Offered by Ignatius of Loyola and Dallas Willard

CATHERINE LOOKER

SSJ, Chestnut Hill College

Abstract: The centuries-old art of spiritual direction continues to be crafted by those who willingly serve as spiritual mentors for countless spiritual seekers who feel drawn by God's grace to engage in the transformative process of spiritual formation. The work of this chapter offers an in-depth consideration of the spiritual guidance offered by two outstanding spiritual guides, Ignatius of Loyola in his sixteenth century spiritual manual, *The Spiritual Exercises,* and Dallas Willard in *Renovation of the Heart* (2002). After establishing the historical and contextual frameworks needed for getting to know each of our spiritual guides, significant attention will be then given to the exploration of five key spiritual movements that can effectively serve as unifying threads for our consideration of the work of our spiritual transformation into Christ-likeness.

Nestled in chapter 6 of *Renovation of the Heart,* Dallas Willard emphasizes the importance of identifying and emulating the wisdom of true spiritual practitioners (e.g., Billy Graham, Teresa of Calcutta, William Law, Martin Luther, Ignatius of Loyola, as he names a few) who have "walked the walk" of following Christ as Willard asks the provocative question: "How did they come to be able to live with 'the Lord always before them?'" Willard goes on to assert in his response: "We learn from them how to do that by making them our close companions on the way" (*Renovation*, 114).[1]

Inspired by Willard's inclusion of Ignatius of Loyola (in particular, in his list of spiritual practitioners), the work of this chapter seeks to explore the spiritual guidance offered by Dallas Willard in the company of Ignatius of Loyola with the assertion they both can serve as viable and relevant companions for contemporary spiritual seekers who desire to engage in the process of spiritual formation and transformation into Christ-likeness.[2] As guides who are skilled in the art of spiritual formation, both Ignatius of Loyola and Dallas Willard, although centuries apart, can invite us to ponder how God offers grace in abundance, not only as God did for each of them, but as God desires to do for each one of us. Furthermore, since Ignatius of Loyola and Dallas Willard can effectively model for us a significant depth of personal authenticity, we can relate to them as real persons, especially since their writings give evidence that they have pondered life's challenges in light of their evolving relationship with Christ. For "at the heart of Christianity, the Christian believer confidently expects to find religious experience: an existential encounter in faith with his [or her] God . . . Moreover, religious experience is not an esoteric event but a dimension of his [or her] ordinary living."[3]

Since the writers in the Christian tradition generally offer their spiritual guidance primarily through the legacy of their classic spiritual texts, the work of this essay revolves around the textual settings offered by *The Spiritual Exercises* of Ignatius of Loyola and *Renovation of the Heart* by Dallas Willard as a way for us to tap into the rich legacies of both of these spiritual guides. The motivating questions of interest in working with excerpts from their selected texts in the context of spiritual formation can be formulated as follows: First, what is their main message regarding the

---

[1] Short titles and parenthetical references are used throughout this chapter for the main Willardian corpus. See Dallas Willard, *Renovation of the Heart: Putting on the Character of Christ* (Colorado Springs: NavPress, 2002), 114.

[2] Dallas Willard frequently clarifies the depth of his meaning regarding spiritual "formation" by adding the word "transformation" to his phrasing, as illustrated in the following example found on page 21 of *Renovation of the Heart:* "The quest for spiritual formation (really, as indicated, spiritual *trans*formation) is in fact an age-old and worldwide one."

[3] William J. Walsh, review of *Discernment of Spirits According to the Life and Teachings of St. Ignatius of Loyola*, by Piet Penning de Vries, *Theological Studies* 34, no. 4 (1973): 727.

essence of spiritual formation in each of their texts? Second, how might they offer guidance to contemporary spiritual seekers who desire spiritual formation in Christ? Third, what might be the experience of contemporary spiritual seekers who may look to Ignatius of Loyola and Dallas Willard as spiritual guides through accessing their spiritual texts, *The Spiritual Exercises* and *Renovation of the Heart,* respectively? Each of their texts reveals a working document, not simply a text to be read and put aside, particularly since *The Spiritual Exercises* and *Renovation of the Heart* are both written in such a way as to invite the reader into a clear response filled with discernment flowing from a desire to embody the teachings of Christ. In particular, their texts have the potential for offering a significant blueprint for guiding spiritual seekers toward fuller and more explicit expression of their spiritual longings. Thus it may be accurately asserted that Ignatius of Loyola and Dallas Willard have the capacity to be relevant, applicable, inspirational, and devotional as they function as spiritual guides via their classic texts that are intended to be, as Willard effectively asserts, "intensely practical" (*Renovation*, 25).[4]

In following the flow of this chapter after these preliminary considerations, there will first be a brief, yet significantly foundational, look at Ignatius of Loyola and Dallas Willard in a way that can help establish some of the needed contextual understandings of their lives and selected works. However, the main work of this essay will attempt to respond to the three areas of interest highlighted above by a consistent focus on our two spiritual guides regarding their message, their guidance, and the experience of contemporary spiritual seekers who reflect on *The Spiritual Exercises* and *Renovation of the Heart,* respectively. In order to reflect on Christian spiritual formation in the company of Ignatius of Loyola and Dallas Willard, five key movements will be offered as unifying threads for our consideration of the work of spiritual transformation as follows: (1) building on graced foundations; (2) experiencing God's healing love and reconciliation;

[4] Staying with his emphasis on the need for a hands-on approach to working with *Renovation of the Heart,* Willard continues: "[This book] aims to help those who are 'seeking the kingdom of God and His righteousness' to find them and to fully live in them" (pgs. 25–26). For a similar assertion regarding the practical use of Ignatius' *Spiritual Exercises,* see George E. Ganss in his introduction to *The Spiritual Exercises of Saint Ignatius: A Translation and a Commentary* (Chicago: Loyola University Press, 1992), where he states, "The present translation is intended for practical use, especially by retreatants, directors" (pg. 10).

(3) discerning the call of Christ Jesus; (4) taking up our cross with Christ Jesus; and (5) learning the ways of God's love.

In tracing these five spiritual movements through *The Spiritual Exercises* and *Renovation of the Heart,* it needs to be noted that there are some significant differences inherent in the paradigms of both medieval and evangelical piety, relevant to Ignatius of Loyola and Dallas Willard, respectively. In an effective summary of such distinctions in the context of dynamics of the spiritual journey, theologian Timothy George makes the case that

> evangelical piety turns upside down the medieval paradigm of a pathway to God. There the journey of faith began with purgation, moved on to illumination, and finally, ended in unification, that is, union with God. In the evangelical understanding, we begin with union with Christ (the new birth) and move on through Word and Spirit to illumination and the process of sanctification until, at last, in heaven we see Christ face to face.[5]

While it is appropriate to acknowledge such key distinctive elements as found in the medieval and evangelical paradigms, the main task of this essay will be to explore the more unifying and fluid aspects of the above-named five key movements of the spiritual journey in the company of our two spiritual guides, Ignatius of Loyola and Dallas Willard. Our explorations into the richness of *The Spiritual Exercises* and *Renovation of the Heart* can offer fruitful reflections and encouragement to contemporary spiritual seekers who find themselves earnestly on the pathways of their own spiritual transformation in whatever "order" they might be drawn to the commonly shared awareness, inherent in both forms of piety, that "we can never earn God's favor and goodwill toward us—[for] that is what is so amazing about grace!"[6]

[5] On these distinctions between medieval and evangelical piety, see Timothy George, introduction to *For All the Saints: Evangelical Theology and Christian Spirituality,* edited by Timothy George and Alister McGrath (Louisville, KY: Westminster John Knox, 2003), 4.

[6] George, *For All the Saints,* 4.

Ignatius of Loyola as Spiritual Guide

To say that Ignatius of Loyola (1491–1556) can be considered as a spiritual guide with experience would be to complement the way that Harvey Egan describes Ignatius in his *Anthology of Christian Mysticism* as follows:

> Ignatius of Loyola became known for his role as ascetic, spiritual director, champion of the poor and sick, reformer of the Church, a counter-reformer, advisor to popes, cardinals, bishops, kings, princes, and other heads of state, founder of the Society of Jesus, leader of men, and initiator of world-wide missionary activity. As educational innovator, his *Spiritual Exercises* changed the course of the history of spirituality from the 16th century to the present day.[7]

And yet, before the shattering of his leg by a cannonball while in battle during his days as a soldier, Ignatius "drove himself toward success, recognition, and esteem . . . [however], neither gambling, womanizing, nor dueling filled the void within his heart."[8] For it was during his time of recuperation from his wounds from the battle at Pamplona that Ignatius was led by God's grace to the path of true conversion and formation in Christ that can be succinctly described as follows:

> True conversion comes when we turn to God, acknowledging that only God can fill our emptiness and that God's love has already been poured out by Jesus. We cannot earn God's love because Jesus gives it to us freely and constantly—if we will open ourselves to it. Ignatius needed to let go and trust God. Only then could God fill the emptiness in his heart.[9]

It is important to note that in the process of his series of conversion experiences from his period of solitude and healing while at Loyola, Ignatius was in the early stages of developing his gift of discernment of spirits, whereas he developed his capacity to stay with certain thoughts and desires and

---

[7] Harvey Egan, *An Anthology of Christian Mysticism* (Collegeville, MN: The Liturgical Press, 1991), 421.

[8] Jacqueline Syrup Bergan and Marie Schwan, *Praying with Ignatius of Loyola*, Companions for the Journey Series (Winona, MN: Saint Mary's Press, 1991), 30.

[9] Bergan and Schwan, *Praying with Ignatius of Loyola*, 30.

then afterward he would notice where they led him interiorly. Gradually, the thoughts of serving Christ as his King brought him great interior joy and lasting peace, and "after his conversion, Ignatius strove to serve the greater glory of the one true ruler of the world: Christ"[10] rather than dedicating himself to an earthly monarch. As George E. Ganss aptly points out in a quote from *The Constitutions of the Society of Jesus,* containing the guiding principles for the Jesuits, the religious order of men later founded by Ignatius,

> God was the center and preoccupation of Ignatius' thoughts, and the object of his special love, and the beloved Person for whom he wanted to do all the little acts which make up daily living. He wanted to be bound irrevocably to God, with the bridges burnt which might lead back to another way of living in which he might have interests other than God—God and [all others] for whom Jesus Christ had shed His blood.[11]

Ignatius of Loyola spent the rest of his life desiring and seeking the greater glory of God in his inspired attempts "to reach a balance of prayer and action, realizing that one without the other puts our spirituality out of harmony."[12]

It was during his time of his conversion, particularly while at Manresa, that Ignatius developed what came to be known as the first draft of *The Spiritual Exercises*, a spiritual manual that was to be frequently revised throughout his life. According to Ignatius' intention, *The Spiritual Exercises* were designed for working along with a spiritual guide.[13] The four weeks into which *The Spiritual Exercises* are divided are "fixed and equal periods only by courtesy, like the days of creation. Each 'week' represents a

---

[10] *Praying with Ignatius of Loyola*, 69.

[11] Ignatius of Loyola, *The Constitutions of the Society of Jesus*, cited by Bergan and Schwan in *Praying with Ignatius of Loyola*, 40.

[12] Bergan and Schwan, *Praying with Ignatius of Loyola*, 86.

[13] See H. Outram Evennett, *The Spirit of the Counter-Reformation*, 4th ed. (Notre Dame: University of Notre Dame Press, 1986), and Evennett's description of the personal approach needed by this "spiritual guide" while giving *The Spiritual Exercises*: "Flexibility, indeed, was to be the main concern of the giver, who was to adapt the technique and the general plan to the particular needs, state, psychology, character, intelligence, stamina, of each individual concerned, without, however, altering the actual of making what meditations were included: the composition of the mental scene, the application of the senses, the subsequent prayer and resolution. This recognition of the separateness and difference of each individual person is surely a high tribute to the perceptive humanity of Saint Ignatius" (pgs. 50–51).

stage—a true week being the optimum duration"[14] with section numbers sequentially bracketed in order to designate the content for each of these weeks.[15] For our purposes here, the main sections of *The Spiritual Exercises* under consideration in this essay can be adequately summarized as follows:

> **The First Principle and Foundation [SE 23]:** Ignatius designed the First Principle and Foundation in order to awaken the spiritual desires of the spiritual seeker [or retreatant].
>
> **The First Week [SE 24–90]:** It is likewise important to note that it is "the loved sinner [that] stands at the center of the First Week which really dwells on love, God's love, which is greater than human sin."[16]
>
> **The Second Week [SE 91–189]:** Given the extensive and Gospel-oriented content of the Second Week, the spiritual seeker is led through prayer and experience into the mysteries of the life of Christ while developing a keener sense of discernment of spirits.
>
> **The Third Week [SE 190–217]:** The "entire paschal mystery grounds the Third Week. Followers, then and now, must choose their response to this encounter with mystery, an encounter that can lead to new depths of compassion, friendship, and love."[17]
>
> **The Fourth Week/*Contemplatio* [SE 218–237]:** The nature of the grace of joy that Ignatius had in mind here can be described as follows: "We are concerned with paschal joy, the joy proper to Easter, the joy which springs from a still more fundamental grace, that of the faith and love that make the Risen Christ, though invisible, the very core of the believer's existence."[18]

---

[14] Evennett, *The Spirit of the Counter-Reformation*, 48.

[15] For the sake of clarity and ease of navigating the material in each of the weeks of *The Spiritual Exercises,* the designation [SE #(s)] will be used throughout this essay for each of the referenced sections of the Ignatian text.

[16] Katherine Dyckman, Mary Garvin, and Elizabeth Liebert, *The Spiritual Exercises Reclaimed: Uncovering Liberating Possibilities for Women* (New York: Paulist Press, 2001), 153.

[17] Dyckman et al., *The Spiritual Exercises Reclaimed*, 217.

[18] Michael Ivens, *Understanding the Spiritual Exercises, Text and Commentary: A Handbook or Retreat Directors* (Trowbridge, Wiltshire: Cromwell Press, 1998), 162.

Thus, the "genius of *The Spiritual Exercises* is that they combined the accumulated spiritual wisdom of the Christian centuries with the direct lessons by [Ignatius] himself."[19] As George E. Ganss so effectively summarizes,

> St. Ignatius [has] a dynamic spirituality which [is] ordered toward both personal spiritual growth and energetic apostolic endeavor. It [is] firmly based on the chief truths in God's revelation, with a particular focus on God's plan for the creation, redemption, and spiritual development of the human beings who use their freedom wisely—that plan of salvation which St. Paul calls "the mystery of Christ."[20]

Dallas Willard as Spiritual Guide

In her insightful article, "A Divine Conspirator," Christine A. Scheller contends that Dallas Willard was most familiar to many Christians from his books, and it is philosophy that is "both his primary vocation and the foundation of his devotional writing."[21] From his long tenure as a professor at the University of Southern California, Willard was known to his students and colleagues for his academic honesty, and he asserts that "while he doesn't believe anyone will be saved except by Jesus, he adds: 'How that works out, probably no one knows.'"[22] And yet, with evidence inherent in Willard's legacy of prolific writings, there is a palpable reassurance at work that Willard sought to make "the search for deeper spirituality and efforts to understand spiritual formation"[23] accessible to contemporary seekers who desire "a renovation of the heart into Christ likeness."[24] One must wonder who could fail to be inspired by a spiritual guide who can say the following: "All scripture is inspired, but some of it is electric. The power of the Holy Spirit hums in the lines so thrillingly that you hardly dare to touch them."[25] Willard's compelling message that there is a need for

---

[19] Evennett, *The Spirit of the Counter-Reformation*, 46.

[20] George E. Ganss, introduction to *Ignatius of Loyola: Spiritual Exercises and Selected Works* (New York: Paulist Press, 1991), 9.

[21] Christine A. Scheller, "A Divine Conspirator," *Christianity Today* 50, no. 9 (2006): 45.

[22] Scheller, "A Divine Conspirator," 46.

[23] Purushotham Francis Burgula, review of *Renovation of the Heart,* by Dallas Willard, *Journal of Youth Ministry* 3, no. 1 (2004): 117.

[24] Burgula, review of *Renovation of the Heart,* 117.

[25] Cornelius Plantinga, "Dr. Willard's Diagnosis," *Christianity Today* 50, no. 9 (2006): 49.

a "thoroughgoing inner transformation through Christ"[26] is one that can draw spiritual seekers who are "out of shape, spiritually speaking."[27] A possible remedy offered for some soul-shaping exercises designed for spiritual fitness may be found in Willard's book *Renovation of the Heart.*

Renovation of the Heart is clearly divided into two major parts with the first part (chapters 1 through 5) dealing with the right understanding of the relationship between human existence and divine operation and the second part (chapters 6 through 13) dealing with the essential dimensions of human personality and how they should be transformed.[28] All through the book, Willard makes the significant claim that "the renovation of the heart into Christ likeness is not something that concerns the heart (spirit, will) alone."[29] Therefore, "it is important for us to understand the idea that we renovate the heart by changing it, but we can't truly transform the heart without changing the other essential parts of the human personality."[30] It is this assertion that leads Willard to effectively develop his VIM schema (vision, intention, and means) as necessary for transformation.[31] Believing that the work of spiritual transformation by necessity involves a community aspect, Willard offers a key clarification of the difference between vessel (traditions and denominations) and treasure (the Great Commission), with a rightful caution to avoid making the vessel the treasure.[32]

Since, according to Willard, the process of spiritual formation involves "those who love and trust Jesus Christ [and] effectively take on his character,"[33] their "outward conformity to His example and His instructions rises toward fullness as their inward sources of action take on the same character as His. They come more and more to share His vision, love, hope, feelings, and habits."[34] Thus, through the work of his book, *Renovation of the Heart,* Willard desires that through "spiritual formation in Christlikeness as the sure outcome of well-directed activities that are

[26] Plantinga, "Dr. Willard's Diagnosis," 50.
[27] Plantinga, "Dr. Willard's Diagnosis," 50.
[28] Burgula, review of *Renovation of the Heart,* 117.
[29] Burgula, review of *Renovation of the Heart,* 117.
[30] Burgula, review of *Renovation of the Heart,* 117.
[31] Burgula, review of *Renovation of the Heart,* 117.
[32] Burgula, review of *Renovation of the Heart,* 117.
[33] Dallas Willard, "The Spirit Is Willing: The Body as a Tool for Spiritual Growth," in *The Great Omission: Reclaiming Jesus's Essential Teachings on Discipleship,* 80–90.
[34] Willard, in *The Great Omission,* 225.

under the personal supervision of Christ and are sustained by all of the instrumentalities of his grace" the benefits offered to what Willard refers to as our "aching world" will be enormous. Given his assertion that "it is only spiritual formation in Christ that makes us at home on earth," Willard then urges us as spiritual seekers to notice that "Christ brings me to the place where I am able to walk beside my neighbor, whoever he or she may be. I am not above them. I am beside them: their servant, living with them through the events common to all of us" (*Renovation*, 255).

Movement One: Building on Graced Foundations

> God who loves us creates us and wants to share life with us forever.[35] —Ignatius of Loyola

> Genuine transformation of the whole person into the goodness and power seen in Jesus and his "Abba" Father—the only transformation adequate to the human self—remains the necessary goal of human life. (*Renovation*, 20)

In pondering the First Principle and Foundation at the beginning of *The Spiritual Exercises,* it seems evident that Ignatius simply and profoundly prioritizes his acknowledgement of the level of God's desire for us. Here Ignatius creates a context of "the sense of creaturehood that underlies the First Principle and Foundation . . . For we are beings of love, created out of love . . . [and] a person must begin the *Exercises* with the awareness of being a creature of love."[36] This sense of creaturehood may seem as basic as "the answer to the catechism question, 'Why did God create me?'"[37] However, a "sense of creaturehood is not just an intellectual realization."[38]

Rather, creaturehood is a deep awareness. In some ways, it comes from our human condition, and in some ways it comes from grace. Creaturehood contains a mixture of feelings involving a feeling of fear and at the same time a feeling of security. Christians know themselves as dependent beings

---

[35] Ignatius of Loyola, *The Spiritual Exercises* [23], in David L. Fleming, *Draw Me into Your Friendship: The Spiritual Exercises, A Literal Translation and a Contemporary Reading* (St. Louis: The Institute of Jesuit Sources, 1994), 27.

[36] John English, *Spiritual Freedom: From an Experience of the Ignatian Exercises to the Art of Spiritual Guidance,* 2nd ed. (Chicago: Loyola Press, 1995), 26.

[37] English, *Spiritual Freedom*, 27.

[38] English, *Spiritual Freedom*, 27.

who are surrounded by love. At the very least, Christians should be sure that they are safe in the arms of their Creator.[39]

Thus, in our growing awareness of ourselves as loved and created by a God, we may come to know our "desirableness,"[40] where "we come to know that [God's] desire makes us desirable, makes us 'the apple of [God's] eye.'"[41] For "such an experience of our creation is the affective first principle and foundation upon which not only the Ignatian *Exercises* rest, but upon which any development of a personal relationship with God must rest."[42] However, as we shall see, there is often difficulty in claiming this degree of "desirableness," since our life histories can hold countless examples of how others did not always see us as so desirable or lovable. As a result, significant interior conflicts can often occur in spiritual seekers who experience degrees of difficulty in believing in their graced identities.

Building on his foundational focus, Ignatius succinctly frames the retreatant's response to the unconditional love of God, our Creator, as follows: "Our love response takes shape in our praise and honor and service of the God of our life."[43] For "the Foundation outlines a vision of life and the most basic criteria for making choices. It says that we live well and attain our ultimate purpose by loving just one thing, or rather some One . . . [For] according to the Foundation, serving God is what makes us happy."[44]

Given that spiritual seekers may struggle with where to begin in pondering the deeper implications of Ignatius' Principle and Foundation in their day-to-day living, some valuable questions[45] for further prayer and reflection in light of Ignatius' foundational premise may be considered:

(1) How would you describe your world and how it influences you?
(2) How do you imagine God?
(3) What is your relationship to others and all of God's creation?

---

[39] English, *Spiritual Freedom*, 27.

[40] William A. Barry, *Paying Attention to God: Discernment in Prayer* (Notre Dame, IN: Ave Maria Press, 1992), 18.

[41] Barry, *Paying Attention to God*, 18.

[42] Barry, *Paying Attention to God*, 18.

[43] Ignatius of Loyola, *The Spiritual Exercises* [23], in Fleming, *Draw Me into Your Friendship*, 27.

[44] Dean Brackley, *The Call to Discernment in Troubled Times: New Perspectives on the Transformative Wisdom of Ignatius of Loyola* (New York: The Crossroad Publishing Company, 2004), 11.

[45] Dyckman et al., *The Spiritual Exercises Reclaimed*, 99.

(4) What is your part in creation?
(5) What are the dominant influences on your sense of God, humans, heaven and earth?
(6) What does it mean to exist in this vast unfolding universe?[46]

In accompaniment with the focus on the wonder of our creation in the image and likeness of God as put forth by Ignatius of Loyola in his First Principle and Foundation [SE 23], spiritual seekers may also greatly profit from the spiritual guidance of Dallas Willard as they reflect and pray with various sections of his *Renovation of the Heart.* At this point in our consideration of our two spiritual guides, it can be instructive to note that where Ignatius offers four paragraphs of concise construction and exhortation at the outset of his *Spiritual Exercises,* Willard more extensively clarifies what he means by the orderly process of spiritual formation in Christ as creatively woven and reinforced all throughout his book. For example, Willard asserts: "Instead of focusing upon what God *can* do, we must humble ourselves to accept the ways he *has chosen* to work with us. [For] these are clearly laid out in the Bible, and especially in the words and person of Jesus" (*Renovation*, 10). For the goal is to

> leave our burdensome ways of heavy labor—especially the "religious ones"—and step into the yoke of training with [Jesus]. This is a way of gentleness and lowliness, a way of soul rest. It is a way of inner transformation that proves pulling his load and carrying his burden with him to be a life that is easy and light. (Matthew 11:28–30). (*Renovation*, 10)

Willard effectively offers what he deems to be essential reflections on each of the six dimensions of the human person in *Renovation of the Heart,* summarized here as follows:

[46] Regarding the importance of considering the evolving universe story in relation to the *Spiritual Exercises,* refer to *The Spiritual Exercises Reclaimed,* where Katherine Dyckman and collaborators, *The Spiritual Exercises Reclaimed,* offer concise and relevant insights regarding the importance of the new cosmology in their chapter 4, "Grounding in Truth," where they assert: "No longer can a human story be told apart from a universe story; the two are inextricably bound together . . . Human beings are radically interconnected with all other creatures" (pg. 97).

> **Thought**—brings before our minds in various ways (including perception and imagination) and enables us to consider them in various respects and trace out their relationships with one another.
>
> **Feeling**—inclines us toward or away from things that come before our minds and thought.
>
> **Will (Spirit, Heart)**—volition or choice, is the exercise of the will the capacity of the person to originate things and events that would not otherwise be or occur.
>
> **Body**—the focal point of our presence in the physical and social world.
>
> **Social Context**—the human self requires rootedness in others.
>
> **Soul**—that dimension of the person that interrelates all of the other dimensions so that they form one life (*Renovation*, 32, 33, 35–37).

In light of these six dimensions, Willard, similarly to Ignatius, acknowledges the holistic nature of the process of spiritual transformation into Christ-likeness as the integration of these six areas requiring consistent attention. No small task for the spiritual seeker "who has been found by Christ" and who places oneself "at the disposal of God!" (*Renovation*, 94).

Movement Two: Experiencing God's Healing Love and Reconciliation

> I raise my mind and think how God our Lord is looking at me.[47]—Ignatius of Loyola
>
> When God stands before us, we stand before him. Refusing to worship him is a way of trying to avoid his face and his eyes. (*Renovation*, 108)

For the spiritual seeker who has allowed Ignatius' First Principle and Foundation to become essential in his or her life, it is important that there

[47] Ganss, *The Spiritual Exercises of Saint Ignatius: A Translation and Commentary*, 48.

has been an "experience of God as the Creator who loves us into existence for community with God."[48] As Ignatius himself asserts, "Our love response takes shape in our praise and honor and service of the God of our life."[49] This awareness helps lead the retreatant from pondering the Principle and Foundation into the spiritual work of the First Week of the Ignatian *Exercises.*

However, apparent progress in this First Week may be slow since "it is often difficult to let our experiences of God's dream and creative love take root in our hearts."[50] What might be the cause of such difficulty? It is likely that a poor self-image can get in the way,[51] while distorted images of God can reveal themselves in people's illusions that "God needs to be placated, and yet that God is really implacable . . . The illusion comes down to the belief that I am rotten to the core and unlovable."[52] For "the fact that we need reassurance about God's love of us sinners indicates that at this stage of our spiritual journey we also labor under an illusion. It is difficult for us to believe in our bones that God loves sinners."[53] It is important to note that Ignatius is not as interested in a detailed list of past sins as much as clear attentiveness to areas of disorder that can serve as the backdrop for everyday decisions that can lead to darkness and desolation.

Thus, it is with a growing spirit of gratitude that we can allow ourselves to stand in the face of God's tenderness and mercy where Ignatius exclaims: "This is an exclamation of wonder and surging emotion, uttered as I reflect on all creatures and wonder how they have allowed me to live and have preserved me in life. The angels: How is it that, although they are the swords of God's justice, they have borne with me, protected me, and prayed for me? The saints: How is it that they have interceded and prayed for me?"[54] As Ignatian scholar, Michael Ivens, so well expresses: "In this

---

[48] William A. Barry, *Letting God Come Close: An Approach to the Ignatian Spiritual Exercises* (Chicago: Loyola Press, 2001), 72.

[49] Ignatius of Loyola, *The Spiritual Exercises* [23], in Fleming, *Draw Me into Your Friendship*, 27.

[50] Barry, *Letting God Come Close*, 72.

[51] Barry, *Letting God Come Close*, 72.

[52] Barry, *Letting God Come Close*, 73.

[53] Barry, *Letting God Come Close*, 76.

[54] Ignatius of Loyola, *The Spiritual Exercises* [60], in Ganss, *The Spiritual Exercises of Saint Ignatius: A Translation and Commentary*, 44.

final point, with its mood of wonder and 'intense affection,' the exercitant [retreatant] is already moving toward the concluding prayer of gratitude."[55]

At the beginning of chapter 3 of his *Renovation of the Heart,* Dallas Willard makes the following astute observation: "One of the greatest obstacles to effective spiritual transformation in Christ today is simple failure to understand and acknowledge the reality of the human situation as it affects Christians and non-Christians alike. We must start from where we really are" (*Renovation,* 45). Similar to where Ignatius of Loyola can exhort me as a retreatant to "raise my mind and think how God our Lord is looking at me,"[56] so too Dallas Willard reinforces that "when God stands before us, we stand before him" (*Renovation,* 108). As Willard effectively emphasizes further while complementing the more concisely expressed spiritual guidance of Ignatius, "The tender soul of a little child shows us how necessary it is to us that we be unobserved in our wrong. The adult carries the same burden—but now so great as to be crushed by it. . . . The so-called 'right to privacy' of which so much is made in contemporary life is in very large measure merely a way of avoiding scrutiny in our wrongdoing" (*Renovation,* 108–09). To illustrate the need for accountability in our quest for transformation, Willard showcases the Twelve Steps used by Alcoholics Anonymous and other similar 12-Step programs that include "the personal and social arrangements in which they are concretely embodied, including a conscious involvement of God in the individual's life."[57]

In light of our need to bring God and others into our process of transformation that contains a plan that complements one's good intentions, Dallas Willard offers what he calls the VIM pattern that includes the essential components of (1) vision; (2) intention; and (3) means. Since Willard rightfully acknowledges that "vim" is a "derivative of the Latin term 'vis,' meaning direction, strength, force, vigor, power, energy, or virtue,"[58] it seems appropriate that this acronym contains the essential elements inherent in our process of being spiritually formed in Christ. The goal of this VIM process is not merely outward conformity to Gospel teachings, but

---

[55] Ivens, *Understanding the Spiritual Exercises,* 58.

[56] Ignatius of Loyola, *The Spiritual Exercises* [75], in Ganss, *The Spiritual Exercises of Saint Ignatius: A Translation and Commentary,* 48.

[57] Ganss, *The Spiritual Exercises of Saint Ignatius: A Translation and Commentary,* 84.

[58] Ganss, *The Spiritual Exercises of Saint Ignatius: A Translation and Commentary,* 85.

rather a progression "to the point where what Jesus himself did and taught would be the natural outflow of who [we] really are 'on the inside.'"[59] More will be said about how the VIM process relates to the glimpse of the kingdom of God that is necessary to proceed while considering Movement Three in the next section of this essay.

Movement Three: Discerning the Call of Christ Jesus

> I ask Jesus our Lord that I might not be deaf to his call in my life and that I might be ready and willing to do what he wants.[60]
> —Ignatius of Loyola

> If we are concerned about our own spiritual formation or that of others, the vision of the kingdom is the place we must start. (*Renovation*, 86)

As we become more aware of our desires in light of God's desires, "we discover what we should do and what we should choose as we grow in our capacity to act and choose. As a result, we find that we are not making a choice after all; rather, the Spirit is constantly disposing us."[61] It seems that before spiritual seekers can authentically consider what more they might do for God, most people "want to experience the closeness and care of God, but hold little hope that God will actually be a felt presence. In other words, some people expect so little of God and have an image of God as being more niggardly than God actually is."[62] To further illustrate this point here, I remember one of my directees named "Carol" saying to me many years ago: "You know, I have come to believe that I have a spirituality of deprivation rather than abundance when it comes to my relationship with God. I often expect so little of God! I think that God wants me, rather, to have a spirituality of abundance where I can expect great and wonderful things of God!"

---

[59] Ganss, *The Spiritual Exercises of Saint Ignatius: A Translation and Commentary*, 86.
[60] Ignatius of Loyola, *The Spiritual Exercises* [91], in Fleming, *Draw Me into Your Friendship*, 83.
[61] English, *Spiritual Freedom*, 35.
[62] Barry, *Letting God Come Close*, 44.

Perhaps it can be most helpful for us to remember in the company of Ignatius that "God always moves first, searching for us."[63] Awareness of our true dependence on God is of greatest importance to facilitate our understanding that "another prerequisite for the freedom that comes from knowing God's love is prayer to the Holy Spirit. We seek what is solely a gift from God."[64] Jesuit John English so well captures the spirit of Ignatius as follows:

> Jesus said, "The Holy Spirit, whom the Father will send in my name, will teach you everything, and remind you of all I have said to you" (John 14:26). He also said, "The truth will make you free" (John 8:31). The basic truth that makes us free is that God loves us with an overwhelming love. It follows that our prayer . . . should ask the Holy Spirit to make us aware of God's love, to help us so "abide in God's love," and to give us the trust to surrender in all freedom to God's loving desire for us.[65]

As indicated, Ignatius' own process of discernment began while he was recuperating at Loyola when he noticed "that two sets of daydreams led to different affective states, and he drew the conclusion that God was leading him toward a new way of life, away from the life of chivalry that gave him so much apparent pleasure."[66] As we, as contemporary spiritual seekers, continue to plumb the depths of our own desires, we may be drawn to notice that "God desires that the actions of each of us be in tune with God's one action; in our best moment, we too desire to be in tune with God's action."[67] This metaphor of being "in tune" with God may be aptly described and enhanced as follows:

> Have you ever experienced a time when you were "in the flow," able to live with relative unambivalence and lack of fear in the "now," attuned to the presence of God? Then you have an idea of what it might be like to be at one with the one action of God. In

[63] English, *Spiritual Freedom*, 41.
[64] English, *Spiritual Freedom*, 42.
[65] English, *Spiritual Freedom*, 42. These Scripture quotations, noted by English, are taken from the New Revised Standard Version (NRSV).
[66] Barry, *Letting God Come Close*, 116.
[67] Barry, *Letting God Come Close* 126.

> such a state you are a contemplative in action. You know that you are in the right place at the right time . . . To be attuned to the one action of God, to [God's] will, is to be extraordinarily free, happy, and fulfilled even in the midst of a world of sorrow and pain.[68]

To the spiritual guide walking with a discerning person, the following sound advice may be appropriate to recall: "When guides are discerning whether good or evil is at work, they should remember that 'you will know them by their fruits' (Matthew 7:20)."[69]

As surprised as we may be that Christ would choose us, it is important to remember that the call "of Christ brings with it further gifts—a soul-expanding generosity; new burning desires for service; and a remarkable confidence in what Christ can do. Jesus Christ, the Only Begotten One, offers us the chance to work at his side. How can we refuse?"[70] "Christ offers personal love, but he offers it in a new way. Jesus is saying 'Come and labor with me.' He is offering companionship."[71] Thus, with the spiritual guidance of Ignatius of Loyola, we seek to understand how we can serve Jesus Christ. "How can we be with Christ, working for the fulfillment of the world?"[72]

As promised and as a fitting complement to Ignatius' clear focus regarding our need to respond wholeheartedly to the call and mission of Christ, it is now that our discussion of Movement Three continues with a closer look at Dallas Willard's VIM process, including vision, intention, and means, with an emphasis on the quality of discernment that involves our clear "intention to be a kingdom person" (*Renovation*, 87). One might ask: How do I know that I am following the call of Christ in my life? What reassurance do I have that I am not just listening to myself and doing what I want? In response to such concerns, Dallas Willard affirms that "in the clear and forceful vision of Jesus and his kingdom, as our personality becomes progressively more reorganized around God and his eternal life, self-denial

---

[68] William A. Barry, *Spiritual Direction and the Encounter with God: A Theological Inquiry* (New York: Paulist Press, 1992), 78.

[69] English, *Spiritual Freedom*, 127.

[70] English, *Spiritual Freedom*, 97.

[71] English, *Spiritual Freedom*, 104–05.

[72] English, *Spiritual Freedom*, 150–51.

moves beyond more or less frequent acts to settled disposition and character" (*Renovation*, 71).

As a practical guide to this progression toward complete identification of our will with God's, Willard offers the following distinctions to be noted: (1) **Surrender**—a person's consent to God's supremacy in all things; (2) **Abandonment**—there is no part of oneself that holds back from God's will; (3) **Contentment**—we are assured that God has done, and will always do, well by us—no matter what; and (4) **Participation**—the accomplishing of God's will in our world (*Renovation*, 150–51). Given the thoroughness of these key four distinctions of complete identification of our will with God, Willard astutely asks what many others may be asking at this point: "Do we then lose ourselves?" (*Renovation*, 156). While responding that it would be impossible for a fully functioning human person not to have a will, Willard reiterates what true spiritual transformation really means when he clarifies that "for the first time to have a will that is fully functional, not at war with itself, and capable of directing all of the parts of the self in harmony with one another under the direction of God" (*Renovation*, 156). The good news is that "for the first time we not only have a fully functioning will, but we also have a clear identity in the eternal kingdom of God and can day by day translate our time into an eternity embedded in our own life and in the lives of those near us. The will of God is not foreign to our will. It is sweetness, life, and strength to us. Our heart sings" (*Renovation*, 156).

Movement Four: Taking Up Our Cross with Jesus

> I continue to pray with the gift of being able to feel sorrow with Jesus in sorrow, to be anguished with Jesus' anguish, and even to experience tears and deep grief because of all the afflictions which Jesus endured for me.[73] —Ignatius of Loyola

> And then [Jesus] uses an absolutely shocking image—one all too familiar to his hearers, but rather hard for us to fully appreciate today. It was that of a man carrying on his back the lumber that would be used to kill him when he arrived at the place of

[73] Ignatius of Loyola, *The Spiritual Exercises* [203], in Fleming, *Draw Me into Your Friendship*, 153.

> execution. "Whoever does not come after me carrying his own cross cannot be my apprentice" (Luke 14:27, par). (*Renovation*, 66)

As spiritual seekers continue to travel with Jesus on the journey that takes him to Jerusalem, they often develop a deepening desire to stay with Jesus on this difficult road that eventually leads to Calvary. Even here the focus remains on the Lord. In asking for such a grace, retreatants "are not seeking to shoulder a heavy burden of guilt, but to ponder a mystery of love—that Jesus could love us enough to suffer and die for us."[74]

In moving more deeply into the contemplative exercises related to Jesus' journey to Calvary as progressively detailed in Ignatius' Third Week, it may be well to recall that these reflections are "intended to help us escape our narrow selves—we die to ourselves. This demands a deeply personal union with Jesus in suffering . . . [We] ask for the grace to be drawn beyond ourselves. In dying to ourselves through union with Christ suffering, we gain strength and courage, freedom and conviction—all those graces that are necessary to do the desire of God."[75] In order to facilitate the depth of one's heartfelt longing for this grace, Ignatius invites each spiritual seeker to "maintain a certain attitude of sorrow and anguish by calling to mind frequently the labors, fatigue, and suffering which Jesus our Lord endured from the time of his birth down to the particular mystery of the Passion which I am presently contemplating."[76]

In order to allow this level of desire of being with Jesus in his suffering to be increasingly connected to areas of suffering experienced by contemporary spiritual seekers, the following questions may prove to be helpful: "(1) What happens as a result of this suffering? (2) How can I learn to suffer for the right reasons and what are they? (3) How can I see meaning in this suffering, leading me to greater faith, hope, and love? (4) How do I identify the value of living with pain and how do I get out of pain that is destructive?"[77] As rightfully noted by the authors of *The Spiritual Exercises Reclaimed:* "Past interpretations of spirituality and theology uncritically

---

[74] Michael Harter, ed., *Hearts on Fire: Praying with Jesuits*, 2nd ed. (St. Louis: The Institute of Jesuit Sources, 2005), 106.

[75] English, *Spiritual Freedom*, 219–20.

[76] Ignatius of Loyola, *The Spiritual Exercises* [206], in Fleming, *Draw Me into Your Friendship*, 155.

[77] Dyckman et al., *The Spiritual Exercises Reclaimed*, 223.

accepted the value of suffering. Today, however, the insights of psychology and liberation theology demand the alleviation of demeaning and unjust suffering and expose the ways people and systems legitimate this kind of oppression."[78]

As an enhancement to what has been observed about the loving labor needed to be present to Jesus in his suffering both on the cross and in our contemporary world, the following points effectively characterize the depths of compassion needed, since "contemplating the passion draws us closer to Christ and deeper into the procession of suffering humanity . . . We discover the divinity hidden in weakness today. We share God's grief over humanity and our wounded earth. We locate our own suffering in a larger context. Finally, we are strengthened for the persecution that befalls all who take the gospel, and life itself, seriously."[79]

While Willard does not try to mitigate Jesus' words in Luke 14:27, he is also quick to point out that "one of the great dangers in the process of spiritual formation is that self-denial and death to self will be taken as but one more technique or 'job' for those who wish to save their life (soul)" (*Renovation*, 67). A key point of emphasis that serves to clarify the meaning of the interior work entailed in the carrying of our cross with Jesus in our daily lives can be summed up by Willard as follows: "This dreary and deadly 'self-denial,' which is all too commonly associated with religion, can be avoided only if the primary fact of our inner being is a loving vision of Jesus and his kingdom. This is where correctly counting the cost comes in" (*Renovation*, 67).

It seems important to note at this point that while Ignatius of Loyola tends to render practices of penance or self-denial as "always seen in terms of my love response to God,"[80] Willard offers an essential vigilance that can be instructive regarding such penitential practices where he asserts: "Practices of 'mortification' can become exercises in more self-righteousness. How often this has happened!" (*Renovation*, 67). Willard extends his caution about how the phrase "death to self" can be interpreted when he makes the following observation: "Self-denial will then externalize itself

[78] Dyckman et al., *The Spiritual Exercises Reclaimed*, 223.
[79] Brackley, *The Call to Discernment in Troubled Times*, 185.
[80] Ignatius of Loyola, *The Spiritual Exercises* [82], in Fleming, *Draw Me into Your Friendship*, 71.

in overt practices of group identity that may seem very sacrificial, but can leave the 'mind of the flesh' in full control. We see this, for example, in many who wear what they regard as plain clothing or who abstain from certain foods" (*Renovation*, 67). Likewise, the authors of *The Spiritual Exercises Reclaimed* echo Willard's rightful caution regarding ascetical practices as follows: "Paying close attention to his [Ignatius'] insight about inner conversion leading to outer asceticism can help keep penances in their rightful place as useful means to a significant goal: assuming one's rightful freedom as called, graced, and missioned."[81]

Perhaps a viable reinterpretation for our times of what it means to "carry one's cross" could rightfully include the following discernment question: "To what am I attached and therefore unconsciously substitute for the source of life?"[82] Even beyond the individual reinterpretation of what it means to "come after Jesus while carrying my own cross" (Luke 14:27, par), it may also be helpful to engage in the communal process of "expanding Ignatius' perspective to include cultural and social systems and the natural environment within which each individual dwells as an interdependent member [in order to uncover] new possibilities for reclaiming asceticism."[83]

The true spirit of such a giving up of one's life as it has been understood before following Jesus can be made clear in the words of Saint Paul to the Philippians where Paul shares his compelling perspective on his desire to be formed into Christ Jesus: "That I may know Him, and the power of His resurrection and the fellowship of His sufferings, being conformed to His death, in order to participate in the life of His resurrection (Philippians 3:10–11)." As Willard appropriately asks: "What are we to say of anyone who thinks they have something more important to do than that?" (*Renovation*, 43).

Movement Five: Learning the Ways of God's Love

> I beg for the grace of being able to enter into the joy and consolation of Jesus as he savors the victory of his risen life.[84]
> —Ignatius of Loyola

---

[81] Dyckman et al., *The Spiritual Exercises Reclaimed*, 75.
[82] Dyckman et al., *The Spiritual Exercises Reclaimed*, 74.
[83] Dyckman et al., *The Spiritual Exercises Reclaimed*, 75.
[84] Ignatius of Loyola, *The Spiritual Exercises* [221], in Fleming, *Draw Me into Your Friendship*, 169.

> Jesus' resurrected presence with us, along with his teaching, assures us of God's care for all who let him be God and let him care for them. "Do not be afraid, little flock' for your Father has chosen gladly to give you the kingdom" (Luke 12:32). (*Renovation*, 70)

Ignatius allows the retreatant to gently move from praying with Christ's passion and death to praying for the grace to know Jesus' joy and consolation in the fullness of his risen life. In order to assist the retreatant in praying for the grace of this intense joy with risen Jesus, Ignatius includes thirteen apparitions [SE 299–311], and this is "a beautiful way of showing how Jesus goes about bringing joy, hope, and confidence to people. All of the Resurrection appearances have the Immanuel theme—the continuation of the Incarnation today. God continues with us and is present to us."[85]

It needs to be noted, however, that a significant number of spiritual seekers often experience unexpected difficulties in praying for this depth of joy with Jesus in "the office of consoler that Christ our Lord exercises."[86] In light of such concerns and challenges, the following reminder can be instructive: "Remember that you are asking for a grace, a personal revelation of Jesus, not something that is in your power to attain on your own. It may take some time before this grace is given. . . . At any rate, be patient with yourself as you contemplate these resurrection scenes and keep insisting with Jesus that you want to share in his joy."[87] For, "to receive the grace of the joy of the resurrection we must accept the full reality of the horror of the crucifixion. Jesus, glorified, still bears the marks of that horror in his hands, feet, and side."[88]

Toward the end of *The Spiritual Exercises*, a spiritual seeker can experience a growing sense of transformative completion by reflecting on Ignatius' Contemplation to Attain Love [SE 230–237] as a way of inviting us to see God working in all creation to 'make all things new' and to respond in loving service.[89] It is important to consider that Ignatius skillfully lays the important groundwork for entering into this *Contemplatio* in "supplying two pre-notes: 'The first is that love ought to manifest itself

---

[85] English, *Spiritual Freedom*, 230.
[86] Ignatius of Loyola, *The Spiritual Exercises* [224], cited by English, *Spiritual Freedom*, 230.
[87] Barry, "What Do I Want in Prayer?," 112–13.
[88] Barry, "What Do I Want in Prayer?," 112.
[89] Brackley, *The Call to Discernment in Troubled Times*, 211.

in deeds rather than in words' [SE 230]. 'The second is that love consists in a mutual sharing of goods, for example, the lover gives and shares with the beloved what he possesses' [SE 231]."[90]

As the spiritual seekers continue their sustained reflections on Ignatius' *Contemplatio*, they are led into four distinct, yet related, "points" that can be simply summarized as follows: (1) **First Point:** I will call back into my memory the gifts I have received—my creation, redemption, and other gifts particular to myself; (2) **Second Point:** I will consider how God dwells in creatures; (3) **Third Point:** I will consider how God labors and works for me in all the creatures on the face of the earth; that is, [God] acts in the manner of one who is laboring; and (4) **Fourth Point:** I will consider how all good things and gifts descend from above.[91]

Beginning with the First Point and after each of the subsequent three points, Ignatius suggests that retreatants "make an offering of themselves in terms of the 'Take, Lord, and Receive' prayer:"[92] "Take, Lord, and receive all my liberty, my memory, my understanding, and all my will—all that I have and possess. You, Lord, have given all that to me. I now give it back to you, O Lord. All of it is yours. Dispose of it according to your will. Give me love of yourself along with your grace, for that is enough for me."[93] If "this offering is approached in the biblical way of a covenant relationship with God, it is much more meaningful."[94]

Willard rightly observes the following: "In laying down my life I must experience much more than 'my strength, my wealth, my power.' . . . The necessary support for giving and forgiving is abundantly supplied by Jesus through the reality of the Kingdom of God that he brings into our lives . . . when we experience cross and tomb, but resurrection is not yet" (*Renovation*, 70). Thus, as one moves through the Paschal Mystery while reflecting on the implications of what it means to have Jesus' resurrected presence with us, Dallas Willard asserts that "it is the love of God,

---

[90] Ignatius of Loyola, *Spiritual Exercises* [230–31], cited by English, *Spiritual Freedom*, 235.

[91] This summary of the four points of Ignatius' Contemplation to Attain Love is based on *The Spiritual Exercises* [234–37], in Ganss, *The Spiritual Exercises of Saint Ignatius: A Translation and Commentary*, 94–95.

[92] English, *Spiritual Freedom*, 237.

[93] Ignatius of Loyola, *The Spiritual Exercises* [234], in Ganss, *The Spiritual Exercises of Saint Ignatius: A Translation and Commentary*, 95.

[94] English, *Spiritual Freedom*, 237.

admiration and confidence in his greatness and goodness, and the regular experience of his care that free us from the burden of 'looking out for ourselves.'"[95]

As a fitting complement to the four points of Ignatius' *Contemplatio*, Willard outlines what he calls "Four Movements Toward Perfect Love" (*Renovation*, 131), which can be summarized as follows: (1) **First Movement of Love**—the acknowledgement that no other source, whether inside or outside of religions, even comes close to what God in Christ shows of love, particularly exemplified in Christ's laying down His life for us (1 John 3:16); (2) **Second Movement of Love**—the acknowledgement that the first great commandment, to love God with all our being, can be fulfilled because of the beauty of God given in Christ; (3) **Third Movement of Love**—the acknowledgement that the first great commandment makes it possible to fulfill the second: love of neighbor as oneself (1 John 4:12); (4) **Fourth Movement of Love**—the acknowledgement that the fellowship of Christ's apprentices in kingdom living is a community of love (John 13:34–35) (*Renovation*, 132). Thus, Willard offers the articulation of these movements of love as a way for us to "live in the community of goodwill from a competent God" with an assurance that "those who live in the fulfillment of God's redemptive love in human life will no longer experience fear" and the [resulting] torment that is incompatible with "living in the full cycle of love" (*Renovation*, 132).

However, love is inextricably bound to joy and peace, according to Willard's reflections on living one's life in the presence of the Risen Lord. Similar in tone to Ignatius of Loyola, Willard asserts that "joy is a basic element of inner transformation into Christlikeness and of the outer life that flows from it . . . [since] full joy is our first line of defense against weakness, failure, and disease of mind and body." Likewise, Willard describes "peace as the rest of will that results from assurance about 'how things will turn out' [since] when 'I am at peace about it,' we say, and this means I am no longer striving, inwardly or outwardly, to save some outcome dear to me or to avoid one that I reject" (*Renovation*, 133–34). When Willard talks about peace with God, he is reflecting on the quality of peace that "comes only from acceptance of his gift of life in his Son (Romans 5:1–2). We are

[95] English, *Spiritual Freedom*, 237.

then assured of the outcome of our life and are no longer trying to justify ourselves before God or others" (*Renovation*, 134).

Closing Reflections

Willard aptly reflects that "spiritual formation is not only formation of the spirit or inner being of the individual, though that is both the process and the outcome, it is formation by the Spirit of God and by the spiritual riches of Christ's continuing incarnation in his people—including most prominently, the treasures of his written and spoken word and the amazing personalities of those in whom he has most fully lived" (*Renovation*, 24). The work of this chapter has been to shed the spotlight on Ignatius and Willard as two viable spiritual guides for our contemporary times, since they have indeed given evidence of having "walked the walk" of following Christ with "the Lord always before them." Thus, "we learn from them how to do that by making them our close companions on the way" (*Renovation*, 114) in our ongoing quest to engage in the process of spiritual formation and transformation into Christ-likeness.[96] As a result, we can be filled with thanks for the lives of Ignatius of Loyola and Dallas Willard, who continue to give testimony to the essence of what it means to "take love itself—God's kind of love—into the depths of our being through spiritual formation [that will] enable us to act lovingly to an extent that will be surprising even to ourselves, at first" (*Renovation*, 24).

In the process of giving thanks for the graces given for being drawn by God in this process of spiritual transformation, spiritual seekers soon realize that these desires "move beyond thanksgiving to thankfully giving ourselves in return—to serve, to love."[97] As Jesuit John English rightfully asserts: "We should move from an attitude of thanks to one of welcome, saying, 'For all that has been, thank you, God. For all that will be, yes!'"[98]

However, given the humanness of our efforts in our quest to "love God with the totality of our being, we know that we do not do it. God loves us,

[96] As already acknowledged earlier in this essay (see footnote #3), Dallas Willard frequently clarifies his meaning of spiritual "formation" in light of "*trans*formation" in *Renovation of the Heart* by emphasizing that "spiritual formation for the Christian basically refers to the Spirit-driven process of forming the inner world of the human self in such a way that it becomes like the inner being of Christ himself" (*Renovation*, 22).

[97] English, *Spiritual Freedom*, 236.

[98] English, *Spiritual Freedom*, 236.

but how can we love God?"[99] And yet, even with the deepening awareness of our own limits in loving God and others, Ignatius encourages that "accordingly, the 'Take, Lord, and Receive' prayer starts from a recognition that God desires to share everything, including the persons of the Trinity," with spiritual seekers.[100] As rightfully articulated in the spirit of Ignatius, "this sharing should continue to grow until the Spirit stirs up in retreatants the longing to live in the present all God's loving acts of the past and share all in Christ's name: 'where two or three are gathered in my name, I am there among them' (Matthew 18:20)."[101]

Thus, the mutual love and intimacy experienced by spiritual seekers at this stage of transformation can be greatly enhanced by praying with Willard's effective paraphrasing of Jesus' Great Commission: "As you go through this world, make apprentices to me from all kinds of people, immerse them in Trinitarian reality, and teach them to do everything I have commanded you" (Mathew 28:19–20). As Willard continues to note: "These instructions are bookended by categorical statements about the plentiful resources for this undertaking: 'I have been given say over everything in heaven and earth' and 'Look, I'm with you every moment, until the work is done' (verses 18, 20)" (*Renovation*, 240). The assurance of "the great cloud of witnesses" who, having gone before us, can offer great reassurance as I desire to "see myself as standing before God our Lord, and also before the angels and saints, who are interceding for me."[102] We are surely not alone in our "joining the mighty project" of God who "wants people like us to become fit enough to follow Jesus inside the 'infinite rule of God,' becoming searchers for his kingdom, agents within it, witnesses to it, and models of it."[103]

---

[99] English, *Spiritual Freedom*, 234.
[100] English, *Spiritual Freedom*, 238.
[101] English, *Spiritual Freedom*, 238.
[102] Ignatius of Loyola, *The Spiritual Exercises* [232], in Ganss, *The Spiritual Exercises of Saint Ignatius: A Translation and Commentary*, 94.
[103] Plantinga, "Dr. Willard's Diagnosis," 50.

6

EMBRACING JESUS IN A FIRST CENTURY CONTEXT

What Can It Teach Us about Spiritual Commitment?

DARRELL L. BOCK

Dallas Theological Seminary

Abstract: This chapter shows that genuine faith in Jesus as life-changing—something that Dallas Willard emphasized—first emerged within second temple Judaism of the first century. After reviewing the unique claims of Jesus in a Jewish context, the chapter surveys the Greco-Roman context, and then offers application.

When I think of Dallas Willard I think of someone who was not afraid to point to Jesus and spiritual commitment in an age when most people are committed to themselves. Dallas was very clear in all of his writings that knowing Jesus is not a hobby, a business transaction one makes and forgets, nor an add-on to life; it is an entry into a journey that God directs in the context of the uniqueness of his person and the enablement of his rule and presence. The Father leads, Jesus mediates and exemplifies, and the Spirit enables. This commitment to Jesus is the goal of this chapter. It deals with unique claims about Jesus within the Second Temple Judaism of the first century, as well as looking at what religious life was like in the first century Greco-Roman world. Such background might seem distant in a journal on spiritual formation, but let me warn you that is not the case. To understand the world in which "decisions" for Jesus were made is to appreciate what it took to receive Jesus and begin the journey with him.

The Jewish Context

Those who study Jesus know that he emphasized the coming of the kingdom of God, the reestablishment of a rule among His people lost by Adam and sought for in Israel. The failure of this rule to gain a consistent response among God's people led to the promise of the prophets that one day God would do a work in the hearts of people. Whether this was called the New Covenant (as in Jeremiah), the Eternal Covenant (as in Isaiah), or simply described (as in Ezekiel), the point was that God would cleanse his people and bring them enablement from within so his rule could now be visible. This inner reading of the Law stands at the core of Matthew 5 and the Sermon on the Mount, where Jesus measures integrity not by the law's letter but by the heart. This is a text Willard developed so well in his key work, *The Divine Conspiracy.* So murder is not the issue; anger is. Adultery is not the issue; lust is. Divorce is not the issue; a commitment before God and his design are. The presence of an oath is not the point; having your word be true is. An eye for an eye in revenge is not the point, but vulnerability in the seeking to serve peace is. Hating your enemy is not the call; loving your enemy is. In all of this, Jesus pushes for human responses that are hardly instinctive, as he argues that disciples are to have a living standard greater than the world.

The pursuit of morality is not what made Jesus controversial. Jesus teaching that we should do unto others what we wish would be done to us was not a new idea. The "golden rule," a name that became attached to this teaching centuries later, is actually echoed in many ancient Greco-Roman and Jewish teachers.[1] His offering of the kingdom in itself was not offensive. It was quite Jewish, even if Jesus' articulation and model of that rule lacked the coercive political power Jews had hoped would come with the new era.

What made Jesus controversial in a Jewish context were his claims of authority. He said the Son of Man had authority to forgive sin (Mark 2:1–12). He called himself Lord of the Sabbath (Mark 2:28). He showed his authority in the temple precincts (Mark 11:15–19). He ruled the wind and the waves (Mark 4:35–41). He changed liturgy to refer not to Passover but himself (Mark 14:22–25). He did not teach like the rabbis. He claimed God

[1] Darrell L. Bock, *Luke 1:1–9:51*, BECNT (Grand Rapids, MI: Baker, 1992), 596–97, documents twelve ancient parallels to this saying.

would vindicate him and give him a seat at the right hand of God (Mark 14:61–62). These are not the claims of a mere prophet. There is more to Jesus' teaching than heralding the promise of God. In proclaiming the kingdom, Jesus also showed himself to be the one who had the authority to bring in the promise. This is why Peter's declaration of Jesus as Messiah and not prophet is a key turning point in the story in the synoptic gospels (Mark 8:26–30). Jesus was central to what God was doing, so central that one could not talk about God's program without mentioning Jesus' role in it.

This feature is what made Jesus' ministry so maddening to many more traditional Jews. They were focused monotheists reacting to a polytheistic world that surrounded them. To be faithful Jews meant living in a peculiar way, following God's law and its practices out of faithfulness and devotion to the one God and his covenant. This included distinctive and unusual practices in the ancient world like circumcision, Sabbath, dietary practices, and issues associated with purity, as well as limiting worship of God to only one temple. Jews focused on the one God, a stumbling block to Greeks and Romans who acknowledged multiple gods.

When Jesus presented and enacted his authority in the midst of declaring the kingdom and performed acts that pointed to divine prerogative, this caused many Jews to step back. Actions, like forgiving sin or ruling over the Sabbath as if he had written the commandment, caused offense. By the time we get to the early church, Paul is indicating to us that Jesus and God are part of the same confession of the one God! Nothing says this as clearly as 1 Corinthians 8:4–6 or the hymn in Philippians 2.[2]

In the Corinthian text, Paul alters the *Shema* of Deuteronomy 6:4. He takes the confession that Israel is to hear and live in the light of understanding that God is one and is Lord and splits those titles, so that God the Father causes the creation and Jesus mediates it. Both the Father and the Son are creators, another divine prerogative.

I will lay out the text so the point is clear:

"Now concerning meat offered to idols,
We know That there is no idol in the world
and there is no God but one.

[2] Translations are the author's.

> For since there are many so-called gods
> Whether in heaven or on earth
> Just as there are many gods and lords,
> But to us, [there is] one God the Father
> from whom are all things and we are for him.
> And one Lord Jesus Christ
> Through whom are all things and we are through him."

There is no doubt Paul alludes to ideas tied to the *Shema* here. The idea that there is one God is distinctive to Judaism in this time. This belief stands in contrast to the many gods of the Greco-Roman world. Yet in this confession of the one God, there is the confession of the Father and Jesus Christ in the same breath. More importantly, Jesus Christ is tied to the creation as creator, not as creature. What is more, in the LXX, the statement in Deuteronomy 6:4 about the one God used the title Lord to describe God. That text reads, "Hear, Israel, The lord our God is one Lord." This title Paul has split to bring in Jesus Christ. Paul is not adding Jesus to a statement about God as a separate figure. That would be ditheism, something Deuteronomy 6 denies. This is what Richard Bauckham rightfully has called "Paul's Christology of Divine Identity."[3] Believers in God's promise through Jesus worship one God, but that God and Lord as Creator entails Father and Jesus Christ. As Bauckham says, "The only possible way to understand Paul as maintaining monotheism is to understand him to be including Jesus in the unique identity of the one God affirmed in the Shema."[4]

In Philippians 2:6–11, the hymn ends with a declaration that every knee shall bow and every tongue in creation will confess that Jesus is Lord to the glory of God. Such worship was reserved in the old era for Israel's God. Even more the language used of Jesus comes from Isaiah 45:23. This Isaianic text comes from a context in which it is the one God of Israel who is set forth as the only true God. This text from Isaiah is one of the clearest declarations of God's uniqueness and sovereignty in the Hebrew Bible. God declares that allegiance will one day be uniquely his. There is no other

[3] Richard Bauckham, *Jesus and the God of Israel: God Crucified and Other Studies on the New Testament's Christology of Divine Identity* (Grand Rapids, MI: Eerdmans, 2008), 212.

[4] Bauckham, *Jesus and the One God*, 213. He goes on to say Jesus is the Lord whom the Shema affirms to be one.

God, nor is there any other savior or judge. The indication of this divine position is the fact that one day everyone will acknowledge this. Every knee will bow and every tongue will confess that God is the Lord and a powerful deliverer. The name given above every name is that which affirms the sovereignty of the Creator God over those whom he rules. There is no other place to go. There is no other one to whom to turn. One day all creation will know and affirm this. That is Isaiah's teaching.

Now Paul was a rabbi. He surely knows this background as he cites this hymn *about Jesus* with its intentional allusion to Isaiah 45. In the hymn, the bowing of the knee and the confessing of the tongue include giving such honor to the Lord Jesus. His work of emptying and death is so in conjunction with the Father, and so rooted in a heavenly origin, that the honor due the God of Israel will come to be given to the one through whom God worked. We see that substituting Jesus in the place of the God of Israel is kosher, justified by the calling and activity of Jesus at God's behest. Note how the hymn makes it clear that God is the one gifting Jesus with this name and role. Jesus does not act, nor does he claim to act, independently of the Father. But they are like a double helix in a piece of DNA, a package deal, operating as an inseparable team to deliver and save with a mighty hand stretched out, ironically, through the death of a frail human who once had been in the presence of God and who afterward was vindicated back to that original position. To see and speak of one is inevitably to speak of and see the other. So the hymn of Philippians 2 summarizes a core confession of who the saving Jesus is.

It is these kinds of understandings that stand behind what it means to acknowledge Jesus as God's promised one. Understanding and trusting Jesus began with how Jesus presented his role in the kingdom in his ministry and extended to the response of worship in the early church for all he had done. To believe in him was not only to acknowledge his work; it was entry into a spiritual walk of faith that appreciated who had done the saving. Spiritual commitment and relationship to God was the product of such faith, something God solidifies by giving his Spirit to seal that identity. The key role of the Spirit is something Romans 6–8 makes clear.

So what is the significance of this Jewish background? It means that to embrace Jesus and his message was to distinguish yourself from Jews who did not see Jesus as sent from God and vindicated by him so that Jesus sat at God's right hand. This view of kingdom and kingship, as Jesus taught, divided families and led to believers being persecuted. The earliest persecutions were led by Jews, such as Saul, who saw the early Jesus followers as people who had made too much of Jesus and not enough of Israel's God. My point is simply that to "come to Jesus" in the first century was to come to him in terms of who he said he was as he performed his work on behalf of God. It was to see Jesus as God's promised One who stood at the center of the arrival of God's deliverance. It also was to declare as a result of Jesus' death and resurrection that one knew not only that Jesus was alive but that he was seated with God at his right hand, sharing in the divine work as an equal to God.

This appreciation of a living, exalted Jesus is clear from Peter's speech about the saving Lord and Christ in Acts 2, no matter how one reads the rest of the speech. Peter in Acts 2:32–36 says it this way:

> This Jesus God raised, of which we are all witnesses. Therefore, exalted to the right hand of God, and having received the promise of the Holy Spirit from the Father, he has poured out what you both see and hear. For David did not ascend into the heavens, but he himself says, ***"The Lord said to my lord, 'Sit at my right hand until I make your enemies a footstool for your feet.'"*** [Psalm 110:1] Therefore let all the house of Israel know beyond a doubt that God has made both Lord and Christ this Jesus whom you crucified.

Salvation now comes through Jesus. The Father works his promise through the One seated with him. The Father delivers the Spirit through the one at his right hand. In all of this, the uniqueness of Jesus is embraced. To many Jews used to God possessing unique glory, such a position for Jesus spoke volumes and challenged much about their common belief. My point is simple. Someone responding to Peter's portrait of the Jesus who delivers embraces a model of kingdom rule that altered how one saw God, even the God of Israel. Such a decision, if we are to use that term, meant a shift of worldviews and led to the charge that followers of Jesus had distorted the Law (Luke 23:2–3). This charge came from leading Jews who could not embrace Jesus' claims of divine prerogative authority nor the idea that a plurality existed within God. In sum, to come to Jesus in a Jewish context was to embrace the fact that God had exalted him and enabled Jesus to become the beneficiary for those who called out in the name of Jesus Christ and received baptism through this name and authority. In Acts 2, we no longer call out to the God of Israel alone, but rather by getting baptized in Jesus Christ's name we understand that God works God's promise inseparably through Jesus as God distributes the gift of the Spirit through the now exalted One. In sum, to believe in Jesus was to believe in this act and what it entailed. Salvation was not merely a transaction; it was a belief that embraced this portrait of Jesus. This saving faith set the stage for the walk of discipleship and commitment to follow out of gratitude for what God had done by his grace.

The Greco-Roman Context

The issue in the Greco-Roman context for someone considering Jesus was completely different. Here the issue was not the exclusivity of God, but a life lived in the context of a pantheon of gods. Whether one thought of the "big twelve" Olympian gods led by Zeus (to the Greeks) and Jupiter (to the Romans) or a plethora of lesser deities, the Greco-Roman world lived in a highly religious context where gods were everywhere and so were the temples honoring them.[5] For example, if one goes to Pompeii today and walks through the Forum area which was frozen in time by the eruption of Vesuvius in AD 79, one will see on the program that four temples are found to surround this central locale of the city. In that forum one finds temples to Vespasian (the emperor), the public lares, Jupiter, and Apollo. The temple of Jupiter stands at the head of the forum. Behind it loomed not too far in the distance Mount Vesuvius. If one walks further away, even a temple to the Egyptian goddess Isis can be found in Pompeii. A house dedicated to a mystery religion also could be found down the street. The ancient world was not like the secular West. The creation was seen as alive and animated with gods and spirits. In the Greco-Roman view, it was best to keep as many of these gods happy as possible. Religion in this world was

---

[5] The twelve tied to Mount Olympus were Zeus/Jupiter, Hera/Juno, Poseidon/Neptune, Athena/Minerva, Apollo, Artemis/Diana, Aphrodite/Venus, Hermes/Mercury, Hephaistos/Vulcan, Ares/Mars, Demeter/Ceres, and Dionysius/Bacchus. The first name in the pairing is the Greek name, while the second is the Roman name for the god. Lesser gods included figures like Pan and the satyrs, not to mention the great emperors whom the culture deified.

not about doctrine but about bargaining, honoring the gods so they would not become displeased with you. Each god had his realm and the need was to be sure as many of them were honored as was possible. Sacrifices were offered in a spirit of what in Latin was called *do et dies* ("I give so you might give"). The attitude was that one should conduct rites before the gods carefully and with respect lest they be offended and act against you. A rite undertaken in a wrong way was to be repeated.

But there is more. These gods were not only related to individuals; they were seen as paying attention to affairs of state. So there were civic cults as well, designed to make sure the gods were honored and the state was protected. Generals did not go to war without offering sacrifices and checking portents in order to be sure the gods favored their cause. Livy (56 BC–AD 17) in his *History* 19.10–14 tells of the story about how the goddess Cybele/Attis was brought from what is Modern Turkey to Rome in 204 BC because hail and other portents of evil had led the city to look for an answer to reverse the sequence of disasters. He notes, "So they began seriously to consider the best means of transferring the image of the goddess to Rome, in order to enjoy as soon as possible the victory which so many omens and oracles portended–from Delphi, from the Sybilline books, and from the inexplicable confidence of Scipio." Her arrival into Rome led to a citywide celebration. The religious calendar, known as the *Fasti*, noted the observance of some 150 religious holidays for the public. That is a religious holiday every three days! The expectation was that faithful citizens would show their respect to the gods on these days. The fate of the city was seen to be associated with participation.

Beyond this there were family gods, known as lars. These little idols occupied a niche in the house that served very much like a family altar. These niches either were carved out in the wall or were wooden cupboards hung there. One can see these niches preserved in Pompeii as well. This part of a house formed a little house chapel, sometimes called the *aedicule*. Every day sacrifices of grain or other simple offerings were made to be sure the gods were honored. Plautus (254–184 BC) in *Aulularia* 1–25 describes the role of the household God in one of his plays as follows:

> THE HOUSEHOLD GOD [emerging from Euclius' house]: So that no one may wonder who I am, I will put it briefly: I am the

> *Lar familiaris* of the house out of which you see me come. I have possessed and watched over this house for years now, already for the father and grandfather of the man who lives in it now . . . He [i.e., the present owner] has only one daughter. She sacrifices incense or wine to me every day, or prays in some way to me again and again, decorating me with garlands.

In the *Fasti*, a work about the annual calendar, Ovid (43 BC–c. AD 17) describes one ancient practice and its rationale, "In older days it was the custom to sit on long benches before the hearth, and it was believed that the gods were present at the meal . . . Even into our own days, a trace of this old custom has survived: a clean vessel bears the food that is sacrificed to Vesta" (6.305–310). A text describing a private cult in Philadelphia in the first century BC notes in lines 12–15 an oath made to the gods about various aspects of one's behavior.[6]

Life in the Greco-Roman world was saturated with religious belief and practice. One could not escape it. Observance and the gods were everywhere. With it was bound up a sense of loyalty to one's state and so to one's neighbor. Religion involving the gods was not a private affair, but a corporate act of identity.

I teach a class on Greco-Roman backgrounds, and when we finish covering Greco-Roman religion I have a discussion class on what students have learned and how this impacts how they read the Scripture. In that discussion, the reactions are consistent. "I had no idea how pervasive religion was then." Another will say, "I thought only the Jews had involved religious ritual to make vivid their relationship to God." Still another common response is, "I had no idea that the gods were tied up in the religion of the state to the degree they were." Here, students are describing the impact of seeing and sensing from the photos we view in class and the ancient texts we read during the semester of how religion in the first century was not a tagalong enterprise. It impacted every area of life daily.

So what does this mean for the Greek, Roman, or other non-Jews who began to consider Jesus? It meant to confess the one God and Jesus entailed

---

[6] The examples of ancient Greco-Roman life come from Hans Klauck's fine survey of the background of the first century and religious practices. See *The Religious Context of Early Christianity: A Guide to Greco-Roman Religion* (Edinburgh: T&T Clark, 2000), 60–61.

leaving all of this other practice behind. It was to opt out of all the social activity that involved the gods. That included leaving activity at the religious temple, in public civic rites, at home before the lars, and including associations with ancestors that were tied to some of the gods of the home. It led to Christians burning their magic books in Ephesus (Acts 19), as well as outsiders calling them "atheists," since they no longer believed in the gods of their neighbors. It meant Paul taught that even though in one sense Christians knew idols were nothing, one should not go to the temple and participate there (1 Cor. 8–10). It involved a confessed break and a comprehensive social separation from their former religious practices. Once again, the mere decision to embrace Jesus and his work as unique meant that one made more than an instant act or a momentary decision.

This act of faith involved a statement about the divine. It affirmed the singularity of believing in the One Creator God and the One Judge he had appointed. Both Peter and Paul say as much in Acts 10 and 17, respectively. Peter in Acts 10:42–43 says, "He [Jesus] commanded us to preach to the people and to warn them that this is the one [Jesus] appointed by God as judge of the living and the dead. About this one all the prophets testify, that everyone who believes in Him receives forgiveness of sins through His name." Note once again how saving authority comes through the name of this exalted one, Jesus. Paul in Acts 17:30b-31 declares, "He [God] now commands all people everywhere to repent, because He has set a day on which He is going to judge the inhabited world in righteousness, by a man whom He designated, having provided proof to everyone by raising Him from the dead." My point is that to believe in Jesus in this context was to "turn from idols to the true God" (1 Thess. 1:9–10). This turning was a social act that not only identified with what God had done through Jesus, but also that one had broken all their former divine relationships. One did not make this move lightly. A decision for Jesus in the first century came with huge ramifications. In a real sense, it was to embrace a reorientation in one's life and walk a new path in rebirth.

Application

As a New Testament scholar and believer, I often hear debates today about whether one is to come to faith and believe that Jesus is Lord *or* Savior. This bifurcation was not distinguished in the New Testament texts I read about faith in coming to God's grace in Jesus. Even more, the context of this confession shows that such a bifurcation was almost culturally impossible for the first century. So this look at the larger context of the first century is instructive, no matter which culture is in view, Jewish or Greco-Roman. You can take your pick. Either way the act of believing in Jesus meant leaving an older way of thinking about God. This faith had Jesus firmly entrenched as the one at God's right hand through whom salvation, judgment, and even worship came. It was because Jesus is Lord, and exalted by God to show it, that salvation can be preached in his name and faith in him launches forgiveness *and* a new life—what the New Testament intentionally calls rebirth.[7] The New Testament never intends us to separate forgiveness from new life. Rather forgiveness leads into new life. God and his grace lead to spiritual commitment in a response of faith. I cannot get there myself. Jesus must give me the forgiveness I so desperately need. He also must enable me by his Spirit to walk the walk. New life is not only about obtaining forgiveness; it is about entering into God's presence as his enabled child. In fact, that entry into new life is the core of the gospel.

So Ephesians 2:8–10 teaches us not only that salvation is by grace through faith, as verses 8–9 teach, but that salvation teaches that we are God's workmanship, created in Christ Jesus for good works that God designed that we might walk in them. The point in this passage is that God saved us so we would live differently in the experience of his grace. It was part of the divine design for transformation. In fact, Titus 2:11–14 says it most clearly:

> For the grace of God bringing salvation to all people has appeared. It [i.e., that grace] trains us to reject godless ways and worldly desires and to live self-controlled, righteous, and godly lives in the present age, as we wait for the happy completion of our hope in the glorious appearing of our great God and Savior, Jesus Christ, who gave himself for us to set us free from every kind of lawlessness and to purify for himself a people who are truly his, who are eager to do good.

---

[7] I have detailed this emphasis on forgiveness and new life in defining the gospel in *Rediscovering the Real Lost Gospel: Rediscovering the Gospel as Good News* (Nashville, TN: Lifeway, 2010). This book is a biblical theology of the gospel, showing how transformed life is at the gospel's core.

The points of Jesus' death were to (1) offer himself for sin and (2) to purify a people to himself who desire to honor God. God's grace gives the enablement that makes this transformation possible. Faith believes God for it.

This hope in the gospel is what Paul called in Romans 1:16–17, "the *power* of God unto salvation." The gospel is about more than salvation; it is about enablement. This power is the reason Paul said he was not ashamed of the gospel. That power is the enablement to be and live like a child of God. God gives that power through the Son in the Spirit. Jesus discussed the sending of the Spirit in the Upper Room (John 14–16). Peter preached about this gift of the Spirit in Acts 2. Paul summarized this enablement as the core of his gospel in Romans. In Romans 4:16–5:5, what did Abraham believe? It was that God could bring life out of two old dead bodies. So in the gospel, God gives life to a spiritually dead body that he not only declares righteous, but also gives enabling life to through the Spirit. So the saving faith of Romans 4 leads into the story of the Spirit's work in Romans 5–8 (see especially 5:5).

Salvation is about a new journey that does not wait on eternity. Rather, eternity comes to us. For when we know the Father and the Son he sent, we have eternal life, not merely a life of duration, but a life rooted in and sent from eternity, a life of quality. Dallas Willard has spent his life writing about this life of quality in his many works, urging us to the spiritual commitment that stands at the core of believing in Jesus.[8] May we walk in that newness of life enabled in our commitment by the very Spirit God, by his grace, gave us through Jesus Christ.

In sum, may we believe God for his grace and receive the power to be who he made us to be. For faith is not a decision of a moment, but an abiding virtue turning to God for a transforming life.

[8] See especially Dallas Willard, *The Great Omission: Reclaiming Jesus's Essential Teachings on Discipleship* (New York: HarperOne, 2006).

7

PUTTING ON CHRIST

Spiritual Formation and the Drama of Discipleship

KEVIN J. VANHOOZER

Trinity Evangelical Divinity School

Abstract: This chapter explores the role of doctrine in creating a disciple's self-understanding and suggests that it is healthy for Christians to think in terms of "acting out" what it means to be "in Christ." This "theodramatic" approach to theology can be viewed as one theologian's attempt to atone for what Dallas Willard calls "the great omission"—namely, the neglect of Jesus' command to "make disciples of all nations."

Dallas Willard has been instrumental in my own growing conviction that the teaching of Christian doctrine is for naught unless it aids and abets the cultivation of disciples—people whose hearts are rightly oriented and who know how to live out the life of Christ in them. But long before Willard called for spiritual formation, C. S. Lewis suggested: "Every Christian is to become a little Christ. The whole purpose of becoming a Christian is simply nothing else."[1] Lewis's call to become little Christs recalls Paul's exhortation to "put off" the old self and "put on" Christ. This chapter explores what this change of costume involves from the perspective of what a "theodramatic" approach to theology that I have developed in *The Drama of Doctrine* and *Faith Speaking Understanding*. I there argue that the role of doctrine is to (1) indicate what is in Christ and (2) direct those in Christ to participate in

[1]C. S. Lewis, *Mere Christianity*, Revised Edition (1952, New York: HarperCollins, 2001), 177.

Christ by playing their parts in the drama of redemption. This theatrical model raises an important issue concerning the disciple's self-understanding: is it healthy for Christians to think in terms of "acting out" what is "in Christ" (their new identities as Christ's disciples) or does this encourage a false sense of self—a "put on"? I respond to this question in four steps where I (1) present a theodramatic anthropology; (2) describe discipleship as the project of growing into/putting on Christ; (3) consider three objections to my previous work about the relationship between persons/roles and role-playing; and (4) respond to the objections by offering a dogmatic description of putting on Christ (i.e., spiritual formation) in soteriological, pneumatological, and eschatological terms.

Introduction: "But We Have *the Mind of Christ*" (1 Cor. 2:16)

"We have *the mind of Christ*." This is an extraordinary declaration, whether one reads it as making a theological or a psychological claim (I think it is both). The apostle Paul is not simply saying that we have the same beliefs, much less the same brainwaves, as the historical Jesus. Disciples are neither carbon nor cerebral copies of Christ. In context, Paul is explaining to the Corinthians why the wise men of this age do not understand the wisdom of God: they cannot accept, or even comprehend, the thoughts of God, much less the wisdom of the cross, because they do not have the Spirit of God (1 Cor. 2:11). Conversely, truly spiritual people—those who have the Spirit—understand how God is reconciling all things to himself through the cross. They have the mind of Christ, at least as concerns the plan of salvation. In a different context, however, Paul issues not a declaration but an exhortation: "Have this mind [of Christ]" (Phil. 2:5). Does the Spirit give us access to Christ's mind or not?[2]

A preliminary question is how people who are not Jesus Christ can have his mind. Is Paul encouraging us to be schizophrenic or, worse,

[2] In the context of 1 Corinthians 2 Paul is arguing against those who claim to be spiritual, and thus in a position to judge him, yet regard the cross as foolishness. The truly spiritual person is the one who discerns the wisdom of God in the cross of Christ through the Spirit, who knows and reveals the mind of God. In the context of Philippians 2, by way of contrast, Paul is addressing those who intellectually understand the cross but need to display the same humility in their corporate life as Christ did in becoming obedient to the point of death on a cross. To have Christ's mind in this context is to have the same dispositions. As we shall see, having the mind of Christ is tied to having the Spirit, and this in turn explains the already/ not-yet character of the Christian life: the Spirit is an eschatological reality.

inadvertently giving us a recipe for hypocrisy? On the contrary: what is ultimately at stake in claiming to have the mind of Christ is our understanding of how we come to be in our own right minds, and how we come increasingly to share in Christ's life. The question of how disciples progressively come to embody the mind of Christ is therefore an appropriate ground on which to negotiate the way forward in the discussion between theology, Christian psychology, and pastoral care, especially if the pastor's prime imperative is to grow mature persons whose maturity is measured by "the stature of the fullness of Christ" (Eph. 4:13).[3] This process of maturation—the post-conversion process of becoming more like Christ, of "growing up . . . into him" (Eph. 4:15)—is what I mean by *drama of discipleship*.[4]

Discipleship is dramatic because it involves both call ("Follow me") and response. Discipleship is dramatic because it is possible to deny one's calling, at least on certain occasions (Peter did it three times). Drama means *doing*, and the assumption is that the disciple is somehow active in his or her becoming like Christ. How much drama is there in the life of an ordinary disciple? According to Paul, there is quite a bit, for those who have been raised with Christ have put to death (put off) the old self and "have put on the new self" (Col. 3:10). What is the nature of the change Paul has in mind in speaking of putting off/putting on? How are we to understand the relationship between having the mind of Christ (1 Cor. 12:16) and being directed to have the mind of Christ (Phil. 2:5)? In particular, to what extent can people change and what contribution, if any, can people make to their own transformation? Pastors and counselors are particularly interested in changes that encourage proper functioning, which is another way of saying, changes that make disciples more like Jesus Christ, the exemplar of true humanity. Our question is not "What must I do to be saved?" but rather "What must I do to be sanctified?" What must I *do* to have the mind of Christ? How does character formation—in this case, coming to have the mind of Christ—actually happen?

---

[3] See James G. Samra, *Being Conformed to Christ in Community: A Study of Maturity, Maturation and the Local Church in the Undisputed Pauline Letters* (London and New York: T&T Clark, 2006).

[4] See also Kevin Vanhoozer, "The Drama of Discipleship: A Vocation of Spiritual Formation," in *Pictures at a Biblical Exhibition: Theological Scenes of the Church's Worship, Witness, and Wisdom* (Downers Grove, IL: InterVarsity Press, 2016).

In the sixteenth century Anabaptists agreed with Luther that Christ, the righteous one, is a *donum*, a gift to the believer. But they went on, beyond Luther, to say that Christ was also an *exemplum*, an example to follow. In response, Lutherans called the idea that a true Christian must follow in Christ's steps "the first article of the Anabaptist heresy,"[5] thereby bequeathing to disciples striving to conform to Christ not one but two theological H-bombs to worry about: heresy and hypocrisy. The latter is a danger when a person's external action (behavior) fails to coincide with a person's internal disposition (heart).

To avoid confusion, we need first to distinguish converting from sanctifying grace. While in one sense conversion is a lifelong process, the grace that transfers sinners from the kingdom of darkness into the kingdom of light marks a definitive break: only God can make the blind see; only God can make dead hearts beat anew. My immediate concern is with counseling Christians—that is, those who have experienced the regenerating work of the Holy Spirit and have responded in faith to the gospel word about Jesus Christ. To be sure, born-again Christians too can suffer from various psychological disorders. Yet even persons who receive a clean bill of psychological health may display a conspicuous lack of conformity to Christ: to be in one's normal mind is not yet to have the mind of Christ.

My primary interest in this chapter is not with people who have certifiable mental illnesses but with everyday Christians who seem to be functioning normally yet are nevertheless dysfunctional insofar as they lack conformity to Christ. How can dysfunctional disciples become people who have the mind (which as we shall see includes the heart) of Christ? From a theological point of view, all of us have sinned (Rom. 3:23) and fallen short of psychological health due to the noetic effects of sin, in particular our tendency to suppress the truth in unrighteousness (Rom. 1:18–21). To the extent that we fail to coincide with our true selves, then, all people, Christians included, need therapy. Discipleship itself is, I submit, a kind of therapy for rightly ordering lives that are still disordered, even after conversion. Stated differently: the drama of discipleship is another way of addressing the dynamics of spiritual formation.

---

[5] Cited in Malcolm B. Yarnell III, *Formation of Christian Doctrine* (Nashville: B&H Academic, 2007), 13.

This chapter examines the "turn to drama" in theology and argues that it yields helpful insights into the process of Christian maturation. But first: what is theodramatic anthropology, and how can it help?

How I Came to Theodramatic Model
(And What It Has to Do With Anthropology and Discipleship)

1. From Speech Acts to Theater Acts

I took one small step (or was it a great leap?) toward viewing Christian life and theology in theodramatic terms when, in thinking about what it means to be biblical, in the context of hermeneutics, I discovered speech acts. The basic idea is that speakers and authors do not merely state facts but use words to *do* other things as well—acts like promising, warning, consoling, insulting, and so forth.[6] It was Paul Ricoeur who first taught me that the language of the Bible owes much more to *parole* (dynamic discourse) than *langue* (static structure). Considered as a closed system, "Language no longer appears as a mediation between minds and things. It constitutes a world of its own."[7] The Bible is not a closed book of signs, sealed off in a world of its own, but a book discourse: *what it says to someone about something in some way at some time for some purpose.* In the case of the Bible, the "someone" is a prophet or apostle (and ultimately God, the divine author), the "to someone" is Israel, early Christians (and ultimately readers today), the "about something" is the good news about the life of God made available to all in the risen Jesus Christ, and the "for some purpose" is salvation, present and future. "Discourse" therefore reminds us that we fail to do justice to the Bible if we focus only on what it says (semantics) to the exclusion of what it does (pragmatics).

Speech act theorists (often philosophers of ordinary language) distinguish between locutionary, illocutionary, and perlocutionary acts (i.e., the distinction between saying something, doing something besides speaking *in* speaking, and bringing something about *by* speaking).[8] The triune God does many things with biblical words, including narrating, promising,

---

[6] The seminal text of speech act philosophy is J. L. Austin's *How to Do Things with Words* (Oxford: Oxford University Press, 1962).

[7] Paul Ricoeur, *Interpretation Theory: Discourse and the Surplus of Meaning* (Fort Worth: Texas Christian University Press, 1976), 6.

[8] Austin may have written the key seminal work, but the most important systematic treatment is probably John Searle's *Speech Acts: An Essay in the Philosophy of Language*

commending, and so on, but Paul tells us that what the Bible is particularly good for is "training in righteousness" (2 Tim. 3:16). What the triune God does in, with, and through the Bible is cultivate mature disciples who come to resemble Jesus Christ. In a word, what God does with the Bible is *make disciples*. And this relates to another aspect of speech acts: the *interlocutionary* act, the idea that discourse is addressed *to someone*.[9] It takes two to interlocute.

Speech acts therefore bring us to the threshold of theater in two ways. First, speech act theory reminds us that language is not merely descriptive but also *performative*. Speakers and authors *do* things with words. This is the thrust of the concept *illocution*: what we do in saying something (e.g., promise). Second, the interlocutionary act is the essence of theater: one person presenting herself to another, communicating something via speech acts and acts that speak a thousand words. Theater is not about physical events (things colliding) but *interpersonal interaction* (people communicating). In retrospect, it seems a fairly straight line from speech acts to the theater: "It is quite correct that the particular vocation of theatre is to explore the consequences of this intuition that 'to say is to do' and 'to do is to say.'"[10]

2. Theodramatic Anthropology

During the same period, I was working on biblical hermeneutics, I was also asked to write an essay on theological anthropology. The timing was providential. I was aware of John Macmurray's argument in *The Self as Agent* that we are better off understanding human persons not with Descartes' "I think" (rationality) but rather with "I do" (agency).[11] In *thinking*, the mind alone is active, but *doing* engages mind and body. What most intrigued me, however, was the notion of the self as *speech* agent.[12] The idea of speech agency allowed me to view the person in relational terms without collapsing personhood into relations. God, of course, is the primary and paradigmatic

(Cambridge: Cambridge University Press, 1969). For an application of speech act theory to biblical interpretation, see Richard S. Briggs, *Words in Action: Speech Act Theory and Biblical Interpretation* (Edinburgh: T&T Clark, 2001).

[9] Ricoeur, *Interpretation Theory*, 14–15.

[10] Ross Chambers, "Le Masque et le miroir: Vers une théorie relationelle du théâtre," *Etudes littéraires* 13 (1980): 402.

[11] John Macmurray, *The Self as Agent* (London: Faber & Faber, 1957)

[12] Vanhoozer, "Human Being, Individual and Social," in *The Cambridge Companion to Christian Doctrine,* edited by Colin Gunton (Cambridge: Cambridge University Press, 1997), 158–88.

speech agent, but—and this is absolutely central to my account—God addresses human creatures who, being in his image, can cry out, or talk back, to God.

Theodramatic anthropology thus begins with the insight that to be a person in God's image is to be a communicative agent in various kinds of communicative relationships with others. Indeed, it is in the process of being dialogically addressed, called by *others*, that the self comes into its *own*. First and foremost, God calls us into being: to be a human person is to be evoked, addressed, and summoned by God.[13] God's address to various individuals (e.g., Adam, Abraham, Moses, David, the prophets) is often a key development in the drama of redemption (cf. Gen. 22:1; 46:2; Ex. 3:4–7; 1 Sam. 3:6). But others—parents, children, neighbors, friends, and so on—call us too. If persons are answerable agents, then one's particular personal *identity* is largely a function of the pattern our responses take to the calls of these others. If our word is our bond, then perhaps we can view persons as communicative agents in various kinds of covenantal relationships. For example, the identity of characters in the Bible, as well as the nation of Israel as a whole, is largely a function of their settled pattern of response to various summons by the word of God.

3. Theodramatic Theology

The next step in my thinking was the realization that Christianity itself is essentially dramatic. The entire story of the Bible concerns God's own self-presentation on the world-stage to address his human creatures. If drama involves interpersonal interaction, then the Bible is *theodramatic* insofar as it concerns the relationship between God in three persons and the world of human persons. In particular, the Bible tells the story of how God creates humanity in his image in order to dwell and have fellowship with them, sharing his light and life in love.[14] The story gets underway with a divine

---

[13] See Alistair I. Mcfadyen, *The Call to Personhood: A Christian Theory of the Individual in Social Relationships* (Cambridge University Press, 1990).

[14] Interestingly, Eugene Peterson suggests that the drama could be construed as centered on spiritual formation. The Spirit forms creation (Gen. 1:1–3), descends on Jesus at his baptism thus anointing him Messiah (Mark 1:9–11), and descends again on his disciples who had gathered according to his instructions in the upper room (Acts 2:1–4). The Spirit is thus involved in creation, salvation, and community building and therefore "is not marginal to the main action, but *is* the main action" ("Spirituality/Spiritual Formation," in the *Dictionary for Theological Interpretation of the Bible*, edited by Kevin J. Vanhoozer [Grand Rapids, MI: Baker, 2005], 767).

promise—"And you shall be my people, and I will be your God" (Jer. 30:22; cf. Gen. 12:2; Ex. 6:7; Lev. 26:21)—and continues with repeated demonstrations of God's covenant faithfulness and steadfast love (Ex. 34:6–7). The meaning of human life is to glorify God (by imaging him) and enjoy him forever (by living in his light and love). Human beings are communicative agents in order to dwell in communion with God and with one another.

The biblical drama of redemption is all about how God makes good on his promise to Adam, Abraham, and others to defeat Satan and reclaim the world as his kingdom and temple. The Bible ultimately treats the wonderful way in which God fulfills his promise and completes his purpose for humanity in and through Jesus Christ. The gospel is the good news that communion with God and one another has been established through the cross and resurrection of Jesus, and has begun to be realized through the Holy Spirit in the church. Indeed, the church is the temple—the special dwelling place of God—and is therefore an ingredient in the climax of the drama.

My book, *The Drama of Doctrine,* argues that the point of theology is to help disciples understand the theodrama in ways that are not merely theoretical but also theatrical.[15] The point is not simply to theorize about the drama, but to participate in it. The important point is that doctrine helps to build up the church by offering *direction* for participating in the drama, for living out the way, truth, and life of Jesus Christ. Obviously the most important speaking and acting part belongs to the triune God: the whole play turns on what God the Father is doing in God the Son through God the Holy Spirit. Nevertheless, members of the church have something to do as well. The task of the disciple is to demonstrate his or her understanding of the drama of redemption by joining in, and to do so in the right heart and spirit. Doctrine thus serves the purpose of helping disciples demonstrate their understanding in practice. Theology here takes on the character of *performance* knowledge.

To speak of performance raises the specter that doctrine directs Christians merely to "play-act" or "role-play" the faith: "To *be* or merely to *pretend* to be: that is the question, for the actor as well as for the would-be disciple," I said.[16] The goal, of course, is to become an integral self, with

[15] Kevin J. Vanhoozer, *The Drama of Doctrine: A Canonical-Linguistic Approach to Christian Theology* (Louisville, KY: Westminster John Knox, 2005).
[16] Vanhoozer, *The Drama of Doctrine*, 365.

no gap between the inner and outer person. I acknowledged the danger of hypocrisy but argued that the way forward is not to abandon the theatrical metaphor but to take it with the utmost seriousness. I then suggested, drawing on the actor and director Constantine Stanislavsky, that the good actor *becomes the role he plays.*[17] The idea is that actors must not simply go through the external motions, but actually experience the emotions or inner state of their character. As we shall see, this claim has provoked, maybe not a storm but at least a tidal spout of criticism (see below).

Doctrine resembles cognitive therapy to the extent that it encourages certain ways of thinking about God, the world, and ourselves. Ultimately, however, doctrine addresses the heart, the seat of our desires and dispositions. It is largely for this reason that I want to include the imagination under "cognitive": the imagination is the kind of thinking that fits parts into larger wholes and discerns meaningful patterns and is in turn grasped (i.e., delighted) by the beauty of the whole. Doctrinal theology helps Christians acquire theodramatic habits of thought whereby we understand persons and events in relation to the broader theodrama of which everything on heaven and on earth is a part: the story of the Father renewing creation in Christ through the Spirit. The drama of doctrine is ultimately a matter of the Christian's most important habits: will we adopt ways of seeing, judging, and acting that form a pattern of right response to God's word and fitting participation in the drama of redemption?[18]

4. The Drama of Discipleship

The role Christians are called to play in the theodrama is that of disciples of Jesus Christ: persons who have the mind of Christ and who know how to embody it at all times and places to everyone. This is the drama of discipleship: discerning and then doing the way of Jesus Christ in particular situations. There is another aspect to the drama of discipleship—namely, the question of how we become the kind of people who not only know what to say and do to embody the mind of Christ, but the kind of people for whom all this comes *naturally*. In *The Drama of Doctrine* I argued that

[17] Vanhoozer, *The Drama of Doctrine*, 366.

[18] Insofar as doctrine is concerned with making disciples, it might also be seen as a form of psychodynamic therapy to the extent that it encourages disciples to internalize dispositions and habits of the heart that lead to right participation in the theodrama (a point I owe to Steve Porter).

doctrine itself is a means of character and spiritual formation insofar as it strips up our false masks (our *persona*) and discloses our true faces: faces that reflect the glory of God; faces that "speak" Christ.

Theodramatic anthropology depicts Christian identity as both gift and task. Gift: God has given Christ to us and us to Christ. This is the gift of the doctrine of union with Christ, which spells out what it means to be in Christ and to partake of all the spiritual blessings that appertain thereunto. Task: Christ calls us to follow him, to become increasingly *more* like him. C. S. Lewis says, "Every Christian is to become a little Christ. The whole purpose of becoming a Christian is simply nothing else."[19] Lewis here echoes Paul's exhortation to "put on" Christ (Rom. 13:14; Gal. 3:27). With this we return to my key question: is putting on Christ a matter of external appearances only? How should disciples "act out" their role as "little Christs"? Does counseling people in our care to think of themselves in theodramatic terms (i.e., as actors in the drama of redemption) exacerbate or resolve the problem of the false self?

Though I talk about disciples in *Drama of Doctrine*, there are no index entries for "disciple" or "discipleship." My main focus there was to describe nature of Christian doctrine, not to prescribe procedures for making Christian disciples. The situation is altogether different in *Faith Speaking Understanding: Performing the Drama of Doctrine*, where there are some sixty index entries under "disciples," including "church as company of," "location in Christ of," and "improvisers of mind of Christ."[20] I there describe discipleship as the project of having the mind of, growing into, or putting on Christ. To have the mind of Christ, I submit, is ultimately a matter of the Spirit illumining renewed minds (Rom. 12:2) and cultivating patterns of embodied wisdom—lived knowledge—hence the drama (embodied action) of discipleship.

Person, Role, and Identity: Three Objections to the Model of Self as Actor

With this background knowledge in hand, we can now return to the main question of the present essay: how might a theodramatic model contribute

[19] Lewis, *Mere Christianity*, 177.

[20] Kevin J. Vanhoozer, *Faith Speaking Understanding: Performing the Drama of Doctrine* (Louisville, KY: Westminster John Knox, 2014).

to our understanding of how sinners with God-denying habits change into persons who respond obediently, like Jesus Christ, to God's call on their lives? According to Cedric Johnson, "Theology speaks of the process of conversion, and psychotherapy deals with how people change."[21] I want to argue, on the contrary, that a theodramatic theology has something to contribute both to our understanding of the process by which a person changes, or rather, matures into Christ, and the process itself. Specifically, my claim is that spiritual formation prepares disciples to play their roles in the drama of redemption, and that doctrinal theology has a role to play in what we could call the *theodramatic formation* of disciples.[22]

But how does *saying* "put on the Lord Jesus Christ" (Rom. 13:14), and explaining this putting on with doctrines like justification by faith, actually help a person change? Is performing doctrine (acting out *what is* "in Christ") a matter of *acting oneself into new ways of thinking* or of *thinking oneself into new ways of acting*?[23] And, regardless of how we answer, does not an emphasis on the drama of discipleship reduce the Christian life to an unhealthy moral activism? This question leads straight to the first of three objections I now want to consider.

1. The "Moralistic" Objection to Putting on Christ (John Coe)

The first objection is one that Reformation Protestants rightly raise. We can state it in the form of a question: Does not an emphasis on *performance* lead to precisely the kind of works righteousness that Paul contrasts to the righteousness of God that comes, in Christ, "from faith to faith" (Rom. 1:17)? Or, does not an emphasis on the disciple's *doing* amount in the end to a kind of moral activism?

I readily grant that moralism is an ever-present danger. If pride is the besetting temptation of saints and sinners alike, we ought to be cautious about commending a course of action that adds fuel to the fire of our fallen inclination toward self-reliance. John Coe defines the temptation to

---

[21] Cedric B. Johnson, "The Process of Change: Sacred and Secular," *The Journal of Psychology and Theology* 5, no. 2 (1997): 103.

[22] Wesley Vander Lugt makes a similar point in the context of his treatment of Christian ethics: "Theatrical formation refers to the preparation, development, and growth of actors toward excellence and a readiness for particular roles and performances." See *Living Theo-Drama: Reimagining Theological Ethics* (Burlington, VT, and Farnham, UK: Ashgate, 2014), 29.

[23] I owe this alternative to E. Stanley Jones, as cited in O. H. Mowrer, "The Role of the Concept of Sin in Psychotherapy," *Journal of Counseling Psychology* 7 (1960): 185–201.

moralism as the mindset behind "the attempt to deal with out spiritual failure, guilt and shame by means of spiritual efforts, by attempting to perfect one's self in the power of the self."[24] On this view, "moralism" is not a good but a bad thing, insofar as it refers to the attempt to make oneself a spiritual person—an actor prepared to walk the way of Jesus Christ—through what ultimately amounts to no more than self-help. Moralism is the illusion that disciples can make do without God's grace. It is the attempt to become good without God. On a strong anti-moralist position, the attempt to imitate Christ is particularly dangerous to the extent that it insinuates human works (moral effort) in the last place it belongs. We cannot put on Christ by our own unaided moral strivings.[25]

The kind of acting I have in mind, however, is more than moral striving. Theodrama is not a technique or a program for self-improvement but a way of conceiving, concentrating on, and participating in what God is doing for us (theodrama = God doing). It involves our doing too, yes, but a doing of a very particular kind: a participation in the doing (and the done) of Jesus Christ. C. S. Lewis comes close to what I have in mind when he asks what we think we are doing when we utter the first two words of the Lord's Prayer: "our Father." In a chapter from *Mere Christianity* entitled "Let's Pretend," Lewis says that what we're doing is "*dressing up as Christ.*"[26] His claim that this is an example of "good pretending" leads to the second objection to my theodramatic proposal I want now to consider.

2. The "Mere Semblance of Virtue" Objection to Putting on Christ (Jennifer Herdt)

How else can we become virtuous *except* by acting the part? Jennifer Herdt criticizes those who worry overmuch about moral activism. The principal concern is that acting virtuously to become virtuous leads either to hypocrisy (the mere semblance of virtue) or pride—a "fruitless assertion

[24] John Coe, "Resisting the Temptation of *Moral* Formation: Opening to *Spiritual* Formation in the Cross and the Spirit," *Journal of Spiritual Formation & Soul Care* 1, no. 1 (2008): 55.

[25] Coe identifies moralism with legalism, and suggests that Paul's concern with the Galatians is not they were relying on works in order to be saved (i.e., justified) but that they were relying on their own works to achieve their sanctification ("Resisting the Temptation of *Moral* Formation," 58–59).

[26] Lewis, *Mere Christianity*, 163 (*emphasis* original).

of human moral agency."[27] In Herdt's words, "Hypocrisy is not a virtue. But is 'putting on virtue,' acting the part of virtue, always a vice?"[28] Aaron Preston makes a similar point in criticism of John Coe, noting that it is a mistake to equate all moral effort with "moralism," the sinful strategy of relying on one's good works instead of God.[29] Dallas Willard is even more succinct: "God is not opposed to effort but to *earning*."[30]

Herdt examines the Protestant idea, represented by Luther, that we should "abandon our own efforts and rely wholly on God's grace to transform us from within"[31] and finds it wanting. For Luther, it seems that "The natural life and the graced life are utterly discontinuous, and the natural aspiration to virtue thus blocks, rather than advances, true Christian righteousness."[32] Herdt thinks Protestants like Luther (and me) betray an exaggerated anxiety over the idea of acquired virtue under the mistaken assumption that we cannot put on virtue, or become the role we play (i.e., disciple of Christ), unless and until God by grace creates a new heart and makes us new creatures. From this Protestant perspective, Herdt contends, to "put on" is to act out what is ultimately nothing more than a sham: external practices cannot transform the inner person; pretending is inauthentic.

Herdt's basic problem with this standard Protestant position is that it seems to prescribe "pure passivity in which human agency is wholly abandoned."[33] Herdt has a healthy respect for Aristotle's view that we acquire virtues "largely by habituation, that is, by acting as if we already possess them."[34] In Herdt's view, "putting on Christ" is best understood "as an imitation of Christ's example through which we are brought into participation in Christ's virtue."[35] The grace of moral transformation works through nature, namely, the ordinary process of learning by imitating. It is as if those who act according to their *better* natures get the grace to go

---

[27] Herdt, *Putting on Virtue: The Legacy of the Splendid Vices* (Chicago: University of Chicago Press, 2008), 1.

[28] Herdt, *Putting on Virtue.*

[29] Aaron Preston, "Redeeming Moral Formation: The Unity of Spiritual and Moral Formation in Willardian Thought," *Journal of Spiritual Formation & Soul Care* 3, no. 2 (2010): 206–29.

[30] Jan Johnson, Keith J. Matthews, and Dallas Willard, *Dallas Willard's Study Guide to* The Divine Conspiracy (San Francisco: HarperOne, 2001), 107.

[31] Herdt, *Putting on Virtue*, 1.

[32] Herdt, *Putting on Virtue*, 15.

[33] Herdt, *Putting on Virtue*, 15.

[34] Herdt, *Putting on Virtue*, 23.

[35] Herdt, *Putting on Virtue*, 2.

on. What begins as pretending ("dressing up") ends up becoming genuine Christlikeness.

Herdt approves of Erasmus's "performance conception" of virtue, according to which "we develop the virtues only by enacting them, and so transform being through doing."[36] Grace works *through* nature to improve it, not *on* nature to transform it. Stated differently, instead of a nature/grace dichotomy Herdt assumes that all forms of human agency are always/already grace-enabled; even people who do not confess Christ can imitate him so long as they are striving to act virtuously. For Herdt, then, putting on Christ is a matter of people acting like Christ, not of ceding moral agency to Christ (as she thinks Luther has done). In Herdt's view, we could be said to have the mind of Christ when we imitate his acts (with or without converting grace).

3. The "Not Becoming the Role" Objection to Theatrically Putting on Christ (Natalie Carnes)

Whereas Herdt complains that I, like other Protestants, too anxiously *distinguish* person and role in order to acknowledge the ever-present threat of hypocrisy, my second critic, Natalie Carnes, attacks from the other direction and complains that I too complacently *conflate* actor and character.

Carnes appeals to one of Gregory of Nyssa's pastoral strategies for helping his congregation interpret Jesus' first beatitude ("Blessed are the poor in spirit, for theirs is the kingdom of heaven"—Matt. 5:3). Gregory encouraged his wealthy and powerful congregants to perform their real-world roles of social prestige as actors perform parts, "knowing that they will eventually hang up their costumes and give up their personas."[37] The antidote to hypocrisy in such social performances is to remember not to confuse who one truly is (a mere mortal) with the role one temporarily plays here on earth: "The man who plays king does not take his symbols of power to say something about who he is as a person."[38] A king who understands the accident of his birth (he might have been born into the house of a commoner),

---

[36] Herdt, *Putting on Virtue*, 128.

[37] Natalie Carnes, "The Mysteries of our Existence: Estrangement and Theatricality," *Modern Theology* 28, no. 3 (2012): 402.

[38] Carnes, "The Mysteries of our Existence," 414.

and the inevitability of his own death can play his royal role "resistantly" (i.e., under protest of its ultimate unreality).

Carnes worries that "recent theater theologians collapse important distinctions between persons and their roles, which is seen particularly in their insistence that actors become their characters."[39] It is true that in *Drama of Doctrine* I urge disciples to become the role they play in order to avoid hypocrisy. Putting on Christ, I argued, is a means of spiritual formation. Carnes, however, sees this as a problematic move that erases the space between actor and role, thereby canceling out the very thing that makes theatrical performance *theatrical*.[40] *Becoming* the role "is precisely what the actor does *not* do."[41] At the end of a performance of *Hamlet*, she reminds us, Kenneth Branagh is not dead. Actors remain distinct from the characters they embody. The *becoming* is only *metaphorical*, for "it is precisely the *not* becoming that distinguishes theatrical performance from other kinds of performance."[42] Hence the way a Christian becomes Christ-like in the performance of doctrine "cannot be the way Kenneth Branagh 'becomes' Hamlet in his performance of that character."[43]

While "putting on Christ" may indeed be a type of performance, Carnes insists that it is not theatrical.[44] For in the context of the theater, the actor and the character the actor puts on are two different persons, not the inside and outside of a single person. In contrast, what is unique about putting on Christ is that "it turns on the performance of a role that discloses and realizes one's personhood."[45] I think Carnes is right in what she affirms but wrong in what she denies. But I am grateful to both Herdt and Carnes for pushing me to think harder about what Paul means by "putting on Christ."

Theodramatic "Putting On":
Doctrine as Cognitive-Affective Therapy for Acting Out What Is in Christ

I want now to respond to my critics by taking my cue from Dorothy Sayers's adage, "The dogma is the drama."[46] In particular, I want to offer a *dogmatic*

---

[39] Carnes, "The Mysteries of our Existence," 404.
[40] "Yet it is precisely that gap between actor and role that defines *theatrical* performance" (Carnes, "Mysteries of Our Existence," 405).
[41] Carnes, "The Mysteries of our Existence," 405.
[42] Carnes, "The Mysteries of our Existence," 405.
[43] Carnes, "The Mysteries of our Existence," 405.
[44] Carnes, "The Mysteries of our Existence," 409.
[45] Carnes, "The Mysteries of our Existence," 410.
[46] Dorothy Sayers, *Creed or Chaos?* (New York: Harcourt, Brace & Co., 1949), 3.

description of putting on Christ, by which I mean an account that takes as its overarching framework the triune economy of God's works. To do so, however, I need to respond to a last objection.

1. The Drama of Discipleship: Toward a Dogmatic Account

When Paul commands his Roman readers to "put on the Lord Jesus Christ" (Rom. 13:14), he is asking them to do more than merely go through the dominical motions. When Paul exhorts his readers, "Have this [Christ's] mind," he is urging them to adopt in their inner being ("spirit") Christ's habitual attitude of humility, his disposition to look to the interests of others before his own (Phil. 2:3–4). Paul asks his readers to put on Christ only because he views them as those who have already been baptized into Christ. Indeed, what was issued as an imperatival command in Romans 13:14 is now stated as indicative fact: "For as many of you as were baptized into Christ have put on Christ" (Gal. 3:27). It appears, then, that baptism has something to do with putting on Christ, but what? The short answer is that water baptism is a sign and sacrament of the believer's baptism with the Holy Spirit, a dramatic elemental representation of our participation, through faith, in Jesus' death and resurrection, and thus of our being born again, made new.

Baptism is a graphic representation of our dying and rising with Christ. It is a moment of high drama in the church, an act fairly dripping with meaning and significance. It is also a clue to what it means to put on Christ. However, some people object that baptism does not represent anything. It is simply something humans do to signal our allegiance to Christ. Indeed, some wonder whether the theodrama as a whole represents something; if it does not, it is not strictly speaking *theatrical*. This is similar to Carnes's criticism, though now transposed from the level of actors and their roles to that of God and his work. No doubt Carnes would protest the idea that the history of redemption is "theatrical." To be sure, God acts, but this in itself does not make God an actor.[47] If God is an actor, what role is he playing? More pointedly, if God is an actor, who is God representing?

It is an excellent question. My answer: when God acts in time he represents *himself*. The drama of redemption dramatically represents, in the

---

[47] Michael Pakaluk is willing to speak of God as acting, but not of God as an actor. See "The Play's Not the Thing," *Edification: The Transdisciplinary Journal of Christian Psychology* 4, no. 1 (2010): 29.

form of the space-time missions of Son and Spirit, the eternal life of the triune God. What God does in time (the "economic" Trinity) corresponds to the way he is in eternity (the "immanent" Trinity). This directly bears on our topic, because the new humanity created in Jesus Christ also corresponds to what God in eternity determined (elected) his human creatures to be: what disciples perform is no socially constructed role but a role for which they were chosen "before the foundation of the world" (Eph. 1:4; cf. Rev. 13:8).

We understand the drama of discipleship, and theodrama in general, only when we see that the divine drama refers to the economy of redemption. Theodrama is not simply a pedagogical tool, much less a colorful way of speaking, but rather a way of giving a properly economic account—what I am referring to as a dogmatic description—of putting on Christ. Putting on Christ is not an exercise in moral striving, something we do, but something made possible only by a prior work of the triune God. Baptism is thus a key scene in the drama of discipleship: on the one hand, only God can bring about our participation in the death and resurrection of Jesus Christ; on the other hand, we participate in our incorporation into Christ precisely by acting out, with water, what God has accomplished through faith, and the Holy Spirit. Baptism dramatically represents our union with Christ, just as God's works in history dramatically represent his eternal plan of salvation.

The Spirit's role in the drama of redemption is essential. As Calvin says, "as long as Christ remains outside of us . . . all that he has suffered and done for the salvation of the human race remains useless" (Institutes III.1.1.). The Spirit is the "giver of life" because he unites us to Christ. It is thanks to the Spirit that the life of Christ is formed within us. The Spirit is the theatrical "dresser" who clothes disciples with the righteousness of Christ (Eph. 4:24; cf. Isa. 61:10), the one who assists disciples with putting on Christ and maintains costume quality throughout the performance.[48] For those who by faith through the Spirit have been united to Christ, putting on Christ is not a fiction (what *if*) but a reality (what *is*). Contra Herdt, disciples do not act like Christ in order to approximate an exemplar *outside* them. Rather, disciples put on Christ *from the inside out.*

[48] I shall say more of the Spirit's role in spiritual formation below.

At the heart of the drama (economy) of redemption is the mission of the Son: Christ's death, resurrection, ascension, and heavenly session. Disciples can act out Christ only if Christ is first in them, and getting disciples into Christ, and Christ into disciples, is arguably the whole point of the Spirit's mission, as well as the climactic Pentecostal scene where God creates a new people. The Holy Spirit is set apart to minister Christ: to witness to Christ; to illumine our minds to receive the knowledge of Christ; to renew our nations to form Christ in us. To be in Christ through the Spirit is to have been transferred into his kingdom (Col. 1:13) and thus to enjoy citizenship in heaven (Phil. 3:20). This change in citizenship may not be empirically verifiable, but it is neither fantasy nor pretense. On the contrary, doctrine is simply the attempt to spell out (indicate) *what is* "in Christ."

Is, the operative term, carries an eschatological charge. To say what is in Christ is to describe what is "already" and "not yet." To put on Christ is therefore to begin to act out *now* our participation in the age *to come*. It is the eschatological qualification what *is* in Christ that gives me the resources to respond to Carnes's objection that I lose what makes a performance theatrical when I say the actor "becomes" the part she plays. Contra Carnes, the theatrical element in the theodrama is not the gap between actor and role but rather the *present representation in earthly, bodily form of what is eternally true in heaven: what is "in Christ."*

In acting out the life of Christ, disciples are neither relying on their moral efforts nor pretending to be something that are not; they are rather participating in what is eschatologically the case, namely, that disciples "are his workmanship, created in Christ Jesus for good works" (Eph. 2:10). As Herman Ridderbos rightly observes, the change of costume—the putting off of the old man and the putting on of the new—is not something we do (a step in our personal *ordo salutis*) but something the triune God has accomplished (an event in the *historia salutis*): "If anyone is in Christ, there is a new creation" (2 Cor. 5:17). What is in Christ—our new humanity—is meant "not first of all in a personal and ethical sense, but in a redemptive-historical, eschatological sense."[49]

[49] Herman Ridderbos, *Paul: An Outline of His Theology* (Grand Rapids, MI: Eerdmans, 1997), 63.

What, however, does it mean to participate in what is eschatologically the case? After all, the costume with which we are clothed—Christ's righteousness—is invisible, as is the Spirit himself. Is participating in what is eschatologically the case a kind of supercharged cognitive therapy, whereby if we simply believe hard enough, we can convince ourselves of a thing's truth? The short answer is that faith is a gift of the Spirit that allows us to apprehend reality. The reality is that, thanks to the Spirit, those who confess Jesus Christ as Lord really do have a share in his life, and this includes his sense of sonship, desire to do God's will, and compassion for others (i.e., his "mind"). Through faith we come not only to believe but also to *experience* the reality of we in Christ and Christ in us. The Spirit ministers the biblical word in so renews our imagination, our ability to both *taste* and *see* the glory and excellence of the unfolding theodrama in which we have been caught up.

To put on the new self, then, is *not* to pretend to be something that we are not; rather, it is to participate in the new humanity that *is*—in Christ. It is through faith, which includes the eschatological imagination—the ability to taste and see the invisible things of God—that people view and experience themselves as citizens of the kingdom of heaven. To put on Christ is to "taste and see" (Psa. 34:8) that one is *already* living in the kingdom of God, which is "the realm of God's action."[50] In putting on Christ, then, disciples enter into a new state of affairs: what eschatologically *is*.

To be in Christ is to be in the process of being restored to true humanity, a process that requires our active involvement. To put on Christ entails acting him out: otherwise, our *doing* would fail to correspond to our *being*. To act out what is in Christ is to be an answerable self who can respond to God's call like Samuel ("Here I am"; 1 Sam. 3:4) and Mary ("Let it be with me according to your word"; Luke 1:38). It takes an eschatologically charged imagination to participate in reality, to taste and see what is already but not yet in Christ.[51] The drama of discipleship is all about

---

[50] Dallas Willard, "The Gospel of the Kingdom and Spiritual Formation," in *The Kingdom Life: A Practical Theology of Discipleship and Spiritual Formation*, edited by Alan Andrews (Colorado Springs: NavPress, 2010), 29.

[51] See also Alison Searle, "Performance, Incarnation, Conversion: Theology and the Future of Imagination," in *Theology and the Future: Evangelical Assertions and Explorations*, edited by Trevor Cairney and David Starling (London and New York: Bloomsbury T&T Clark, 2014), 208: "Imagination is the aspect of human nature or identity that enables us to envisage the eschatological future that God has promised."

acting out—dramatically representing in earthbound bodies and everyday practices—the new humanity that is in heaven, which is to say, in Christ. Let me now call upon two witnesses to help further clarify my case.

2. N. T. Wright: Forming Christian Character

Christians have been cast, called, and clothed "in Christ" by the triune God to be actors in the drama of redemption. That they are part of the play, the divine comedy of the Christ, is by grace alone. However, precisely because they have been cast, disciples have a role to play. Paul says they have put Christ on, and yet he also directs them to put on Christ. It remains to be seen whether what actors have to do—to become the role they have been assigned by acting out—involves a kind of moral effort. Stated differently, is spiritual formation simply a matter of character (moral, virtue) formation, as we saw Herdt earlier maintain? This is a subtle query, because people are always in the process of some kind of spiritual formation in the sense that the things we typically do shape our character and eventually form our heart. How is acting in the theodrama any different?

N. T. Wright has written a book from the perspectives of New Testament studies on how Christians become virtuous: *After You Believe: Why Christian Character Matters*. The central thing that is supposed to happen "after you believe" is the transformation of character.[52] Character is transformed by having a goal, deciding what steps to take to attain the goal, and then making sure those steps become habitual, a way of walking (Wright says "second nature"[53]). So far, so Aristotle. If this were all Wright had to say, he would be in Herdt's camp, an advocate of the idea that virtue comes to those who work hardest at it. But it is not all he has to say.

The drama of discipleship concerns a very particular kind of spiritual formation—namely, the Holy Spirit's formation of Christ's life in disciples.[54] Central to Wright's account is his insistence that Jesus came not simply to provide an example but to inaugurate God's new creation (i.e., new humanity). The "new humanity" (Eph. 4:24; Col. 3:10) has already

[52] N. T. Wright, *After You Believe: Why Christian Character Matters* (New York: HarperOne, 2010), 26.

[53] Wright, *After You Believe*, 29.

[54] Preston helpfully summarizes Willard's threefold distinction of the meaning of spiritual formation ("Redeeming Moral Formation," 212).

begun in Jesus' resurrection. For lack of a better term, we could perhaps refer to the distinctive virtues of Jesus—the habits of mind that comprise Christlikeness—as *kingdom virtues.* Virtues such as humility and compassion are hyper-ethical, going beyond earthly systems of morality. Kingdom virtues are the fruit of the Holy Spirit, the first fruit of the saints' eternal life. To put on Christ is to embody the mind of Christ and practice the kingdom virtues. Such a life is shaped "*by God's promised future*" and lived "*within the ongoing story of God's people.*"[55] This, after all, is God's missionary purpose, the point of the whole drama: to bring heaven—the place where God's will is freely and joyfully done—down to earth. Christian living in the present "consists of anticipating this ultimate reality through the Spirit-led, habit-forming, truly human practice of faith, hope, and love."[56] To put on virtue is to live in ways that anticipate the life in the age to come. In my terms, to put on Christ is to act Christ out in the power of the Holy Spirit.

Wright invokes the concept of "eschatological authenticity," which is a matter of practicing now what we will have fully only in the future, "a God-given 'second nature': The authenticity that really matters is living in according with the genuine human being God is calling you to become."[57] Christian character formation—putting on the kingdom virtues—is a matter of progressively becoming on earth what one already is in heaven (in Christ). Christian doctrine helps disciples to perceive what is (eschatologically) the case. This is perhaps what Paul means by speaking of transformation through the renewal of our minds (Rom. 12:2). Such transformation involves letting the word of Christ dwell richly in us (Col. 3:16) so that we can imaginatively indwell the drama of redemption. In addition to dressing us in Christ, the Holy Spirit also illumines our minds, lighting the stage of our inner being, so that we can apprehend through faith the contours of the true story of the world, a drama in which we have lines to say and things to do. The renewal of our minds means cultivating habits of good theodramatic judgment—becoming actors who know what to say and do to be like Christ.

Wright argues that Paul has thoroughly Christianized the ancient pagan (Aristotle's) theory of virtue, not just because it features humility

---

[55] Wright, *After You Believe*, 57. Italics original.
[56] Wright, *After You Believe*, 67.
[57] Wright, *After You Believe*, 108.

but also because it locates us in the story of Jesus Christ: "To be formed by this capital-S Story is to be formed as a Christian."[58] To put on Christ is thus to inhabit his story (cf. Paul "I have been crucified with Christ. It is no longer I who live but Christ who lives in me"—Gal. 2:20). Doctrine, in deepening our understanding of the story—the identity of its protagonists, the meaning of its most important events—helps disciples better understand what God is doing in Christ so that they can act out their new humanity as it were by second nature.[59]

3. Robert Roberts: Practicing Pauline Psychotherapy

My second ally, Robert Roberts, articulates a Christian psychology via Pauline theology without explicit reference to secular psychology—or theater, for that matter.[60] His essay nevertheless converges with the main thrust of what I am calling the drama of discipleship, not least because Roberts too focuses on "acting out" what is in Christ. In particular, Roberts focuses on the role of the disciple in acting out the new personality—a new disposition; a new pattern of response to the call of God and others—they have been given in Christ (Eph. 2:15; 4:24; Col. 3:10): "The effort to live the new and healthy life is reframed as yielding oneself to what one already is in Christ."[61] It is one thing for the paralytic to believe he has been healed, quite another to get up and walk. In getting up and walking, he is not *pretending* to be whole; on the contrary, he is acting out the gift of his new Christ-given capacities. Similarly, disciples must take up their behavioral beds and *walk* (John 5:8). To walk in newness of life (Rom. 6:4) "is just to start performing the kind of actions . . . that are characteristic of the new self."[62] It is no good having legs (or spirits) made new unless one puts them into action.

---

[58] Wright, *After You Believe*, 261.

[59] Loyal readers of Dallas Willard may be wondering if theodramatic therapy ever gets beyond the V of Willard's V-I-M framework for spiritual formation: vision—intention—means (see Dallas Willard, *Renovation of the Heart* [Colorado Springs: NavPress, 2002], chap. 5). The short answer is that theodrama is more than vision because it involves a way of relating to others in the world. I address the question of intention and means in the Conclusion in connection with the heart.

[60] Robert C. Roberts, "Outline of Pauline Psychotherapy," in *Care for the Soul: Exploring the Intersection of Psychology and Theology,* edited by Mark McMinn and T. R. Phillips, (Downers Grove: InterVarsity Press, 2001), 134–63.

[61] Roberts, "Outline of Pauline Psychotherapy," 140.

[62] Roberts, "Outline of Pauline Psychotherapy," 141–42.

Roberts notes that the clothing metaphor ("put on . . . compassionate hearts, kindness" and so on—Col. 3:12–14) suggests "that Pauline therapeutic action is best thought of not as aspiring after an ideal, but as exploiting a perfection already present."[63] *The theatrical is the therapeutic*—but only if the disciple is "in Christ" by grace through faith. Roberts's key insight is "that psychological dysfunction corresponds to a failure to put on one's new self as created in Jesus Christ."[64] This is a failure of what we might call the cognitive-affective-eschatological imagination. Central to Pauline psychotherapy "will be teaching clients that they have been re-created in Jesus Christ."[65] Yes! And this is precisely the task of Christian doctrine: to say *what is in Christ*. Roberts is not discounting secular psychotherapies all together, only trying "to see how far we can go without major importations from outside our tradition."[66] In my terms, he is offering a properly dogmatic account of how people become more like Christ.

In Roberts's view, the church should be the primary place where disciples learn to put on Christ. Wright agrees: it is in community that we learn, from diverse examples—the great cloud of witnesses—what discipleship looks like in particular situations, and it is in community that we practice virtue. The theatrical—in this case, acting out what is in Christ in company with other disciples—is indeed the therapeutic. Doing church means participating in corporate communicative activities—praying, fellowship, hearing the word of God, celebrating the Lord's Supper—that train disciples in right covenantal relationships. Merely pretending to be virtuous is not the same as putting on Christ: "Pretending is a way of not working at it. And working at it is what counts."[67] This thought returns us to Paul: "work out your own salvation with fear and trembling, for it is God who works in you" (Phil. 2:12–13). Disciples become their true selves when they act *from the inside out*, conforming to what God has already done to transform them. Disciples do not dissemble but rather bear witness to the truth when they bring their existential reality into correspondence with their eschatological reality "in Christ."

---

[63] Roberts, "Outline of Pauline Psychotherapy," 142.
[64] Roberts, "Outline of Pauline Psychotherapy," 149.
[65] Roberts, "Outline of Pauline Psychotherapy," 149.
[66] Roberts, "Outline of Pauline Psychotherapy," 161.
[67] Wright, *After You Believe*, 275.

Conclusion: "But We Have the Mind of Christ"

The challenge of pastoral counseling is to help disciples grow into their new selves as communicative agents in new covenantal relationship, not simply to believe that they are "in Christ" but actually to act out the life of Christ in them. Doctrine plays a therapeutic role in the process of sanctification in setting forth in speech *what is in* Christ: the truth of our new identity. Yet this doctrinal renewing of the mind also requires a robust eschatological imagination (i.e., faith) that enables disciples not only to perceive but also to feel the truth of their *already/not yet* union with Christ.

Imitating Christ is not a matter of pretending or play-acting but of participating in something real: the theodrama or, as Dallas Willard calls it, the kingdom of God becoming present on earth as it is in heaven. The disciple is an actor in God's drama of redemption, a person who exhibits his or her knowledge of God through a living interaction with God and others.[68] What distinguishes putting on Christ from the practice of other moral virtues is the unique inner preparation of the disciple-actor. To act from the inside out means that spiritual formation is first and foremost a matter of the heart. The Holy Spirit creates a "clean heart" and illumines our minds to understand the word of God, but it falls to the disciple to trust the word of Christ by stepping out and putting it into practice. This too is a demonstration of the reality that is in Christ. Whenever two or more disciples are gathered to "do Christ," they become living parables of the kingdom of God.

1. "Sense of the Heart"

Many psychological problems stem from a denial of reality. For example, various status anxieties (i.e., the feeling that one is never good enough or has not yet done enough) stem from the failure to appreciate one's status in Christ. People who put on Christ to cast off their false selves and grow into their true selves. Is it enough, however, simply to be told about our new humanity? In the final analysis, is Christian doctrine simply a variation on the theme of cognitive therapy? Is information alone sufficient unto sanctification? I have argued that because the dogma is the drama, the theatrical

[68] Dallas Willard, *Living in Christ's Presence: Final Words on Heaven and the Kingdom of God* (Downers Grove, IL: InterVarsity, 2014), 9–22.

is the therapeutic: in directing us to what is in Christ, Christian doctrine not only tells but shows, and in showing addresses not only the mind but also the imagination and the heart—what Jonathan Edwards calls the affections, the deep springs of all human action.

What is in Christ has both cognitive and affective content, and the Holy Spirit ministers understanding of this reality by giving disciples the eschatological imagination to grasp the biblical words that bear witness to it. Does such an imaginative appropriation of an eschatological truth count as an instance of what C. S. Lewis calls a "good pretending"? We need to proceed cautiously here: that believers have a share in Christ's life is no mere pretense. I submit that what Lewis calls "good pretending" is a case of seeing and tasting the "not yet" in terms of the "already." In keeping with my theatrical model, perhaps it would be more accurate to speak of good *presenting*. When disciples act out Christ they display their performance knowledge inasmuch as they are living out on an earthly stage the truth of the heavenly blessings they have in Christ (Eph. 1:3).

Putting on Christ requires what Jonathan Edwards calls spiritual perception: a perception not only of the truth but also of the goodness and beauty of what is in Christ. The Holy Spirit gives us a "new sense of the heart" (Edwards) that enables us not only to see but also to taste and experience the goodness of the gospel, thus arousing our holy affections and producing new habits of holy practices.[69] The drama of discipleship is ultimately the story of how the Spirit engrafts us into the new humanity in Christ and thus draws us into the very life and kingdom of God. What Edwards calls spiritual perception I am calling the eschatological imagination: the ability to see (think) and taste (feel) our individual lives as caught up in the triune drama of the Christ.

The goal of this doctrinal therapy is to saturate disciples in the knowledge and understanding of what God is doing in Christ through the Spirit to the point that they can demonstrate their understanding by freely embodying the mind of Christ everywhere, at all times, and to everyone as it were by second nature. To put on Christ is ultimately a form of performance knowledge. The prerequisite for right performance is the indwelling word and Spirit

---

[69] See Michael J. McClymond and Gerald R. McDermott, *The Theology of Jonathan Edwards* (Oxford: Oxford University Press, 2012), 316.

of Christ. This is the primary work of converting grace: the donation of a new disposition, a new orientation of the heart.[70] Pastors and counselors serve as secondary means of grace by practicing cognitive-affective therapy, helping disciples to see, feel, judge, and act theodramatically. Though the terminology of theodrama may be new, the insight that doctrine serves a pastoral purpose is not.[71] Christian doctrine, when deployed wisely, is itself a kind of cognitive-affective-eschatological therapy that renews the mind by directing the eyes of our hearts to perceive and appreciate what is in Christ and then to act out what we have come to see and love.

2. Intent of the Heart

To put on Christ involves more (but not less) than changing external behavior. Most radically, it involves a transformation at the source of behavior: the heart. Here, too, the notion of theodrama can help. Most people think about themselves as the heroes of their own stories. If they are Christian, they may allow God into their lives. To say "what is in Christ" is to reverse this way of looking at things. My life is not my own, nor is my story: rather, as a follower of Jesus Christ I have been cast as a supporting player in God's story, a story made flesh each time two or three disciples manifest the kingdom of God in what they do and say. Spiritual formation and discipleship are about people coming to see the world, and themselves, in theodramatic terms, and to be so ravished by this vision that their heartfelt desire and intent is to live for Christ and his kingdom rather than for oneself and one's fiefdom.[72]

3. Habits of the Heart

Let me conclude by suggesting three practical means of theodramatic therapy, three tried and true means of grace: reading Scripture, prayer, and corporate worship.

---

[70] See further Sean Michael Lucas, *God's Grand Design: The Theological Vision of Jonathan Edwards* (Wheaton: Crossway, 2011), chap. 8.

[71] See, for example, Ashish J. Naidu, *Transformed in Christ: Christology and the Christian Life in John Chrysostom* (Eugene, OR: Pickwick Publications, 2012).

[72] For a reflection on the role of the heart in spiritual formation (and a reference to the "inner preparation" of actors in their craft), see Bill Hull, "Spiritual Formation from the Inside Out," in *The Kingdom Life*, 107–38.

Reading Scripture. The drama of discipleship is a matter of acting out what is in Christ. This means acting out what is inside us: the word and Spirit of Christ. Paul exhorts the church at Colossae "Let the word of Christ dwell in you richly" (Col. 3:16). When the Spirit impresses the words of Scripture on our hearts, we have a better grasp of who we are in Christ. Hence, one of the most important habits for disciples to cultivate is reading and studying the Bible: "the more you do it the more it will form the habits of mind and heart, soul and body, which will slowly but surely form your character into the likeness of Christ Jesus."[73] The Spirit renews our minds by rehearsing what has happened in the theodrama and enabling us to see and savor its beauty or "excellency."[74] The drama of discipleship concerns the way in which biblical words make our hearts willing captives to the living Word, Jesus Christ.[75]

Prayer. Prayer is the second means of theodramatic therapy, and this for several reasons. First, it is the quintessential theological act. To pray is to enter into theodrama by speaking lines to God. Second, unlike doctrine, which can be spoken in the third person, prayer is a second-person (singular or plural) address to God, and thus insinuates a person more fully into the drama of discipleship. Third, when disciples pray the way Jesus taught them ("Our Father . . ."), petitioning God for the coming of his kingdom, they not only repeat Jesus' words but also speak Christ's mind. Fourth, prayer is a tonic of reality: there is no better way to reset one's priorities and to see ourselves as we are before God.[76] Finally, prayer is perhaps the best means for the inner preparation of the disciple/actor: it was through prayer, fellowship with God, that Jesus readied himself for the role he had been called to play—"Not my will but yours be done" (Luke 22:42).

Corporate worship. The third and final means of theodramatic therapy is shared worship.[77] Scripture may be the soul of theology, but doxology is the

---

[73] Wright, *After You Believe*, 262.

[74] McClymond and McDermott, *The Theology of Jonathan Edwards*, 378.

[75] Edwards thought that reading Scripture can be an occasion of divine illumination: "the Spirit uses the Word to stir the holy affections of God's people" (Lucas, *God's Grand Design*, 143).

[76] Cf. C. S. Lewis: "Now the moment of prayer is for me . . . the awareness, the re-awakened awareness, that this 'real world' and 'real self' are very far from being rock-bottom realities" (*Letters to Malcolm: Chiefly on Prayer* [New York: Harcourt, Brace & World, 1964], 81).

[77] Wright, *After You Believe*, 278–80.

soul's embodiment: "present your bodies as a living sacrifice" (Rom. 12:1). There is perhaps no more theatrical (or therapeutic) theodramatic act than sharing the Lord's Supper. The central action—breaking and taking the bread; pouring and passing the wine—not only recapitulates what Christ has done but also, in the doing in remembrance of him, *performs* it. Communicants enact the communion they have with one another in Christ: "Such worship is the central performance that trains and rehearses us for the rest of our lives."[78] Even Carnes grants the formative power of worship, though she would deny that what we do in worship is theatrical: "But seen both as participating in eschatological reality and as disclosing who we are, worship breaks the person-role distinction that characterizes theatrical performance."[79] By way of contrast, I see the Lord's Supper as an eminently theatrical act that performs on earth the new creation as it is in heaven.

In conclusion, while Scripture and doctrine provide the script and the direction for understanding the truth, goodness, and beauty of the drama of the Christ, prayer and worship are ways personally to participate in it. While theology sets forth in speech the truth of Christ, corporate worship displays in living color, not only when the church is at table but whenever two or three are gathered in Christ's name, acting out the new humanity that is ours in Christ—performing interactive parables of the kingdom. Each day affords disciples opportunities to act out what is in Christ by presenting their bodies as living sacrifices. Through reading Scripture, learning doctrine, praying, and doing church, disciples sharpen their spiritual perception and strengthen godly habits, thereby disposing themselves to embody the mind of Christ as it were by second (spiritual) nature. These are but some of the forms of cognitive-affective therapy that open the eyes of our hearts to the eschatological *is*, the new humanity in Jesus Christ that is already ours: "But *we have* the mind of Christ" (1 Cor. 2:16).[80]

---

[78] Shannon Craiggo-Snell, *The Empty Church: Theater, Theology, and Bodily Hope* (Oxford: Oxford University Press, 2014), 5.

[79] Carnes, "Mysteries of Our Existence," 408.

[80] I wish to thank Paul Maxwell for helping me think through the issues and for steering me in the right bibliographic direction, and Steve Porter for his astute comments on an earlier draft.

8

LEARNING FROM JESUS TO LIVE IN THE MANNER JESUS WOULD IF HE WERE I

Biblical Grounding for Willard's Proposal Regarding Jesus' Humanity

KLAUS ISSLER

Talbot School of Theology

Abstract: "How *would* Jesus live your life, with your personality, with your talents, with your life experiences, within your life context, if he were you?" is a question posed by Dallas Willard in *The Divine Conspiracy*. How is it possible for Jesus Christ, Second Person of the Trinity, to know about living a really human life with all of its heartache and struggles? The chapter presents the biblical teaching for Jesus' authentic human experience, that Jesus is our genuine example and is the unique one who can show us the way into kingdom living. After addressing concerns that have been raised about emphasizing the example of Jesus, the NT data affirming Jesus' authentic human experience are presented, along with some potential objections. The main claim defended is that Jesus lived normally within his own human power, relying predominantly on the divine resources of the Father and the Holy Spirit, while using his own divine power infrequently. The chapter concludes with a few implications for practice, living within our personal human condition as Jesus did, and living beyond our human limitations as Jesus did.

The invitation for each of Jesus' apprentices, according to Dallas Willard, is "learning from Jesus to live my life as if he would live my life if he were I" (*The Divine Conspiracy*, 283, 285).[1] But how is that possible since Jesus is God? Can Jesus really know what it is like to live as a human? Did Jesus genuinely struggle against the challenges of life just like us? Or, in Jesus' common life with us, did Jesus have access to a power unique to him and unavailable to believers today? The chapter responds negatively to this last question and presents the biblical teaching for Jesus' authentic human experience, that Jesus is our genuine example for how to live the Christian life. Willard clarifies, "I am not necessarily learning to do everything [Jesus] did, but I am learning how to do everything I do in the manner that he did all that he did. . . . My discipleship to Jesus is, within clearly definable limits, not a matter of what I do, but of how I do it" (*The Divine Conspiracy*, 284).

The main point of the chapter is to provide the specific biblical basis supporting this claim by Willard. At a few points in the chapter, more particular comments by Willard will be included where relevant to the discussion. After addressing concerns that have been raised about emphasizing the example of Jesus, I clarify the importance of Jesus' humanity and then present the NT data affirming Jesus' authentic human experience. The chapter concludes with some practical implications. Willard asserts, "Concretely, we intend to live in the kingdom of God by intending to obey the precise example and teachings of Jesus" (*Renovation of the Heart*, 87).

The Importance of the Humanity of Jesus

At a general level, it is difficult to deny Jesus' humanity at the obvious points: he was embodied (e.g., he was thirsty, Matt. 25:35; hungry, Matt. 4:2; weary, John 4:6; and he died, John 19:30–34). He experienced a full range of emotions (e.g., weeping, Luke 19:41; compassion, Mark 6:34; righteous anger, Mark 3:5; frustration, Matt. 17:17; being troubled in spirit, Matt. 26:37). Many who encountered him, especially the religious leaders, regarded

[1] Short titles and parenthetical references are used throughout for the Willardian corpus. See *Hearing God: Developing a Conversational Relationship with God*, 3rd ed. (Downers Grove, IL: InterVarsity Press, 1999); *The Spirit of the Disciplines: Understanding How God Changes Lives* (New York: HarperCollins, 1988); *The Divine Conspiracy: Rediscovering Our Hidden Life in God* (New York: HarperCollins, 1997); *Renovation of the Heart: Putting on the Character of Christ* (Colorado Springs: NavPress, 2002); *Knowing Christ Today: Why We Can Trust Spiritual Knowledge* (New York: HarperCollins, 2009).

Jesus as *nothing more than human*, not as some kind of alien or superhero from outer space. To paraphrase the Nazareth folk with whom he grew up, "It's just Jesus, no one special" (Mark 6:3). Furthermore, Jesus was tempted (Matt. 4: 1–11)—a characteristic which Scripture denies of God (James 1:13)—yet without sinning (Heb. 4:15).

Orthodoxy affirms that Jesus' humanity was a critical factor for our salvation. Millard Erickson notes, "If, however, Jesus was not really one of us, humanity has not been united with deity, and we cannot be saved. For the validity of the work accomplished in Christ's death, or at least its applicability to us as human beings, depends upon the reality of his humanity, just as the efficacy of it depends upon the genuineness of his deity."[2] Regarding God's design of human nature, Bernard Ramm clarifies, "In the very act of the creation the possibility of a future incarnation was made possible. If humankind is produced in the image of God then there is some of that image in God. Hence God can become incarnate."[3] Furthermore, Paul's comparison between Adam and Christ bears testimony to the humanity of Jesus (Rom. 5:12–21; 1 Cor. 15:20–22 and 45–49).[4] Through his experiences and suffering as a human, Jesus became our sympathetic high priest (Heb. 2:10–17, 4:15–16, 5:8–10), one who now intercedes for us (Rom. 8:34). Thus, Jesus is like us.

In becoming incarnate, our Lord Jesus Christ—as one person—is both fully divine and fully human. Although this study emphasizes what is commonly shared between Jesus Christ and all believers, there is no denial that Jesus is also unique and different from us; he is not *merely* human. The thrust of the current project is to draw out implications of an orthodox Christology for practical Christian living. The purpose is not to diminish the doctrine of Christ's deity but rather to enrich our doctrine of sanctification and Christian living. By offering a refinement of our understanding of Jesus Christ we can then benefit from the Bible's teaching that Jesus is our genuine example. Yet, as we delve into this mystery—to honor our

---

[2] Millard Erickson, *Christian Theology* (Grand Rapids, MI: Baker, 1985), 706.

[3] Bernard Ramm, *An Evangelical Christology* (Nashville: Thomas Nelson, 1985), 53. Furthermore, Ramm explains, "In the humanity of Jesus Christ God has revealed what it is to be a true person. Hence a Christian anthropology can be constructed only from a Christology," 77.

[4] Did Jesus fulfill a *moral* obligation by defeating Satan *in his humanity* as the Second Adam, since the First Adam surrendered his rightful role (e.g., Heb. 2:14–15)?

Lord's full humanity—we must do so cautiously so as not to diminish his full deity.[5]

Is Jesus Our Example?

A clear understanding that Jesus lived a genuinely human life does not seem to be a common *practical* article of faith among Christians. Despite the popular appeal for the "What Would Jesus Do?" slogan, down deep believers tend to let Jesus' deity trump his humanity. For example, how do you think most believers would answer the following questions?

"How could Jesus know the thoughts of others?" "Because he was God."
"How could Jesus resist temptation and live without sin?" "Because he was God."
"How could Jesus perform miracles?" "Because he was God."
"How could Jesus forgive his enemies while being tortured on the cross?" "Because he was God."

It is obvious that *if* Jesus normally relied on his own divine power in living his life and engaging in ministry while on earth, then humans *cannot* emulate Jesus' normal example.

Scholarly Reluctance about Jesus' Human Example

Some biblical scholars are not convinced that the NT writers actually present Jesus' life on earth as an example for believers, and argue that instead of imitation, the NT always stresses allegiance and obedience to the *risen* Lord. For example, Wilhelm Michaelis claimed of the verb "to imitate": "There is thus no thought of an imitation, whether outward or inward, of the earthly life of Jesus in either individual features or total impress. The call for an *imitatio Christi* finds no support in the statements of Paul."[6] Others claim that Jesus' command to follow him (e.g., John 8:12, 10:27) cannot be

---

[5] The study works with the canonical New Testament texts and within the basic boundary conditions for orthodox theological inquiry as set down by the Chalcedonian Definition (AD 451).

[6] Wilhelm Michaelis, "Mimeomai," *Theological Dictionary of the New Testament*, IV, edited by Gerhard Kittel, translated by Geoffrey Bromiley (Grand Rapids, MI: Eerdmans, 1967), 672. In a footnote, Michaelis quotes Martin Dibelius: "The qualities to be imitated are not the virtues of a human person but the properties of the divine person."

a call to imitation, but rather a call to be a loyal disciple of the Lord Jesus. To propose such a claim, an alleged distinction must be made between the word "to follow" (*akoloutheo*), which occurs only in the Gospels and Acts, and "to imitate" (*mimeomai*), occurring only in the epistles. Yet, Kevin Giles notes, "The contrast between the Gospels and the Epistles in relation to imitating Christ is therefore, in essence, not one of emphasis or theme but only one of terminology."[7]

Marguerite Shuster raises legitimate concerns about studying Jesus as our example, "My fundamental point is that what we need, and what the NT offers us, is first and foremost, not an example, but a Savior. My major caveat with respect to imitation themes is that they tend to obscure that fundamental point."[8] Of course any exclusive focus on the example of Jesus effectively truncates the genuine gospel. Sanctification must never be reduced to our own moral effort. It is a process in which God the Spirit works, and in which we cooperate, attending to what is in our power to do, sustained by God's power (e.g., Eph. 4:17–24; Phil. 2:12–13). Yet, once Jesus is affirmed as our Savior and our High Priest, can Jesus also serve as our example to imitate?[9]

Ralph Martin, in his often-cited study on Philippians 2:5–11, claims that the exaltation of Christ is the focus of Paul's exhortation not his life on earth.

> The Apostolic summons is not: Follow Jesus by doing as He did—*an impossible feat in any case,* for who can be a "second Christ" who quits His heavenly glory and dies in shame and is taken up into the throne of the universe? The appeal and injunction to the

---

[7] Kevin Giles, "'*Imitatio Christi*' in the New Testament," *The Reformed Theological Review* 38, no. 3 (September—December 1979): 69. Based on his reading of the two standard German monographs of the subject, Giles explains that "H. D. Betz [*Nachfolge und Nachahmung Jesu Christi im Neuen Testament*, Tübingen: Mohr Siebeck, 1967] and A. Schulz [*Nachfolgen und Nachahmen,* Munich: Koesel-Verlag, 1962] carefully study these two motifs and after having analyzed each independently come to the conclusion that in substance the meaning of both is the same" (69, note #22).

[8] Marguerite Shuster, "The Use and Misuse of the Idea of the Imitation of Christ," *Ex Auditu* 14 (1998): 74. Yet focusing on Jesus as a moral exemplar need not lead us doctrinally astray to embrace a moral influence atonement theory. For a survey of moral example atonement theories, see Alister McGrath, *Christian Theology* (Oxford: Blackwell, 1997), 407–12.

[9] Marguerite Shuster also raises two other helpful points to consider for our study (1) the misuse of the concept of imitation, particularly the selectivity of what is considered for imitation and what is ignored, and (2) that we exclude from consideration the distinctive cultural forms of that day that Jesus practiced. "Use and Misuse," 74.

> Philippians in their pride and selfishness are rather: Become in your conduct and church relationships the type of persons who, by that kenosis, death and exaltation of the Lord of glory, have a place in His body, the Church.[10]

Martin seems to confuse the *tasks* of Jesus' vocation, which are unique, with the *manner* in which he lived to carry out his vocation. We do not emulate his mission, and our missional tasks will vary among us, but we can emulate Jesus' manner of living.

Moreover, Joseph Hellerman has argued that Paul intentionally turns upside down the normal Roman honor motif in Philippi, which highlighted a continuing *upward* movement of the career ladder of external success.

> I maintain that Paul, in his portrayal of Jesus in [Phil. 2] verses 6–8, has taken Rome's *cursus* ideology and turned it on its head, so to speak, as he presents Christ descending a *cursus pudorum* ("a succession or race of ignominies") from equality with God, to the status of a slave, to the physical and social death of public crucifixion. . . . The presentation, I suggest, was intended by Paul . . . to encourage persons in the church who possessed some degree of honor or status in the broader social world of the colony to utilize their status, after the analogy of Jesus, in the service of others.[11]

Jesus' human life accomplished much more than being our example, yet his example for believers cannot be ignored.

As long as such ambiguity and ambivalence remains about this critical teaching of Jesus' human example, it will be difficult for believers to make much progress in responding to Jesus' invitation to "learn from me" (Matt. 11:29) that Willard proposes. Consider Alan Spence's explanation for such scholarly reluctance:

---

[10] Ralph Martin, *A Hymn of Christ: Philippians 2:5–11 in Recent Interpretation and in the Setting of Early Christian Worship* (Downers Grove, IL: InterVarsity, 1997), 290–91. Italics added.

[11] Joseph Hellerman, *Reconstructing Honor in Roman Philippi: Carmen Christi as Cursus Pudorum*, SNTS Monograph 132 (Cambridge: Cambridge University, 2005), 1–2.

> The difficulty seems to lie in an inability to conceive of the incarnate Christ as "normative man." Although those who hold to his divine sonship are usually quick to affirm his true humanity, there has, nevertheless, been in the past an unwillingness to give due weight to the Gospel testimony to his growth in grace, wisdom and knowledge; to his continual need of divine comfort and empowering through the Holy Spirit; and consequently to the implication that as man he stood just as we do, a creature totally dependent on his God.[12]

Table 1: Selected Lines of Evidence for Jesus as Our Example
(listed in order of presentation in the chapter; in bold key paragraph for topic)

	From Jesus' Own Words	Paul	General Epistles
As Our Example	**John 13:12-17** Matt. 20:26-28, Mark 10:42-45, Luke 22:24-27, John 13:34-35; John 15:12-13 Matt. 11:29	**Phil. 2:4-11;** Rom. 6:11; 15:3, 7; 1 Cor. 11:1; 2 Cor. 1:5; Eph. 5:2, 25, 29; Col. 3:13; *Implicit* 1 Thess. 1:6	**Heb. 12:1-11** **1 Peter 2:18-25** 1 Peter 4:1, (1 Peter 5:2-3) 1 John 2:5-6, 3:3, 16 *Implicit:* Heb. 4:15

Biblical Evidence for Jesus' Example

In searching the biblical data for Jesus' example, first we look at the Gospels, and then the rest of the NT (see Table 1). The most direct comment from Jesus' own words occurs when he washed the disciples' feet (John 13:12–17): "I have given you an example, that you also should do as I have done for you" (John 13:15). In this declaration, note also the comparison "as I have done to you." This remarkable "just as" pattern can be observed in other passages, in which the disciples (then and now) are encouraged to live as Jesus did. For example, see Matthew 20:26–28: "It shall not be so among you. But whoever would be great among you must be your servant, and whoever would be first among you must be your slave, *even as* the Son of Man came not to be served but to serve, and to give his life as a ransom for many" (italics added). Discussing the parallel passage in Mark 10:45, R. T. France states, "But we must not forget that this crucial verse, however great its soteriological implications, occurs in the context as a model for

[12] Alan Spence, "Christ's Humanity and Ours: John Owen," in *Persons, Divine and Human*, edited by Christoph Schwöbel and Colin E. Gunton (Edinburgh: T&T Clark, 1991), 75.

Jesus' disciples to follow. . . . They, too, must serve rather than be served."[13] In the Gospels, two particular topics surface using this "just as" pattern: servanthood (Matt. 20:26–28; Luke 22:24–27; John 13:13–15) and love (John 13:34–35; John 15:12–13). In addition, Jesus uses the phrase "learn from me" in his invitation to weary disciples in Matthew 11:29.

The key passages on Jesus' example in the Epistles are Philippians 2:4–11, Hebrews 12: 1–11, and 1 Peter 2:18–25. The previously noted "just as" pattern in which believers are encouraged to live as Jesus did also is used in the rest of the New Testament (Rom. 6:11, 15:3,7; 2 Cor. 1:5; Eph. 5:2, 25, 29; Phil. 2:5; Col. 3:13; 1 Thess. 1:6; Heb. 4:15; 1 Pet. 4:1; 1 John 2:6, 3:3, 3:16). For example, see Philippians 2:5, "Have this mind among yourselves, which is yours in Christ Jesus," and 1 John 2:6, "Whoever says he abides in him ought to walk in the same way in which he walked." Furthermore, Paul urged believers to imitate his own example (1 Cor. 4:16–17, 11:1; Phil. 3:17; 1 Thess. 1:6; 2 Thess. 3:7–9 and 1 Tim. 1:16), just as he imitated the example of Jesus (1 Cor. 11:1, cf. 1 Thess. 1:6).

Likewise, the apostle Peter exhorted elders to serve as examples: "Shepherd the flock of God that is among you . . . not *domineereing over* those in your charge, but being examples to the flock" (1 Pet. 5:2–3, italics added). Peter alludes to Jesus' own teaching and example of servanthood, using the same phrase Jesus did, "lord it over," as recorded in the synoptic Gospels (Matt. 20:25, Mark 10:42, Luke 22:25).

The biblical evidence is fairly clear that Jesus, particularly in his earthly life, is an example for us. Another related issue concerns to what extent did Jesus live within his humanity, to which we turn next.

By What Divine Power Did Jesus Live and Minister?

Some might wonder, why worry about the *source* of Jesus' supernatural power? Does it really matter? If we hold to supernatural theism, then Jesus' supernatural life and his ministry of miracles actually occurred and touched the lives of many in his day, regardless of whether he used his own divine power or relied on the supernatural power of the Father and the Holy Spirit. Yet the critical issue raised in this chapter is whether Jesus can be our *example*, including his supernaturally oriented lifestyle. William

[13] R. T. France, *The Gospel of Mark, NIGTC* (Grand Rapids, MI: Eerdmans, 2002), 421.

Barry admits, "If Jesus is superhuman, then I can admire him, but I do not have to take seriously his call to emulate him. I can never be a superhuman being."[14]

Possible Options

Jesus had access to two possible sources of divine power: either (a) his own divine power, or (b) the divine resources of the Father and the Holy Spirit. Four logical positions are possible along this spectrum:

- #1. Never dependent on the divine resources of the Father and Holy Spirit and exclusively using his own divine power;
- #2. Infrequently dependent on the divine resources of the Father and Holy Spirit and predominantly using his own divine power;
- #3. Predominantly dependent on divine resources of the Father and Holy Spirit and infrequently using his own divine power; or
- #4. Exclusively dependent on divine resources of the Father and Holy Spirit, and never using his own divine power.

The Scripture provides clear evidence of some form of dependence on the divine resources of the Father and Holy Spirit, so option #1 is eliminated. The question is to what extent did Jesus rely on the Father and the Spirit, so the main choices are among options #2, #3, or #4.

The main divide on this point whether Jesus' dependency was infrequent and basically unnecessary (option #2) or was Jesus' dependence on the norm of his life on earth (either option #3 or option #4). I suspect Willard would opt for the latter case of the essential role of dependence on divine resources throughout Jesus' life, with which I agree.

Between the latter two options, it will be easier to present an argument for the weaker claim of option #3 (predominantly dependent) than the stronger claim of option #4 (exclusively dependent).[15] Specifically, Jesus lived normally within his own human power, relying predominantly on

---

[14] William Barry, *Letting God Come Close* (Chicago: Loyal, 2001), 111.

[15] Defending the exclusively dependent thesis requires some sort of accounting for the occasions on which Jesus apparently did make use of his own divine power. These occasions are infrequent (e.g., forgiving sins, the transfiguration), but are part of the evidence pool and cannot be simply disregarded. I think reasonable answers can be supplied for these occasions, but since I am presenting evidence for the predominantly thesis, this additional discussion is beyond the scope of this article.

the divine resources of the Father and the Holy Spirit, while using his own divine power infrequently.

This claim regarding Jesus' predominant dependence on God, especially the Holy Spirit, is not new. According to Alan Spence, Puritan theologian John Owen (1616–1683) "regarded [Jesus'] life as man among us as the prototype of Christian existence, and as continually empowered, comforted and sanctified by the Holy Spirit."[16] R. A. Torrey (1856–1928), likewise attempting to articulate only *What the Bible Teaches*, claimed that "[Jesus] lived, thought, worked, taught, conquered sin and won victories for God in the power of that same Spirit whom we all may have."[17] In 1991, Gerald Hawthorne published the sole academic monograph given wholly to discussing the relationship of the Spirit in the life of Jesus.

> Without denying the reality of the incarnation, or that God became a man, it is the purpose of this book, nevertheless, to argue for the reality of Jesus' humanness and that as such he was not aided to rise above and conquer temptations *as God*, but rather as a man whose will was set to do the will of God. His sinlessness was nothing other than the continued obedience to the Father and to the Father's will.[18]

Yet in light of the scholarly reluctance and the continuing popular confusion regarding Jesus living as a genuine human, there seems to be a contemporary need for a new hearing of the biblical witness to Jesus' humanity and example for us in living the Christian life.

The argument for Jesus predominantly living within his humanity while depending on God is developed from biblical evidence within three categories indicating that (a) Jesus depended on the Father, (b) Jesus depended

---

[16] Spence, "John Owen," 75.

[17] R. A. Torrey, *What the Bible Teaches* (Old Tappan, NJ: Fleming Revell, 1898), book 3, (chapter 9), 289.

[18] Gerald Hawthorne, *The Presence and the Power: The Significance of the Holy Spirit in the Life and Ministry of Jesus* (Dallas: Word, 1991; reprint, Eugene, OR: Wipf and Stock), p. 96, n. 94. Hawthorne's book was the stimulating inspiration that launched me toward my own continuing investigation of Jesus' humanity and example. Hawthorne appears to defend option #4. Others devote only a portion of their book on this topic, such as James Dunn, *Jesus and the Spirit* (Grand Rapids, MI: Eerdmans, 1975). For a recent proposal to develop a Trinitarian "Spirit Christology" in which the Spirit is presented as having a more prominent role within the Trinity, see Myk Habets, *The Anointed Son: A Trinitarian Spirit Christology* (Eugene, OR: Pickwick, 2010).

on the Holy Spirit, and (c) Jesus exercised his own faith and trust in God. Table 2 gives an overview of the selected passages that will be cited in the discussion so one can see how these align with the three categories. We will move from the Gospels to the Epistles, and begin with *explicit* biblical support, followed by implicit evidence supplementing the main explicit argument. A few Scripture references from the Gospel of John seem to be a less explicit indication of Jesus' reliance on the Father. Otherwise, verses in the implicit category assume the principle that Jesus practiced what he preached. That is, in any teaching to his disciples to rely on available divine resources, Jesus is sharing the results of his own personal dependence pattern while living in his humanity. These teachings confirm the explicit support. Willard explains, "If we are to exercise the word and rule of God in ways regarded as spectacular by human beings, Jesus is our model, as always. . . . [God] will do this in a way that is suitable to our lives and his calling for us" (*Hearing God*, 136). Now we turn to what the New Testament teaches about Jesus as our example.

Table 2: Selected Lines of Evidence for Jesus' Dependence on God (Listed in Order of Presentation in the Chapter)

	From Jesus' Own Words	Gospels-Acts Authors	Paul	General Epistles
Depend on the Father	John 5:19, 30; 8:28–29, 42; 12:27–28, 49–50; 14:10, 31; 15:9–10; 16:32; 17:7–8; Matt. 26:52–54; *Implicit:* John 7:28–29; 14:24; 17:18			
Depend on the Spirit	Luke 4:16–21; Matt. 12:28 (Luke 11:20) *Implicit:* John 7:37–38; Mark 13:11 (Luke 12:15) Matt. 10:19–10; Luke 12:11–12; Matt. 12:31–32; Luke 12:10, Matt. 26:41; Mark 14:38; "power" Mark 5:30; Luke 8:46; (Acts 1:8)	John 3:34; Matt. 4:1; Mark 1:12; Luke 4:1, 14; Luke 10:21; Acts 1:2, 10:38 *Implicit*: parallel John the Baptist: Luke 1:15, 80 & Jesus Luke 1:35, 2:40; Baptism: Matt. 3:16, Mark 1:10; Luke 3:22; "power" Luke 5:17, Luke 6:19		Heb. 9:14
Jesus' Faith in God	*Implicit*: Mark 9:23; Matt. 6:30 [Luke 12:28]; 8:26, 14:31, 16:8, 17:20; Luke 17:6		Possibly: *pistis Christou*: (faith of Christ) Rom. 3:22, 26, Gal. 2:16 [2x], 2:20, 3:22; Eph. 3:12, Phil. 3:9	Heb. 12:1–6

Dependence on the Father

There are multiple occurrences of Jesus' own declaration of his complete dependence on the Father in the Gospel of John.

> ". . . for all that I heard from my Father I have made known to you." (John 15:15)
>
> "Truly truly, I say to you, *the Son can do nothing on his own accord*, but only what he sees the Father doing. For whatever the Father does, the Son does likewise." (John 5:19, italics added)
>
> "When you have lifted up the Son of Man, then you will know that I am he, and that I do nothing on my own authority, but speak just as the Father taught me. And he who sent me is with me. He has not left me alone, for I always do the things that are pleasing to him.'" (John 8:28–29)
>
> "Do you not believe that I am in the Father, and that the Father is in me? The words I say to you I do not speak on my own authority, but *the Father, who dwells in me, does his work.*" (John 14:10, italics added)

Similar declarations appear also in John 5:30, 8:42, 12:49–50, 14:10, 31; 15:9–10, 16:32, 17:7–8, and 17: 8–8. Carson comments on John 17:7: "The strange way of putting the last point—that everything you have given me comes from you . . . carefully emphasizes Jesus' dependence upon his Father."[19]

Later in the Gospel, Jesus develops a parallel between his dependency on the Father as the analogy for how his disciples will depend on him. For example, we can compare John 5:19 quoted above with John 15:5; "I am the vine, you are the branches. Whoever abides in me and I in him, he it is that bears much fruit, for apart from me *you can do nothing*" (italics added). Jesus depends on the Father, and then he desires that believers experience the same kind of dependence on himself.[20]

Following Jesus' prayer in Gethsemane and during his arrest he offers a remark about his dependence on the Father. After Peter lops off an ear of a

---

[19] D. A. Carson, *The Gospel According to John*, Pillar NTC (Grand Rapids, MI: Eerdmans, 1991), 559–60.

[20] Believers are to abide *in* Christ as subsequent NT teaching emphasizes (e.g., Col. 3:15–17). Yet we still direct our prayer requests to the Father in the name of Jesus (e.g., John 15: 7, 16; 16:23, John 14:14; Matt. 6:9; e.g., Eph. 3:14).

soldier, Jesus commands Peter to put his sword down and announces, "Do you think I cannot appeal to my Father, and he will at once send me more than twelve legions of angels?" (Matt. 26:53; cf. John 12:27). Implicit references of dependence on the Father include John 7:28–29, 14:24, and 17:18.

Dependence on the Spirit—Explicit

Willard affirms that "When we inwardly experience the heavenly sweetness and power of life—the love, joy, and peace—that Jesus knew, that is the work of the Spirit."[21]

1. Explicit References from Jesus' Own Words. Only a few references from Jesus' own lips offer explicit support, but these are profound. Near the beginning of his public ministry, Jesus is the guest synagogue speaker in his hometown of Nazareth (Luke 4:16–21). He startles his hearers, after reading a prophetic passage from Isaiah 61:1–2 and states, "Today this Scripture has been fulfilled in your hearing" (Luke 4:21). He thus announces "himself to be the bearer of . . . God's new age of salvation" being the one who has received the "anointing with God's Spirit."[22]

Later in his ministry, Jesus makes an explicit declaration about relying on the Spirit for his exorcisms, from Matthew 12:28: "But if it is by the Spirit of God that I cast out demons, then the kingdom of God has come upon you"[23] (Matt. 12:28; "finger of God" Luke 11:20[24]). Beasley-Murray notes that this saying "gives Jesus' own explanation of his exorcisms: they are performed not by his own power but by the power of God, i.e., by the Spirit of God, and since the defeat of the evil power is a feature of the end time, they show that the kingdom of God has appeared in his activity."[25] This is the initial evidence from Jesus' own words. Later will be added implicit evidence from Jesus' own words and teachings that can indicate a reference to his own life experience.

---

[21] Dallas Willard, *The Great Omission: Reclaiming Jesus's Essential Teachings on Discipleship* (New York: HarperCollins, 2006), 27.

[22] Darrell Bock, *Luke 1:1–9:50, Baker Exegetical Commentary on the New Testament* (Grand Rapids, MI: Baker, 1994), 407.

[23] Note that Jesus employs the plural "demons," indicating this deliverance as well as others was done by the power of the Holy Spirit.

[24] D. A. Carson states, "Luke 11:20 has 'the finger of God' instead of 'the Spirit of God.' Possibly the latter is original . . . , but the matter is of little consequence since they both refer to the same thing (cf. Exod. 8:19; Deut. 9:10; Ps 8:3)." "Matthew," *The Expositor's Bible Commentary*, vol. 9, edited by Frank E. Gaebelein (Grand Rapids, MI: Zondervan, 1981), 289.

[25] G. R. Beasley-Murray, "Jesus and the Spirit," in *Melanges Bibliques en homage au R. P. Beda Rigaux,* edited by A. Deschamps and A. de Hallelaneux (Gembloux: Duculot, 1970), 471.

2. Explicit Evidence from the Gospel Writers and Acts. John records Jesus as receiving the Spirit without measure (John 3:34). The various descriptions of Jesus' wilderness temptation experience include specific mention of the Holy Spirit's direct involvement (Matt. 4:1, Mark 1:12, Luke 4:1, 14; cf. Rom. 8:14, Gal. 5:18). One time Luke describes Jesus as "full of joy through the Holy Spirit" (Luke 10:21).

In the book of Acts, we learn that Jesus' final teaching to his disciples before his ascension was accomplished "through the Holy Spirit" (Acts 1:2). Then, in a sermon to the Gentile Cornelius and his household, Peter offered a summary statement of the ministry of Jesus: "How God anointed Jesus of Nazareth with the Holy Spirit and with power; how he went about doing good and healing all who were oppressed by the devil, for God was with him" (Acts 10:38).

3. Explicit Evidence from the Epistles. One passage in this category, Hebrews 9:14, offers a distinctive comment regarding Jesus' experience of the passion and his death: "how much more will the blood of Christ, who through the eternal Spirit offered himself without blemish to God, purify our conscience. . . ." Lane explains:

> The fact that his offering was made *dia pneumatos aiôniou*, "through the eternal Spirit," implies that he had been divinely empowered and sustained in his office. The formulation does not occur elsewhere in the NT or early Christian literature, but it may be understood as a designation for the Holy Spirit. A reference to the Spirit is appropriate in a section under the influence of Isaiah, where the Servant of the Lord is qualified for his task by the Spirit of God. (Isa 42:1, 61:1)[26]

These are the explicit references in the NT.[27] Now we turn to implicit references to Jesus and the Holy Spirit.[28]

---

[26] William L. Lane, *Hebrews 9–13*, Word Biblical Commentary, vol. 47B (Dallas: Word, 1991), 240.

[27] Two other passages mention Jesus and the Spirit that seem to relate to his resurrection, but there are challenges in interpretation, so these will be passed over but noted here, 1 Tim. 3:16 and 1 Pet. 3:18.

[28] For a recent and fairly comprehensive treatment on the doctrine of the Holy Spirit, see Graham Cole, *He Who Gives Life: The Doctrine of the Holy Spirit* (Wheaton, IL: Crossway, 2007).

Dependence on the Spirit—Implicit

1. Implicit Evidence from Jesus' Own Words. In the Gospels and early in Acts, Jesus makes claims about the ministry of the Holy Spirit. Can we infer that these claims are based on his own relational dependence on the Spirit? In John 7: 37–38, Jesus cries out in a loud voice, "If anyone thirsts, let him come to me and drink. Whoever believes in me, as the Scripture has said, '*Out of his hear will flow rivers of living water*'" (italics added). Verse 39 identifies the Spirit as Jesus point of reference.

Another teaching is that the Spirit would help believers in tight spots. "And when they bring you to trial and deliver you over, do not be anxious beforehand what are to say, but say whatever is given you in htat hour, for it is not you who speak, but the Holy Spirit" (Mark 13:11).[29] I. Howard Marshall comments that "the Spirit gives guidance regarding both the general form of a speech and the actual content."[30] It is likely that this particular teaching was based on Jesus' own experience (e.g., Acts 1:2). Willard comments, "A major point of this book is that the still small voice—or the interior or inner voice, as it is also called—is the preferred and most valuable form of individualized communication for God's purposes. God usually addresses individually those who walk with him in a mature, personal relationship using this inner voice, proclaiming and showing forth the reality of the kingdom of God" (*Hearing God*, 89).

Jesus' reference to the blasphemy of the Holy Spirit (Matt. 12:31–32, Luke 12:10) indicates how important Jesus viewed the ministry of the Holy Spirit. Donald Hagner explains:

> Given Matthew's Christological interests and the unique and central position held by Jesus throughout the Gospel, one may understandably be surprised that Matthew has not said the reverse of what stands in the text, i.e., that blasphemy against the Spirit is forgivable but not that against the Son of Man. The

---

[29] In Luke 12:15, describing the same context, it is Jesus himself who gives the wisdom. Related passages mentioning the Holy Spirit as the source: Matt. 10:19–20 and Luke 12:11–12. The critique is rehearsing some kind of response to officials solely on our own without the aid of the Spirit (so, I. H. Marshall, *Commentary on Luke* [Grand Rapids, MI: Eerdmans, 1978], 768).

[30] I. Howard Marshall, *Commentary on Luke* (Grand Rapids, MI: Eerdmans, 1978), 520. For example, see Luke 2:26 and Acts 16:6 for cases of believers listening to the Holy Spirit (cf. 1 Cor. 2:12–13).

> gravity of the blasphemy against the Spirit, however, depends upon the Holy Spirit as the fundamental dynamic that stands behind and makes possible the entire messianic ministry of Jesus itself. . . . The failure to understand Jesus is yet forgivable but not the outright rejection of the saving power of God through the Spirit exhibited in the direct overthrow of the kingdom of Satan.[31]

Finally, a saying that may be the most telling of Jesus' relation to the Spirit is "The Spirit indeed is willing, but the flesh is weak" (Matt. 26:41; Mark 14:38). The common view of Jesus' statement to the three sleeping disciples in Gethsemane is about the continuing internal struggle within human nature, between the human spirit against the weak physical body. If this were so, Jesus' preceding words ("Stay awake and pray that you may not come into the time of trial") would then be a challenge to muster more human effort to override their bodily weakness so they could pray.

Another interpretation sees the contrast as one between relying on divine power of the Holy "Spirit," rather than solely relying on human resources ("flesh"), which can never stand alone against the assaults of Satan. Jesus made similar contrasts between the divine sphere and human sphere elsewhere (John 3:6, 6:63), which have OT precedent in Isaiah 31:1, 3 contrasting an Egyptian alliance ("flesh") against relying on the Lord God ("Spirit"; see also Psa. 51:11–12). Is not Jesus giving the three disciples the secret to his own victory in the garden? William Lane comments on Mark 14:38, "Spiritual wakefulness and prayer in full dependence upon divine help provide the only adequate preparation for crisis. . . . Jesus prepared for his own intense trial through vigilance and prayer, and thus gave to the disciples and to the Church the model for the proper resistance of eschatological temptation."[32] Jesus' comment here furnishes a fairly clear inference of his own dependence on the Holy Spirit and its implications as a teaching for all believers for all times.[33]

---

[31] Donald Hagner, *Matthew 1–13*, Word Biblical Commentary, vol. 33A (Dallas: Word, 1993), 348.

[32] William L. Lane, *The Gospel of Mark*, NICNT (Grand Rapids, MI: Eerdmans, 1974), 520–21.

[33] Hawthorne groups a number of additional implicit references to Jesus and the Spirit, (*The Presence*, 115): (a) Acting with authority (*exousia*): Mark 1:22/Matt. 7:29/Luke 4:32; Mark 1:27/Luke 4:36; Mark 2:10/Matt. 9:6/Luke 4:36; Mark 2:12/Matt. 9:6/Luke 5:24; Mark 11:29–30,

2. Implicit Evidence from the Gospel Writers and Acts. James Dunn suggests a parallel between John the Baptist and Jesus implying that if John, the Forerunner was filled by the Spirit from birth (Luke 1:15, 17) would it not be correct to imply that this was the case for Jesus, the Spirit-Anointed One, whose very birth was miraculously accomplished by the Spirit (Matt. 1:20, Luke 1:35). It is quite probable, though not certain, that Luke means us to understand that Jesus was every bit as full of the Holy Spirit as John was (1:15), and that Jesus' growth in wisdom and grace was due to his possession of the Spirit (2.40, 52); the link between the Spirit and divine sonship (and filial consciousness) would also be a pointer in this direction (1.35; 2.49; 3.22; cf. Rom 8.15–16; Gal 4.6).[34]

The important event of Jesus' baptism and commissioning is a full Trinitarian event, with the Spirit resting on Jesus (Matt. 3:16, Mark 1:10, Luke 3:22).

There are also some key references using the term "power" and indicating Jesus as an agent of God's power. Luke 4:14 specifically makes the connection between the Holy Spirit and power: "Jesus returned to Galilee in the power of the Spirit." In some verses, only the term "power" is used, for example Luke 5:17: "And the power of the Lord was with him to heal" (see also Luke 6:19, 8:46, Mark 5:30; comments by the crowd, Matt. 14:12, Luke 4:36). Nolland explains

> The reference to "power" (*dynamis*) [in Luke 5:17] links back to [Luke] 4:14 and prepares the way for the coming references to tangible power proceeding from Jesus (6:19, 8:44 [8:46]): the power that flows out of Jesus and brings healing is the power of God himself . . . It is more likely that Luke is continuing to clarify what it means for Jesus to have become through the descent

33/Matt. 21:23–34, 27/Luke 20: 2, 8; (b) Being perceived by the people as a prophet: Mark 6:15–16/Luke 9:8–9; Mark 8:28/Matt. 16:14/Luke 9:19; Mark 14:65/Matt. 26:68; see also Matt. 21:11, 46; Luke 7:16, 39, 24:19; (c) Perceiving himself as a prophet [and also more than a prophet]: Mark 6:4/Matt. 13:57/Luke 4:24; 13:33; cf. Matt. 23:31–38; Luke 11:47–51.

[34] James D. G. Dunn, *Baptism in the Spirit* (London: SCM, 1970), 24. See also Max Turner, *The Holy Spirit and Spiritual Gifts in the New Testament and Church Today* (Peabody, MA: Hendrikson, 1996), 25: "If the Baptist's own experience of the Spirit was itself an eschatological novum, Jesus' surpasses it. Gerd Schneider explains: 'Jesus is not merely filled with the Spirit, like John, rather his very being is attributed to the Spirit.'"

> of the Spirit the repository of the power of God (3:22; 4:1, 14, 18–19; 6:19; 8:44).[35]

Mark 5:30 clues us in to Jesus thoughts after the woman with the hemorrhage touched him: "Immediately aware that power had gone forth from him, Jesus turned about in the crowd and said, 'Who touched my clothes?'" (also, Luke 8:46). Lane notes:

> Jesus possesses the power of God as the representative of the Father. Nevertheless, the Father remains in control of his own power. The healing of the woman occurred through God's free and gracious decision to bestow upon her the power that was active in Jesus. By an act of sovereign will God [the Father or the Spirit?] determined to honor the woman's faith in spite of the fact that it was tinged with ideas which bordered on magic.[36]

Finally, Acts 10:38, mentioned earlier in the chapter, makes the comment "how God anointed Jesus of Nazareth with the Holy Spirit and power." Furthermore, is not Jesus' familiar challenge to the disciples before his ascension an experience he also had of the Spirit at his baptism? "But you will receive power when the Holy Spirit comes on you, and you will be my witnesses" (Acts 1:8).

Jesus Exercised Faith/Trust in God—Explicit

Having looked at dependence on the Father, and dependence on the Spirit, we now look at the third category of evidence to be explored. We learn that Jesus himself expressed faith and trust in God during his earthly sojourn by examining first explicit and then implicit references.

That Jesus experienced his own faith in God did not cross the minds of some translators of Hebrews 12:2, so they inserted an "our" in the text where there is none in the Greek manuscripts: "looking to Jesus the founder and perfecter of *our* faith" (italics added). We can trace that view at least as far back as Aquinas, who believed Jesus had the full beatific vision of God in the cradle as a new infant, eliminating any need for faith in God. Gerald O'Collins notes:

[35] John Nolland, *Luke 1–9:20*, Word Biblical Commentary, vol. 35A (Dallas: Word, 1989), 234.
[36] Lane, *Mark*, 192–93.

> Aquinas and the subsequent Catholic theological tradition held that in his human mind Jesus enjoyed the beatific vision and hence lived by sight, not by faith. Aquinas expressed classically this thesis: "When the divine reality is not hidden from sight, there is no point in faith. From the first moment of his conception Christ had the full vision of God in his essence . . . Therefore he could not have had faith" (*Summa Theologiae*, 3a. 7. 3 resp.).[37]

Commentators now approach Hebrews 12:2 with fresh eyes. William Lane explains Hebrews 12:2: "Fixing our eyes on Jesus the founder and perfecter of faith":

> The poignant description as a whole points to Jesus as the perfect embodiment of faith, who exercised faith heroically. By bringing faith to complete expression, he enabled others to follow his example. The phrase reiterates and makes explicit what was affirmed with a quotation from Scripture in [Hebrews] 2:13, that Jesus in his earthly life was the perfect exemplar of trust in God.[38]

Donald Hagner adds, "[Jesus] is not only the basis, means, and fulfillment of faith, but in his life he also exemplifies the same principle of faith that we saw in the paragons of [Hebrews] chapter 11."[39]

Jesus Exercised Faith/Trust in God—Implicit

1. Implicit Evidence from Jesus' Own Words. In the Gospel account of the healing of the demonized son, some commentators suggest that Jesus' reply to the father's request in Mark 9:23 is both a challenge to the father, and also a testimony of his own life of faith, "And Jesus said to him, 'If you can!' All things are possible for the one who believes." Sharyn Dowd explains, "Jesus is not merely an example to be imitated, but a leader to be followed. It is likely, then, that 'the one who believes' in 9:23 is deliberately

---

[37] Cited by Gerald O'Collins, *Christology* (Oxford: Oxford University, 1995), 254–55.
[38] Lane, *Hebrews*, 412.
[39] Donald Hagner, *Hebrews*, NIBC (Peabody, MA: Hendrickson, 1990), 212.

ambiguous. Jesus has faith and he calls the father to have faith."[40] O'Collins agrees, "[Jesus] speaks about faith as an insider, one who knows personally what the life of faith is and wants to share it with others (see 2 Cor. 4:13)."[41]

If Jesus was such an insider as a man of faith himself, then perhaps when he criticizes the disciples for their lack of faith (e.g., Matt. 6:30 [cf. Luke 12:28], 8:26, 14:31, 16:8, 17:20; *oligopistoi* "little faiths"), he is actually speaking as one who experientially knows what he is talking about. Ian Wallis notes, "The disciples may have been ineffectual . . . owing to their *oligopistia* ["little faith"], but Jesus was successful because he demonstrated that faith . . . a faith which all who intend to fulfill Christ's commission must demonstrate."[42] Perhaps from his own early developmental experience of faith and trust in God Jesus learned that even small trust in God can accomplish great things, "If you have faith as small as a mustard seed, you can . . ." (Matt. 17:20, Luke 17:6, cf. Mark 11:12, 1 Cor. 13:2).

2. Implicit Evidence from Paul's Epistles. On the topic of Jesus' faith, possible support also comes from a reconsideration of how the Greek phrase *pistis Christou* should be translated. The phrase appears seven times in Paul's letters (Rom. 3:22, 26, Gal. 2:16 [2x], 2:20, 3:22; Eph. 3:12, and Phil. 3:9), as well as in Acts 3:16 and Revelation 14:12. The traditional translation has been as an *objective* genitive ("faith *in* Christ"). Note that there is general agreement that believers must place their faith *in* Jesus, as taught in other NT passages (e.g., John 3:16, Acts 20:21, Col. 1:4, 1 John 3:23). The debate concerns whether the genitive noun (Jesus, or Son of God) is either objective or subjective. More commentators are recognizing the legitimacy of the phrase as a subjective genitive—that is, "faith [or faithfulness] *of* Jesus," that Jesus himself experienced faith in God.[43] In *Renovation of the Heart,*

---

[40] Sharyn Dowd, *Prayer, Power, and the Problem of Suffering: Mark 11:22–25 in the Context of Markan Theology,* SBLDS 105 (Atlanta: Scholars Press, 1986), 111.

[41] O'Collins, *Christology,* 261.

[42] Ian Wallis, *The Faith of Jesus Christ in Early Christian Traditions,* SNTS 84 (Cambridge: Cambridge University Press, 1995), 36.

[43] For a summary of the grammatical options, see Daniel Wallace, *An Exegetical Syntax of the New Testament* (Grand Rapids, MI: Zondervan, 1996), 115–16. For further treatment on this important issue, see Richard B. Hays, *The Faith of Jesus,* 2nd ed. (Grand Rapids, MI: Eerdmans, 2001). Compare also the discussions of Romans 3:22–26 by Douglas Moo, who opts for the objective genitive view ("in Christ"), and Richard Hays, who opts for the subjective genitive view ("of Christ"). Douglas Moo, *The Epistle to the Romans* (Grand Rapids, MI: Eerdmans, 1996), 224–43; Richard Hays, "Pistis in Romans 3.25: Neglected Evidence for the 'Faithfulness of Christ?,'" *New Testament Studies* 39 (1993): 478–80.

Willard quotes Galatians 2:20 with a subjective genitive "by the faith of the Son of God" (143). Wallis concludes his monograph on the faith of Jesus:

> It is the conviction of the present author that interest in Jesus' faith was an unfortunate and unnecessary casualty of early Christological controversy, in which its significance was determined more in terms of what it conceded to rival positions rather than of what it contributed to our knowledge of God and humanity of Jesus Christ. . . . Certainly, Jesus' faith does seem to provide a point of departure for Christology which is rooted in common human experience and which explores his theological significance through reflection upon his human being in relation to God.[44]

The explicit and implicit biblical data offer sufficient cumulative evidence of Jesus' authentic human experience, as he relied on divine resources to live a supernaturally empowered lifestyle. He thus offers to believers a genuine example in his common life to us. But is Jesus only like us, just human? To that issue we turn next.

Differences between Jesus and Us: Potential Objections

Jesus shares a common humanity with us since believers, having been regenerated, now share the same human nature as Jesus does and as Adam and Eve did at creation. Let us consider some differences.

Uniqueness of Jesus and the Spirit

Is the Holy Spirit's ministry unique to Jesus as the Anointed One/Messiah, or does the Holy Spirit also empower Jesus to live his earthly life in a manner similar to how the Spirit works with believers as well? Although the same Spirit that indwelt Jesus indwells all believers, John 3:34 indicates that Jesus had a greater measure of the Spirit. This may have been due to Jesus' unique role as the divine-human Messiah that required the full measure of the Spirit's ministry (John 3:36). Or, this greater measure may also have been the consequence of Jesus' complete dependence on the Father and his life of holiness, which permitted a full measure of the Spirit in Jesus' life and

---

[44] Wallis, *The Faith of Jesus Christ*, 221.

ministry. Sadly, our faith and life in holiness are limited, being hindered by doubt and unbelief as we are still in the process of being conformed to the image of the Son. Our honest prayer can be that of the man in Mark 9: "I believe; help my unbelief!" (Mark 9:24). Jesus teaches that it is possible to grow in greater dependence on God so we can emulate more and more of his life and ministry (e.g., Mark 11: 22–25; John 13:12–17, 14:12–14).

Supernatural Elements in Jesus' Life

Are not the supernatural elements of Jesus' life sourced in his own divine power? Note that most of the supernaturally-oriented activities of Jesus were not unique to him alone, but were also performed by "mere" humans, which supplies additional evidence for the dependency proposal.

(1) Miracles.[45] Both the OT and NT record miracles done by mere humans—not in their own human power, but sourced in the power of God, that were similar to those Jesus performed, for example: (a) raising the dead (2 Kings 4:8–37; Acts 9:36–42), (b) curing a leper (2 Kings 5:1–15), (c) healing the lame (Acts 3:1–10), (d) making an axe head float on water (2 Kings 6:4–7), (e) multiplying food (2 Kings 4:42–44), (f) walking on water for a brief time (Matt. 14:28–30), and (g) healing the sick and casting out demons by means of Paul's handkerchief and clothes (cf. Acts 19:11–12).

(2) Jesus' knowledge. How did Jesus convey God's authoritative message and have knowledge of the thoughts of others (e.g., Matt. 12:25, Luke 11:17; Luke 6:8)? Daniel reported and interpreted the dream of King Nebuchadnezzar (Dan. 2:1–49), and Peter knew the secret sin of Ananias and Sapphira (Acts 5:1–11).

(3) Jesus' temptability and impeccability (sinlessness). Jesus is human, but also uniquely divine. Scripture explicitly teaches that Jesus was tempted (didactic material: Heb. 2:18, 4:15; life examples narrated in the Gospels, e.g., Matt. 4:1–11, 16:23, 26:38–46). Yet James teaches that God cannot be

---

[45] Oliver Crisp's recent insightful studies in Christology are worth consulting. Oliver Crisp, *Divinity and Humanity* (Cambridge: Cambridge University, 2007), 25, conveys the scholarly consensus in labeling the view that Jesus performed his miracles by the power of the Spirit—the view held by John Owen and what is being presented in this chapter—as the "non-conventional view on this matter." See also Crisp, *God Incarnate: Explorations in Christology* (Edinburgh: T&T Clark, 2009).

tempted by evil (James 1:13). The teaching about Jesus' sinlessness claims that either he *could* not sin (or that he *would* not sin; Scripture only explicitly teaches that Jesus *did* not sin).

Bruce Ware offers a helpful analogy to clarify that Jesus did not rely on his divine powers to resist temptation and be sinless.[46] Imagine a man who wishes to swim across the English Channel from England to France. After much training, he hires a boat to go alongside to rescue him in case he is overcome with weariness or cramps. Being nearby, the crew in the boat would not permit him to drown. On the day of the swim, he launches out, perseveres against the cold water, the waves, the weather, and triumphantly reaches the other shore. So we ask: Why *could* the swimmer not have drowned? Because of the boat. But why *did* the swimmer not drown? Because he swam and finished his course. Accordingly, why *could* Jesus not have sinned? Because of his deity. But why did Jesus not sin? Because he resisted the temptations in his humanity, relying on God's powerful grace. The answers to these two questions must be kept distinct.

Yet, we still need to give some explanation for Jesus' inner psychological orientation and motivation. That Jesus fought against temptation is obvious, particularly in Gethsemane (even sweating blood, Luke 22:44; Heb. 12:4). No matter which incarnational model one holds, all must address this seeming paradox: Jesus could not sin, yet Jesus felt the genuine struggle of being tempted. (I do not think anyone would view the struggle in Gethsemane as just an amazing dramatic performance worthy of an Academy Award.) If Jesus knew he was God, which he did, why did he need to struggle against temptations? Resolving the temptability issue requires more space than can be allotted here, but suffice it to suggest one possible resolution. We can affirm that Jesus could not actually sin—that it was not a *metaphysical* possibility—if we also can affirm that it was an *epistemic* possibility.[47] That is, within Jesus' own understanding and perception

[46] Bruce Ware, "The Man Christ Jesus," *Journal of the Evangelical Theological Society* 53, no. 1 (March 2010): 5–18. Ware presented his affirmation of Jesus' dependence on the Father and the Spirit in "Christ's Atonement: A Work of the Trinity," in *Jesus in Trinitarian Perspective: An Introductory Christology*,edited by Fred Sanders and Klaus Issler (Nashville: B&H Publishing, 2007), 156–88. For a helpful historical study of issues related to Jesus' temptation and impeccability, see John McKinley, *Tempted for Us: Theological Models and the Practical Relevance of Christ's Impeccability and Temptation* (Milton Keynes, UK: Paternoster, 2009).

[47] See Thomas Morris *The Logic of God Incarnate* (1986; repr., Eugene, OR: Wipf & Stock, 2001), 147–48: "We have said that it seems to be a conceptual truth that, in some

of reality during his state of humiliation, it could be inferred that Jesus knew he was God but that he was *not certain* whether, as the theanthropic person (the God-man), it might be possible for him to sin. He could have inferred that as God, he could not sin. But the factor of also being human may have led to some uncertainty about that deduction.

Thus Jesus, with some uncertainty, chose to face the temptations as if he might be able to sin. Armchair theologians down through church history have wrestled with this issue and have had some disagreement about whether Jesus could have sinned or not, though the most common evangelical view is that Jesus could not have sinned. One could imagine that the Holy Spirit, his divine Tutor, may never have offered a definitive response to Jesus' question on that particular theological matter.[48] And Jesus did not have these learned tomes we have today to ponder the matter. Thus he struggled to resist temptation.

Furthermore, due to his formed heart of holiness, Jesus was much more painfully aware of the evil attacking him than we are. And he resisted every temptation, requiring greater intentionality in effort and reliance on divine help; believers are usually more clueless and less intentional (e.g., Heb. 12:3–4).

(4) Jesus' sinless life. Was this *solely* the result of his deity, or is it possible for a human person to live without sinning? First, human nature is not essentially corrupt or sinful (e.g., Gen. 1:31). Sinful propensities are a feature added on since the Fall. For a brief period of time Adam and Eve lived without sinning. Also, the Bible promises that all believers in the future eternal state, although still being human, will live continuously without sin (Rom. 8:17, 28–30; 1 Cor. 15: 50–57; Rev. 21:4, 27), sustained by the indwelling Spirit who indwells us forever (John 14:16). Being regenerated,

---

sense, temptation requires the possibility of sinning. On reflection, we can see that it is the *epistemic* possibility of sinning rather than a broadly logical, or metaphysical, or even physical possibility that is conceptually linked to temptation. . . . Jesus could be tempted to sin just in case it was epistemically possible for him that he sin."

[48] One important factor that may have contributed to Jesus being able to live fully in his humanity without having to run personal interference to restrain his divine attributes (especially omnipresence, omniscience, and omnipotence) was that the Holy Spirit, who indwelled and filled Jesus, acted as the dynamic "firewall" to Jesus' divine mind so that his divine knowledge remained dormant in Jesus' "subconscious" mind, and so that other aspects of Jesus' infinite divine nature could not encroach on his finite human nature. Thus, the Holy Spirit played a key active role to help sustain certain aspects of Jesus' hypostatic union during the challenging earthly phase of his first coming.

believers now have a new heart (Ezek. 36: 25–27) and have been freed from the power of sin (Rom. 6: 6–7, 11–12, 18). Yet believers take with them into their new life in God's family all of their sinful habits and propensities, and sadly we may continue to maintain and learn new sin patterns even as Christians. But we are commanded to walk in Christlike ways through the power of God's grace working in us—"ought" implies "can" in God's grace. Jesus demonstrated the possibility for regenerated humans to live sinlessly, becoming another "Adam" of a new God-oriented human race (1 Cor. 15:45–49).

Jesus' life makes the point that living sinlessly is *theoretically* possible for regenerated humans through God's power. The NT conveys an expectation and hope for believers that we can be transformed and sin less and less, as we rely on the Holy Spirit (Gal. 5:16; cf. 1 Cor. 10:13; 1 Pet. 2:21–23). Willard notes, "And that will enable us to walk increasingly in the wholeness, holiness, and power of the kingdom of the heavens. No one need live in spiritual and personal defeat. A life of victory over sin and circumstance is accessible to all" (*Renovation of the Heart*, 11).

Jesus' Deity and Messianic Mission

One may wonder if a predominantly depended thesis is affirmed, is there any Scriptural evidence in the Gospels to be marshaled to support Jesus' deity? Although the proposal affirms that each miracle is done by the power of the Spirit, the cumulative effect of the miracles, in combination with the other evidences, still point to Jesus' deity as well as his unique and distinctive Messianic mission (e.g., Matt. 11:3–5). Various standard evidences can be cited for his deity, as mentioned at the beginning of the chapter: Jesus received worship (e.g., Matt. 28:9, 16; John 20:28), his self-claims (e.g., Matt. 22:42–45; John 8:58–59), use of "Lord" (e.g., Luke 2:11; John 20:28), and the testimony of Gospel writers (John 1:1, 18). Also, evidence of Jesus' messianic mission as the Christ proves that Jesus is more than just a prophet (e.g., Luke 4:16–21; Matt. 16:16; Mark 10:45; Luke 4:41). Thus, despite the veiling of Jesus' deity during the Incarnation, there is sufficient manifestation of his divine person that still shines through clearly, for, as Jesus teaches, "Whoever has seen me has seen the Father" (John 14:9).

Some Practical Implications

That Jesus lived an authentic human existence is a weighty matter to ponder, for our theology, and especially for our daily life. Let us consider some implications along two trajectories and then suggest a few exercises.

Living WITHIN Our Personal Human Context as Jesus Did

Busyness hinders a life with God. H. J. Cadbury notes, "We can hardly make a picture of Jesus' life and that of his contemporaries that will be too casual for the facts."[49] What challenges me is the seemingly casual manner of Jesus' own life as portrayed in the Gospels, yet my own lifestyle is much too busy, as a recovering workaholic. Some Christian leaders tend toward over commitment of activities, which not only hinders our walk with God but also sets a bad example for others. Not only do we need physical rest, but our hearts also need space to listen to God. Willard suggests that solitude is the foundational spiritual discipline. "Solitude frees us. . . . The normal course of day-to-day human interactions locks us into patterns of feeling, thought, and action that are geared to a world set against God. Nothing but solitude can allow the development of freedom from the ingrained behaviors that hinder our integration into God's order" (*The Spirit of the Disciplines*, 160).[50]

Living BEYOND Our Human Limitations as Jesus Did

Yet Jesus also shows us the way to live a kingdom lifestyle, as Willard has pointed out. "The eternal life that begins with confidence in Jesus is a life in his present kingdom, now on earth and available to all" (*The Divine Conspiracy*, xvii). And a key divine resource is God the Holy Spirit who moves

> within our souls and especially our minds. To present the person of Jesus and the reality of his kingdom. . . . After we receive the new life, the Spirit continues to move upon and within us to enable us to do the kinds of works Jesus did (through "gifts" of

---

[49] H. J. Cadbury, *The Peril of Modernising Jesus* (London: SPCK, 1962), 124, cited in Robert J. Banks, *The Tyranny of Time* (Downers Grove, IL: InterVarsity, 1983), 80.

[50] For helpful guidance on developing a conversational relationship with God, see Willard's *Hearing God* and Klaus Issler, *Wasting Time with God: A Spirituality of Friendship with God* (Downers Grove, IL: InterVarsity, 2001), 151–82.

> the Spirit) and to grow the kind of inward character that manifests itself in the "fruit" or outcome of the Spirit in our outward life: love, joy, peace, longsuffering, and similar traits of Christ (Gal 2:23–25). (*The Divine Conspiracy*, 348)

As Jesus depended on the divine resource of the Father and the Spirit, so must we if we wish to live a Jesus-like life.[51]

Suggested Exercises

Consider three exercises to ponder the key theme of Jesus' dependence on God:

#1. From Table 2 and in reference to the extended discussion, select a Scripture passage that intrigued you. Perhaps take some time to study the passage further in its context. Then meditate on the passage for a week or so and listen to the Spirit's moving within.

#2. If you wish an experiential presentation of Jesus' authentic human experience, watch the movie, *Jesus*, starring Jeremy Sitso (1999, 174 minutes; a CBS mini-series). Invite some friends or family to join you. I was initially put off by the "humanness" of Jesus in the film. Yet I have since come to appreciate this as a distinctive contribution of the film. Not all in the film is theologically accurate—but no film can do that.

#3. Refer to Dallas Willard's *The Divine Conspiracy*, and read the section in which the invitation is posed: "I am learning from Jesus to live my life as if he would live my life if he were I" (283–85). Ponder, how would Jesus live my life, do my job, raise my kids, relate to my friends and family, if he were I? The point is not about how Jesus himself would work at a job like mine or be a parent. But, *if he were I*—being sensitive to my personality, to my talents and gifts, having had my experiential background with all the particular highs and lows—how would Jesus live my life, do my job, live within my life context? Dallas shares a bit of his own reflections on

---

[51] As one means to stretch one's God confidence, see J. P. Moreland and Klaus Issler, *In Search of a Confident Faith: Overcoming Barriers to Trust in God*, (Downers Grove, IL: InterVarsity), 2008.

being a professor at a research university. What insights come to mind to try out this week?[52]

Jesus is my hero. Although fully God, the Second Person of the Trinity, he voluntarily came to earth, adding on a human nature, just like you and me, willing to limit his earthly life and experience all the joys and the sorrows as a human, just like you and me. Jesus lived *within* his personal human context. And, Jesus lived *beyond* his human limitations, predominantly relying on the divine resources of the Father and the Holy Spirit, to show us how we can live as he did. Jesus raises the bar for what is possible when one lives in dependence on divine resources. Willard clarifies, "But what we can do with [mechanical, electrical, or atomic power] is still very small compared to what we could do acting in union with God himself, who created and ultimately controls all other forces" (*The Divine Conspiracy*, 22–23).

One of my purposes has been to attend to the scholarly reluctance and the popular confusion about Jesus' example. There is sufficient biblical evidence to support this claim that Jesus did predominantly live a human life, dependent on the divine resources of God.[53] Perhaps we can now leave such challenges behind and give greater practical attention to Willard's challenge: How *would* Jesus live your life, with your personality, with your talents, within your life context, if he were you?

"But you will receive power when the Holy Spirit comes on you;
and you will be my witnesses in Jerusalem, and in all Judea and Samaria,
and to the end of the earth."

(Acts 1:8)

---

[52] Willard suggests that "if [Jesus] were to come today as he did then, he could carry out his mission through most any decent and useful occupation. . . . In other words, if he were come today he could very well do what you do" (*The Divine Conspiracy*, 14).

[53] The chapter is a revision of much of the material in "Jesus' Example: Prototype of the Dependent, Spirit-Filled Life," in *Jesus in Trinitarian Perspective: An Introductory Christology*, edited by Fred Sanders and Klaus Issler (Nashville: B&H Publishing, 2007), 189–225. The chapter will become part of a forthcoming book, tentatively titled, *Mind the Gap, Seven Formation Themes for Deeper Discipleship into Jesus.*

ENACTING WILLARD

9

RETHINKING THE KINGDOM OF GOD

The Work of Dallas Willard and Some Applications to Psychotherapeutic Practice[1]

JOHN ORTBERG

Menlo Church

Abstract: Most of Dallas Willard's work on spiritual life can be said to center around the notion of the kingdom of God. This chapter examines his view of the Gospel as being essentially the proclamation of the radical availability of the kingdom of God in the person and teachings of Jesus, as opposed to what Willard sometimes called "the gospel of sin management." This is discussed particularly in light of the possibility of human transformation implied in the notion of the gospel of the kingdom. This, in turn, requires a certain understanding of the psychological nature of human change, and so involves an examination of the nature and purpose of what are sometimes called spiritual disciplines. The effect of this body of work on the life of the author, as well as some implications for the practice of psychotherapy, are also discussed.

For close to fifty years, Dallas Willard taught philosophy—primarily to graduate students—at the University of Southern California, where he also

[1] This present chapter is a revised version of "Rethinking the Kingdom of God: The Work of Dallas Willard and Some Applications to Psychotherapeutic Practice," *Journal of Psychology and Christianity* 14, no. 4 (1995): 306–17. Permission granted.

served for some time as the head of the department. As a graduate student, he had discovered the writings of Edmund Husserl, and despite some initial resistance from the faculty under whom he worked at the time, he was interested in and influenced by Husserl's approach to phenomenology from there on out.

However, he became better known in religious circles for his teaching and writing on the nature of spiritual life. Given his interest in spiritual disciplines and his involvement in philosophy, one might guess that he was, say, an East Coast Episcopalian. In fact, he grew up in Baptist circles in rural Missouri, and among other distinctions he was an ordained Southern Baptist preacher. In his early life, he was shaped by at least two powerful influences. One was the fact that he was a voluminous reader. He began to find that in reading great practitioners of the spiritual life, certain ideas and practices occurred over and over, even though the lives he was reading about were widely separated by time, geography, and even denominational tradition. (He spoke once of this under the general educational principle that "if you aim at depth, you'll get breadth thrown in as well. If you aim only at breadth, you'll get neither depth or breadth." Trace any great flowering of spiritual life back far enough and you'll find the same roots.)

The other influence is more difficult to articulate, but it involved a certain openness to the *experience* (as opposed to simply the belief *in* a God), which left Willard with a settled conviction that, in fact, God's reality was not only true but inescapable.

Central Concept: The Kingdom of God

"Spirituality" has become something of a topic de jure in American publishing circles in general and in evangelicalism in particular. But it is a little misleading to speak of Willard's primary interest lying in the field of spirituality. To a large extent, popular writings on spirituality have come to emphasize primarily the notion that there is an interior aspect to human existence, and that spirituality mainly involves attending to interiority (see, for example, Moore, 1992). On this score, Willard had relatively little to say.

His primary interest might be said to have centered around the Gospel of the kingdom of God. More to the point, his interest was in clarifying and elucidating the simple fact that the Gospel that Jesus preached is simply nothing other than the Gospel that the kingdom of God is now available in and through the life, teaching, death, and resurrection of Jesus. There is no other Gospel beside the Gospel of the kingdom. This means Willard spent a great deal of time trying not so much to understand new things, as to rethink things others thought they understand but had become largely distorted. For instance, the fact that the Gospel is about the availability of the kingdom requires fresh thought on salvation. (Often in evangelicalism salvation has come to mean nothing more than the means of getting into heaven, or what Willard sometimes called "the gospel of sin management.") It also means that serious thought has to be given to psychology, in the broad sense of wise thought about the nature of human change processes. This is turn leads to an understanding of the nature and purpose of spiritual disciplines, and their connection to enjoying life in the kingdom.

Willard's interests revolved around what Paul Hiebert has talked about as "middle range" issues (Hiebert, 1982); they are not addressed to technical discussions by contemporary theologians, but they are informed enough by theology and philosophy so that they also do not fit into the purely popular category.

Willard's critique of contemporary evangelical understandings of the Gospel is that it has been largely reduced to defining the "minimal entrance requirements" for getting into heaven. Those in the theologically conservative wing of the church are likely to think of the Gospel as an arrangement whereby they can secure an eternal reward for giving the correct response to the critical question. Such an understanding leads to debates as to whether the minimal criteria are set at a low level (for instance, "grace alone") or at a high level (for instance, "obeying Christ's lordship"), but on *both* sides of the debate is a shared assumption that "to be saved" is synonymous with "having satisfied the minimal criteria for getting into heaven." In either case, the Gospel becomes largely divorced from everyday life. In other words, contemporary evangelicals, when they hear the word "salvation," give it substantially different content than it was given by its New Testament writers and hearers. The Gospel is not the offer of minimal entrance criteria for heaven; it is the offer of life from above, which begins now, for ordinary human beings. So he writes,

> We must . . . engage in a radical rethinking of the Christian concept of salvation . . . One specific errant concept has done

> inestimable harm to the church and God's purposes with us—and that is the concept that has restricted the Christian idea of salvation to *mere forgiveness of sins* . . . Salvation as conceived today is far removed from what it was in the beginnings of Christianity and only by correcting it can God's grace in salvation be returned to the concrete embodied existence of our human personalities." (*The Spirit of the Disciplines*, 32–33, italics original)[2]

To regain a more accurate New Testament understanding of salvation, Willard focuses on the synoptic summaries of Jesus' message, typified by Mark 1:15: "The time is fulfilled. The kingdom of God is at hand. Repent and believe the good news." Thus the notion of salvation is dependent on a correct grasp of the nature of the kingdom of God.

The Kingdom of Transformation

Willard's theological thinking on the nature of the kingdom was probably influenced as much by George Ladd (cf. 1964) as anyone. But his primary concern lies in the degree to and the means by which it is possible for human beings to experience this kingdom kind of life on earth. A statement of Frank Laubach (another influence) would be typical of Willard's thought:

> For do you not see that God is trying experiments with human lives. That is why there are so many of them. He has one billion seven hundred million experiments going around the world at this moment. And His question is, "How far will this man and that woman allow me to carry this hour?"[3]

The good news, then, is that through the life, teachings, death, and resurrection of Jesus, it is now possible for ordinary human beings to live in the presence and under the reign of God. It includes the offer of life after death but it is more than that: "the simple and wholly adequate word for salvation in the New Testament is 'life'" (*The Spirit of the Disciplines*, 37).

[2] Short titles and parenthetical references are used throughout this chapter for the following books by Dallas Willard. *Hearing God: Developing a Conversational Relationship with God*, 3rd ed. (Downers Grove, IL: InterVarsity Press, 1999); *The Spirit of the Disciplines: Understanding How God Changes Lives* (New York: HarperCollins, 1988).

[3] Frank C. Laubach, *Letters by a Modern Mystic* (New York: Student Volunteer Movement, 1937), 14.

This is the pearl of great price for which any sane person would gladly sacrifice anything else. As Jeremias notes, this "parable is generally understood as expressing the demand of Jesus for complete self-surrender. In reality, it is 'completely misunderstood if it is interpreted as an imperious call to heroic action.' The key words are rather ἀπὸ τῆς χαρᾶς" (which is translated, in his joy).[4]

The Kingdom and a "Strategy for Transformation"

In general, most of Willard's work on spiritual life could be put in two categories: (1) an attempt to gain clarity on what the Gospel really is, on what the "life from above" offered by God is actually about; and (2) an attempt to clarify a realistic, practical strategy, informed by general wisdom about spiritual life and the nature of human beings as embodied spiritual creatures, whereby people can progressively enter into the life for which they were intended. This latter area—which he sometimes speaks about as an attempt to make practical theology *practical*—is the place most closely related to psychologists.

Several other authors have suggested that evangelical theology and practice have been too heavily influenced by psychology (Guiness, 1992; Wells, 1993). Willard argues, somewhat to the contrary, that precisely what has been lacking in evangelical practice in our day is a psychologically informed approach to spiritual transformation.

This does not mean, of course, simply baptizing whatever the latest therapeutic trends happen to be. It is not an argument for a heavier use of Jungian archetypes or analytic therapy within the church. In particular, it does not mean that theological categories are to be re-interpreted in terms of pop psychology—defining sin, for example, as a lack of self-esteem (cf. Plantinga, 1995). Rather, it is a suggestion that contemporary evangelical spiritual practice ("what Christians were normally told to do, the standard advice given to churchgoers") is not bringing about significant, concrete transformation of human lives. And that the reason for this is that it fails to "do justice to the nature of human personality, embodied incarnate" (*The Spirit of the Disciplines,* 18).

---

[4] Joachim Jeremias, *The Parables of Jesus*, 2nd rev. ed. (New York: Charles Scribner's Sons, 1972), 200.

In this sense, wise writings on spiritual life have always been intensely psychological. They are intrinsically dependent for their success on accurate insight into the nature of human identity and change; on the relationship between thoughts, feelings, and behaviors; and in particular on the mind-body problem. Willard cites writers such as Teresa of Avila (for instance, *Interior Castle*, 1961), Evelyn Underhill (1890), and Frances de Sales (1989) as examples of astute students of the processes of human change, and notes that Thomas Aquinas devoted 170 pages of the *Summa Theologica* to the cultivation of "holy habits."

It is because his work is so ruthlessly centered on life that in one sense Willard is not interested in "spirituality" at all. The extent to which his writing is of interest only to people who normally buy books on such topics would be an indictment of its failure.

Personal Impact

Willard's *The Spirit of the Disciplines* has been, with the exception of the Bible, by far the most influential book I have ever read. I read it at a time when I was frustrated by a sense of stagnation and a lack of deep change in my life in general and a sense of spiritual health in particular. And the sentence that was especially striking (and hope-giving) was essentially the thesis of the book:

> [W]e can become like Christ by doing one thing—by following him in the overall style of life he chose for himself . . . We can, through faith and grace, become like Christ by practicing the types of activities that he himself practiced in order to remain constantly at home in the fellowship of his Father. (*The Spirit of the Disciplines*, ix)

A distinction from learning theory can be helpful here. It is the difference between "training" to do something and "trying" to do something. There is of course a deep connection between the idea of being a "disciple" and of practicing certain "disciplines" (see Dunn, 1992).

My own experience before reading *The Spirit of the Disciplines* involved periodic attempts to "try harder" to pursue a "life of discipleship," followed by inevitable periods of frustration and inattention. For the first time, I came to understand discipleship as a way of life realistically designed to bring about spiritual empowerment.

Some definitions may be helpful (these are essentially from Willard, and are a typical combination of informed spirituality and non-technical language):

Discipline: Any activity that I can do by direct effort which, over time, will enable me to do what I *cannot* now do by direct effort. (This definition involves a basic understanding of disciplines across the spectrum of human activity, from athletics to art to academics, and by extension to spiritual life as well.)

Disciplined Person: Someone who is able to do what needs to be done when it needs to be done. (This definition has the advantage of illustrating that disciplines are means, not ends.) A disciplined person is not one who "does lots of disciplines," but one who is able to respond effectively. A disciplined basketball player is not one who practices 1,000 free throws a day, but one who is able to make them when they need to be made in a game. A spiritually disciplined person, then, is marked not by the lavish practice of religious exercises, but by the ability to love, to speak truth, and so on.

This understanding of the nature of spiritual life was enormously helpful in two ways. One was that it gave hope. I had reached a point where I did not know how significant, authentic transformation was really possible, and of course clients with low hope are poor risks (Beck, 1989). Here was someone who had gone farther down the road and had seen a light I could not see.

More than that, though, was an understanding that there were actually things that I could *do* through which I could eventually become a changed person. This opened up a whole world of thought and (more importantly) practice about the nature of spiritual life. I began to pursue solitude. The first time I went to spend a day alone I had a long list of things to pray for, but I'd prayed through the whole thing in about an hour. I had said pretty much everything I could think of to God, and he hadn't said anything back that I was aware of, and I wished one of us was more talkative.

So, not knowing how to "do" solitude, I just walked along the ocean. And there, with no agenda or list, I began to learn the process by which it is possible to accept the fact that God may really be speaking. I began to sense the possibility of becoming "detached" from the system of approval and reward that was governing my life. I began to sense from watching the ocean and the pelicans that the same Creator who had formed and taken joy in them had some sort of design in mind for me, and that to fail to pursue it was a kind of sin.

I began to experiment with fasting as a way to gain some measure of liberation from appetites. I began to practice silence (at least occasionally), and learned how such a vast amount of what I said was wholly or at least partially devoted to impression management ("I hardly ever watch TV, but . . ."; "I don't believe in gossip, but . . ."; "I like him a lot, but . . ."). I grew aware of my need for help, and entered into a confessional relationship with a trusted friend.

I came to realize that although I had been around prayer my whole life, I did not know how to pray in the way that Jesus did, so that it would feed my soul the way that food nourished my body. So for a year I prayed that God would send someone to teach me to pray, and eventually that prayer was answered as well.

One of the greatest gifts to come out of all this I hesitate to mention, except that this section is supposed to be personal, and that has been getting to know Dallas Willard himself. The circle of people who have been influenced by his life is a very wide one, and to spend much time with him at all was to recognize that he was a person who had entered a long way into a life most of us only loiter at the edges of. More than his writings and thought, helpful as those are, were his simplicity and humility and ability to attend to the moment and to whomever he was with that brought hope that such a life as Jesus promises really is possible.

We were at a restaurant some time ago, and my six-year-old kept interrupting our conversation with information about Michael Jordan. Finally, in exasperation I asked him to keep quiet, and Dallas said: "Don't worry about quieting him; he's the most important person at this table." It's difficult to write about this without making it sound like a clever saying. But it was not meant to be a clever statement; it was simply offered as an observation about the way things really appeared to him.

Interdisciplinary Dialogue

At several points, Willard's discoveries about God's kingdom and human nature offer meaningful dialogue with the practice of psychotherapy.

What Is the Potential for Application to the Practice of Psychotherapy?

A key facet of Willard's thinking involves the significance of the body. He sometimes uses the analogy of God's relationship to creation in Genesis 1: "God speaks, and it is so"; God has direct, unmediated power.

God has created human beings to have their own little spheres in which they have a similar kind of power, and that sphere is their body. People have direct, unmediated power over the movement of their bodies. This power is not unlimited, of course, and is subject to change over time and can be changed by certain practices.

A failure to appreciate the significance of human beings as *embodied* creatures, with all that means about the nature of physically ingrained patterns of thought and feelings, is what has often kept evangelicals from recognizing the nature of the process by which human transformation takes place. (It also lies behind much of the superficiality in fields like pop psychology and self-help literature.)

This understanding means that Christian spirituality will inevitably be *ascetic* spirituality, when properly understood. "Indeed, given what we have already seen about the nature of human life, any religion must be in some significant degree ascetic—admitted or not, consistent or not" (*The Spirit of the Disciplines*, 136). Asceticism is not a denial of the goodness of creation or physical existence, it is a recognition that spiritual transformation requires spiritual training, in particular that for human beings that training must inevitably revolve around human bodies.

There is another challenge here for psychologists. It is in the development of what might be called a psychologically sound theology of redemption, for a kind of "psychology of sanctification."

> We need an understanding that can guide us into constant interaction with the Kingdom of God as a real part of our daily lives, an *ongoing spiritual presence* that is at the same time a *psychological reality*. In other words, we must develop a psychologically sound theology of the spiritual life and its disciplines to guide us." (*The Spirit of the Disciplines*, xx, italics original)

This means coming to grips with the fact that for theology to address human life means it must address—clearly, intentionally, and accurately—processes we have come to compartmentalize as psychological. This is worth a lengthy quotation:

> This concern to understand the fundamental parts and processes of the human self and its redemption—biblical psychology—remains an unrelenting preoccupation of the Christian community . . . We customarily think of Paul as a great theologian, not as a master psychologist. But he clearly perceived and explained the fundamental structures and processes of the human self related to its well-being, its corruption, and its redemption. His letter to the Romans can never be fully appreciated unless it is read as, among other things, a treatise on social and individual psychology. The fact that he viewed his doctrine of redemption as a doctrine of the transformation of the self required him to be a psychologist. In fact, our ability to imagine that a great theologian would not at the same time be a profound psychologies, a profound theorist of human life, shows how far off-course our thinking is today . . . Paul's fundamental psycho-theological insight has to do with the nature of the human body as a bearer of active tendencies to evil and to good. In other words, it had to do with *spirituality* and *habit.* (*The Spirit of the Disciplines*, 112–13, italics original)

Another way in which psychologists could be helpful is in providing a contemporary language to describe the disciplines which have always been used by people wise in spiritual life. The basic practices are ancient, and yet somehow need to be re-discovered and contextualized in every generation.

This has already been done once in the twentieth century, in Alcoholics Anonymous. Growing out of the Oxford Group movement, which in turn was heavily influenced by Pietism and Wesleyanism, much of the power of AA comes from the use of practices like self-examination, confession, surrender of the will, penance, and so on, but described in the language of the recovery movement, and for the purpose of sobriety rather than life in the kingdom of God.

In fact, so basic and universal are these practices that one of the key figures in AA, a Jesuit priest who became a spiritual mentor to one of the co-founders, originally sought him out because he was certain AA had been consciously founded on the Spiritual Exercises of St. Ignatius. What is needed is a way of doing "life as discipleship" similar to what in monastic communities was called a "rule of life," or what in AA is referred to as the twelve steps or "working the program," but which is accessible to contemporary men and women who are interested in the kind of life Jesus offered.

To What Population (People and Presenting Problems) Is the Concept Most Appropriate?

Very often—even among churched populations—interest in "spirituality" or "spiritual formation" is restricted to a subset of people: generally academically inclined, fairly verbal, capable of intense introspection (not far from the archetypal good candidate for therapy). Involvement in "spiritual disciplines" would be restricted to those interested in advanced spirituality; a kind of eschatological extra-credit work.

However, by definition, a correct understanding of the nature of spiritual life will be helpful to all people because its "program" consists simply of whatever will be helpful to a given individual taking the next step in the direction of spiritual life. It may be helpful here to "think backwards" about spiritual life. Often people approach spiritual disciplines as things to be practiced and mastered for their own sake—that in "mastering" fasting, or solitude, I am demonstrating my spirituality.

In fact, the first question is: "Am I gaining an increasingly clear picture of what life in the kingdom (or true righteousness) really looks like?" A distorted understanding of spiritual maturity has led to a substantial amount of the misery of the human race.

The second question is: "What are the particular barriers that keep me from living this kingdom kind of life?" They will vary widely from one person to another, and within a single person from one time to another. They may include such things as busyness, resentment, laziness, or self-preoccupation.

Only when I have a measure of clarity on the first two questions can I ask the third: "What are the practices, experiences, and relationships I can engage in to help me overcome these barriers and enter more fully into life?" Some of those activities will almost surely involve central disciplines such as solitude and silence; some of them may involve much less "spiritual-sounding" ones like driving in the slow lane for a month, eating my favorite foods once a week, or adding another hour of sleep each night. They may even involve therapy.

Seen in this light, it becomes clear that " . . . the disciplines *have no value in themselves*. The aim and substance of spiritual life is not fasting, prayer, hymn singing, frugal living, and so forth. Rather, it is the effective and fully enjoyment of active love of God and humankind . . . The need for extensive practice of a given discipline is an indication of our *weakness*, not our strength" (*The Spirit of the Disciplines*, 138, italics original). This brings us to one sense in which finding the "appropriate population" becomes very critical for practices in spiritual life. They are appropriate only for people who are coming to have a progressively clearer understanding of the nature of spiritual life, and have a real (though not perfect or unmixed) hunger for it. For people with distorted notions about this, attempts at "spiritual growth" are likely to leave them in worse shape than they were when they started. The New Testament term for them was often "Pharisee," and of course they are not by a long shot all dead yet.

How Does It Mesh with Your Existing Theoretical Framework?

My own understanding of psychotherapy (which was suspended some time ago when I went into an alternate field) would have moderate leanings in cognitive directions, although it seems to me that the role of emotion tends to be underplayed (notwithstanding more recent discussions of "hot cognitions" and increased attention to affect) and a good deal of material tends to get smuggled in under the term "rational."

There are some interesting parallels here with Willard's thought, however. Perhaps the primary one relates to the notion of "faith." In evangelical thought, the notion of "saving faith" is largely understood as being about a single fact: if you believe that Jesus died for your sins so you're forgiven based on what he did rather than your works, this belief constitutes "saving faith." (Rarely would it be expressed quite like this, but it comes to the same thing.) For Willard, however, faith is much more tied to cognitive processes in general. He sometimes puts it like this: it is possible to violate your "beliefs," but never your "ideas about the way things are," or your "mental map." This is similar to what Mahoney (1991) calls one's "core processes."

Take an example. When I see a police car nearby, I drive differently than I otherwise might. If I always saw police cars, I'd be a different driver. If I truly believed they were omnipresent, it would make a difference.

Do I believe that God is omnipresent? In one sense, I do. It is part of my creed. I affirm it. However, when I look at the way I live my life, it is quite apparent by my actions that at the deepest level, at the level of my core process or mental map, I do not yet fully trust in the fact that God is omnipresent. If I did, my life would look different (imagine for a moment what your day would have looked like had God been physically, visibly present with you all day.)

Take another example. I believe both in the law of gravity and also in Jesus' teaching that "it is better to give than receive." But when I look at my actions, it is apparent that my trust in gravity runs much deeper than my trust that giving is better than receiving. I never violate the law of gravity. I don't walk out of a seventh-story window, or let go of a cup of coffee thinking that this time perhaps it will float weightlessly by my side. I don't have to "work hard" to believe in gravity. I don't have to drum up willpower to demonstrate my faith in it. My actions tell me I have utter trust that the law of gravity is true. My actions also tell me that I have less than utter trust in the notion that its better to give than receive, because often I behave as if receiving is better.

The faith that the biblical writers invite us into—the faith that transforms life—is clearly faith at this deepest level of mental map or core processes. It is much more than believing something about Jesus. It is, in a sense, simply to believe that Jesus got it right. That he was right about everything.

I think this also has something to say about the notion that there is a dichotomy or a tension between "faith" and "works." I think that notion holds only if "faith" is understood as "belief that Jesus died for my sins which gets me into heaven apart from any works." However, if faith involves coming to trust that what Jesus taught is simply true, then "works" flow out of such trust as inevitably as my "works" demonstrate that I "trust" in the law of gravity. Works are not opposed to faith; they are an inevitable result of it.

Here is a case where careful reflection on "cognition" has something to say about a truer understanding of faith. Having said this, I suspect that in general Willard's thought would be suggestive to a Christian practitioner of psychotherapy whatever their particular orientation would be.

Do You See Parallels in the Existing Psychological Literature?

One of the most important areas of overlap between Willard's work and literature in the field of psychology has to do with the nature and detection of human change (cf. Bugental, 1988; Luborsky, Crits-Christoph, Mintz, & Auerbach, 1988; Seligman, 1990). Spurred on partly by changes in the health care industry, the search continues to identify demonstrable change in human beings tied to concrete therapeutic interventions (Mahoney, 1991).

Literature on therapeutic intervention itself is, according to Willard, one of the major factors in an increase of interest in spiritual disciplines during recent years:

> [This (deeper interest in)] the classical spiritual disciplines was also produced by the growth of psychology, and of Christian psychology in particular, as a profession and as a body of knowledge. *Here was an event of major importance for the twentieth-century American church.* Psychologists, in the very nature of their work, are required to face the *realities* of the Christian soul—all dogmas, professions, and rituals aside-and to propose means of doing something about persons' problems. But this is exactly what the spiritual overseer of past ages tried to do, and though it was not widely studied in the 1960s or 1970s, there is an ocean of literature that relates such work to the earlier recognized disciplines for the spiritual life.
>
> The psychologist's work-indeed, the mere presence of the psychologist in the context of Christian institutions-made it clear to Christians of all denominations and all theological orientations that their "faith and practice" did not necessarily bring peace or health of mind and soul, much less a robust growth toward mature Christlikeness. (*The Spirit of the Disciplines*, 20, italics added)

Of special interest in this regard would be attempts to discern the influence of religion such as the body of literature that has grown up around Allport's writings on intrinsic/extrinsic religiosity (Allport, 1950; Malony, 1985). Attempts of an outside field such as psychology to find discernable differences that the practice of faith makes forces those inside the community of faith to recognize that the "difference" may be far more superficial than they have been accustomed to thinking. It brings, in a sense, a measure of accountability to the church's teachings on spiritual life.

The classical term for the ability of human beings to change while retaining their identity, used by William James in *Principles of Psychology* (1890), is "plasticity": "the possession of a structure weak enough to yield to an influence, but strong enough not to yield all at once. Each relatively stable phase of equilibrium in such a structure is marked by what we may call a new set of habits . . . the phenomena of habit in living beings are due to the plasticity of the organic materials of which their bodies are composed" (pg. xx).

Mahoney (1991), in his work on human change processes, has noted that while therapists (and spiritual directors) often lament the difficulty of change in human beings, in fact such difficulty is a good thing. If human beings did not have a strong core of beliefs, values, feelings, and habits, they would in fact have no sense of identity or continuity.

He goes on to contrast approaches to therapy based on their assumptions about plasticity. At the pessimistic end he places psychoanalytic thought (at least as it involves human development after the first five or six years of life). At the other end he places classical behaviorists, who believe that with proper manipulation of environment almost any change is possible. Willard would be—as G. K. Chesterton (1908) once wrote Christianity inevitably must be—at once "wildly pessimistic" and "wildly optimistic" about the possibilities for human change.

Mahoney (1991) also talks about three questions lying at the heart of education and psychotherapy: 1. Can humans change? 2. Can humans help humans change? 3. Are some forms of help better than others? He notes that these questions are central not only for psychology but also other fields, such as education. His entire work revolves around seeking to demonstrate that people can change, that they can help each other change, and that some forms of help are better than others.

However, I think that Willard would insist that these questions have always been at the heart of people who write about spiritual life. They serve to show the fundamental overlap between writings on "spiritual life" and writings in psychology, which has largely to do with the issue of change.

What Are Some Ethical Reasons to Practice (or to Avoid the Use of) This Concept in Psychotherapy?

In general, ethical issues involving psychotherapists who practice out of their commitment to the kingdom of God and the use of time-tested practice of disciplines for spiritual life would be covered under standard discussions of psychotherapy and the religiously committed patient-clarification of values, informed consent, appropriate use of power, clearly agreed upon joint goals, and so on (Bergin, 1980).

Furthermore, there is a tension here between realized and future eschatology that has ethical implications. In Willard's writings, there is a heavy emphasis on the radical present availability of the kingdom of God, particularly because this has been neglected. The danger would be talking of this in such a compelling way that people might get the notion that a radically transformed life could be entered easily or quickly. Hope and the compelling nature of such a vision need to be balanced with honest, authentic acknowledgement of human pain, the continued existence of "other kingdoms," and the slow and laborious task generally involved in change. And, of course, the kingdom must be understood as an end in itself, not a means to greater power or influence or success in life (see Acts 8, for example). It is not a magical way of by-passing human suffering through power which is available on command for healing or financial desires.

Finally, there is one other sense in which ethical considerations come into play. These considerations come not so much from the APA but from another and older body; they address not so much the therapeutic practice of the psychotherapist but here or his responsibility as a steward of a gift. It seems appropriate to let Willard have the last word:

> At this point in history, every leader among those who identify with Christ as Lord must ask himself or herself: "How can I justify *not* leading my people into the practice of disciplines for the spiritual life that would enable them to reign in their lives by Christ Jesus? How can I fail to give them this opportunity? How can I justify not giving myself to those practices until I am a spiritual powerhouse, the angels of God evidently ascending and descending upon me in my place?" (*The Spirit of the Disciplines*, 246)

REFERENCES

Allport, G. (1950). *The individual and his religion.* New York: Macmillan.
Beck, A. (1989). *Love is never enough: How couples can overcome misunderstandings, resolve conflicts, and solve relationship problems through cognitive therapy.* New York: HarperCollins.
Bergin, A. E. (1980). Psychotherapy and religious values. *Journal of Consulting and Clinical Psychology, 48*: 98.
Bugental, J. F. T. (1988). What is "failure" in psychotherapy? *Psychotherapy, 25*: 532–535.
Chesterton, G. K. (1908). *Orthodoxy.* London: William Clowes and Sons.
de Sales, F. (1989). *Introduction to the devout life,* John Ryan (trans.). New York: Doubleday.
Dunn, J. D. G. (1992). *Jesus' call to discipleship.* Cambridge: Cambridge University Press.
Foster, R. (1979). *The celebration of discipline.* San Francisco, Harper & Row.
Guiness, O. (1992). *The American hour.* New York: Free Press.
Hiebert, P. (1982). The flaw of the excluded middle. *Missiology: An International Review 10,* no. 1 (January 1982).
James, W. (1890). *The principles of psychology.* New York: Holt.
Jeremias, J. (1972). *The parables of Jesus.* New York: Charles Scribner's Sons.
Ladd, G. (1964). *Jesus and the kingdom.* New York: Harper and Row.
Laubach, F. C. (1937). *Letters by a modern mystic.* New York: Student volunteer Movement.
Luborsky, L., Crits-Christoph, P., Mintz, J., & Auerbach, A. (1988). *Who will benefit from psychotherapy?* New York: Basic Books.
Mahoney, M. (1991). *Human change processes: The scientific foundations of psychotherapy.* San Francisco: Basic Books.
Malony, H. N. (1985). Assessing religious maturity. In *Psychotherapy and the religiously committed patient,* M. Stern (ed.) New York: Haworth Press.
Moore, T. (1992). *Care of the soul.* San Francisco: HarperCollins.
Plantinga, C. (1995). *Not the way it's supposed to be: A breviary of sin.* Grand Rapids, MI: Eerdmans.
Seligman, M. (1990). *Learned optimism.* New York: Simon and Schuster.
Teresa of Avila. (1961). *Interior castle.* Garden City, NY: Doubleday.
Underhill, E. (1890) *Mysticism.* New York: Doubleday.
Wells, D. (1993). *No place for truth: Or, whatever happened to evangelical* theology? Grand Rapids, MI: Eerdmans.
Willard, D. (1984). *In search of guidance.* Ventura, CA: Regal Books.
Willard, D. (1988). *The spirit of the disciplines.* San Francisco: Harper & Row.

10

A TRIBUTE TO DALLAS WILLARD

My Favorite Psychologist

GARY W. MOON

Westmont College

Abstract: Modern psychology, pastoral counseling. and even Christian counseling seem to have developed a form of amnesia concerning soul care's classical past. With few exceptions, these disciplines have been prone to adapt existing secular theories as opposed to developing theory and practice that arise from Christian theology. As a result, invisible, immeasurable things like soul and spirit are often left out of the classroom and training labs. In this essay we will briefly discuss this history and then turn attention to three lessons learned from the "psychologist," Dallas Willard, concerning his views of: (1) the components of the person, (2) the process of transformation, and (3) the implications to the field of Jesus' being very smart. It is argued that these are three important pillars for the development of a Christian psychology.

One might find it odd that I would refer to the philosopher and theologian Dallas Willard as my favorite *psychologist*. But if a person traces the roots of modern psychology back through the centuries, it becomes easier to see him as one of that discipline's best modern-day practitioners.

In the late 1970s I began studying psychology at a major southern university. While I did not know it at the time, Dallas Willard had also majored in psychology at a much smaller and decidedly more sober institution about 120 miles north. I also did not know that just over ten years prior to my first undergraduate class in psychology, the university I was attending had offered Dallas a job teaching in their philosophy department. But when another suitor institution offered a reduced teaching load—one more conducive to the writing he wanted to pursue—he took that job instead and began his storied career as a philosopher at the University of Southern California.

In the History and Systems course at my undergraduate institution, we used a thick textbook that devoted about 95 percent of its attention to modern psychology, which the authors claimed sprang to life in the laboratory of Wilhelm Wundt in 1879. Forty-eight of the fifty psychologists working as professors in the department echoed the same sentiments; the other two were closer to retirement than they knew.

During the halcyon days of behaviorism, the prevailing feeling was that not much worth considering within the discipline of psychology had happened before the late 1800s. I never paused to ponder how it would have sounded if the literature department of the same institution had been telling the students, "No need to read Homer, Shakespeare or Dostoyevsky; real literature goes back only to the modernist writers of the early 20th century."

Years after graduating from that university and completing doctoral studies in clinical psychology at another institution, I was listening to a gifted communicator as he unpacked Norman Rockwell's famous painting *Breaking Home Ties*. At some point in the middle of his discussion, I had an epiphany concerning the history of psychology and the debate over which ideas should be kept in and which culled out. The storyteller described the Rockwell classic:

> See the face of the young man. It is a canvas for excitement, anticipation. He stares out, wide-eyed, into the distance. An oversized red tie rests on the outside of a crisp white shirt. A brightly-colored triangular banner featuring the words "State University" decorates his battered suitcase. He looks like Huck Finn on Easter Sunday.
>
> But look at the other figure, probably the boy's father. He's sitting beside his son on the running board of a dirt-caked truck. The man's face is weathered and leathery-brown. He is wearing the

> faded denim overalls of a farmer. He stares downcast at the dusty ground, tenderly holding his son's hat in his hand, perhaps as a way somehow to hold on to the boy a little longer. A large red handkerchief hangs down from an oak barrel as a signal for the next train to stop.

While the speaker was using the image to help a roomful of church leaders representing a small, rural denomination grieve a lost generation—a generation of young people who went off to college and never returned home, the image helped me process what had happened to the discipline of psychology.

Rural America and that particular Christian denomination were not the only "fathers" who have seen their "children" leave. Psychology (and subsequently pastoral and professional counseling) also left "home"—the ancient traditions of soul care—to seek new insights and opportunities in the "city"—methods of modern psychotherapy.

Hurding, Gorsuch, Benner, and LeShan provide interesting overviews that illuminate the migration of modern psychology from its home as a discipline of soul care practices to its present-day dwelling place in the city—or at least the suburbs—as a science of behavior.[1]

Gorsuch and LeShan remind us that psychology distanced itself from the practices of soul care and its parents, philosophy, and religion, when it turned toward the "hard sciences" as role models in the late 1900s. Much was gained, but much was also lost.

Psychology prospered in the "city." It won a place in the academy—usually a few doors down from the biology department (if you get to anthropology, you have gone too far). Hundreds of new divisions, schools, and departments were spawned. Scores of new academic journals were launched. National organizations, some with considerable political clout, were initiated. Human behavior was squeezed under a microscope and studied from the outside in. For many students of the modern discipline of psychology, life on the farm was a dim memory.

---

[1] See R. F. Hurding, *The Tree of Healing* (Grand Rapids, MI: Zondervan, 1985); R. L. Gorsuch, "Psychology and Religion, Beliefs, and Values," *Journal of Psychology and Christianity* 5, no. 2 (1986), 39–44; D. G. Benner, *Psychotherapy and the Spiritual Quest* (Grand Rapids, MI: Baker, 1988); and L. LeShan, *The Dilemma of Psychology* (New York: Dutton, 1990).

But even with all the success, many look back with a sad nostalgia. Thomas Oden is one of these. He is arguably the most outspoken critic of modern pastoral counseling and professional Christian counseling and has made numerous assertions that these have lost touch with their historical roots. Oden, in his book *Care of Souls in the Classic Tradition,* provides a striking graphic to support his claim that pastoral counseling in particular has also left the farm and has "fallen into a pervasive amnesia toward its own classical pastoral past."[2]

Oden selected ten key figures in classical pastoral care: Cyprian, Tertullian, Chrysostom, Augustine, Gregory the Great, Luther, Calvin, George Herbert, Richard Baxter, and Jeremy Taylor. He then checked the number of times they were referenced in seven standard works of pastoral theology in the nineteenth century. He found that each of these texts unfailingly quoted at least six of the ten classic figures he had selected, and in all he found 314 references to them. He then selected seven representative twentieth-century pastoral writers and conducted a similar indexing procedure. What he found was mind-boggling. There were no references, none, to the classic figures. However, there were 330 references to the city-dwelling friends of their older brother, psychology: Freud (109), Jung (45), Rogers (101), Fromm (27), Sullivan (22), and Berne (26). With this research, undeniable credibility is added to his bold-faced assertion that "pastoral counseling has become in many cases little more than a thoughtless mimic of the most current psychological trends."

While these surveys conducted by Oden have a specific focus on pastoral counseling, he and others make parallel observations concerning the youngest brother, professional Christian counseling. David Benner reflects on the wide variety of approaches to Christian counseling and determines that, with only two possible exceptions, "none of the other approaches have been explicitly developed from Christian theology. Rather, they are adapted forms of existing secular theories which the authors argue are consistent with Christian truth."[3] A friend of mine who is less diplomatic than Benner puts it like this: "It seems to me that a lot of Christian counseling/psychology is sacred glaze brushed onto a secular ham."

---

[2] Thomas C. Oden, *Care of Souls in the Classic Tradition* (Philadelphia: Fortress Press, 1984).

[3] D. G. Benner, ed., *Baker Encyclopedia of Psychology* (Grand Rapids, MI: Baker, 1985).

Leslie D. Weatherhead, using less picturesque speech, states:

> Psychology has its place as material medicine has, but neither is to be regarded as a substitute for the dynamic spiritual energy which the Church of the first century knew. We are trying to make do with both, because we are not prepared to pay the price which a healing Church costs. We pretend that the first-century healing miracles are being repeated by psychotherapeutic treatments. We interview a patient for two hundred separate hours, and then rejoice when he does not limp quite so badly. The Apostles could say, 'In the name of Jesus Christ, rise and walk![4]

By the late 1980s, after having completed doctoral studies and finding myself suddenly immersed in private practice, I began to experience a growing disillusionment with a psychology that would embrace the laboratory rat while ignoring the celestial soul. It was not that I did not appreciate the rich contributions the discipline had to offer; I just wanted to know more about areas where it was often silent and sometimes condescending. I had also begun to wonder why I was selling the fruit of modern psychology to those who came to me in distress while I was drinking the wine of Christian spiritual formation to ease my own pain.

It was precisely at the height of this internal questioning that I discovered Dallas Willard's book, *The Spirit of the Disciplines: Understanding How God Changes Lives*.[5] After a slow reading that took almost three months, I came to the conclusion that this "amateur" theologian and professional philosopher knew more about the soul than any psychologist (literally "soul-ologist") I had ever encountered. And his focus was not on helping people limp less; he was teaching people how to rise up and walk "with God."

Within a couple of years of discovering Dallas, I invited him to come to the university where I was teaching to give a lecture series that was to celebrate the launch of something we were calling the Institute of Clinical Theology. I was shocked when he agreed to come and completely bewildered when he would not set a fee for his talks. While visiting with Dallas in our home, I discovered that this mere lad of fifty-five was the most

---

[4] Leslie D. Weatherhead, *The Transforming Friendship* (London: Epworth Press, 1928).

[5] Dallas Willard, *The Spirit of the Disciplines: Understanding How God Changes Lives* (San Francisco: Harper, 1988).

authentic and genuine follower of Jesus that I had ever met. I was drawn to live as he lived, to know Jesus as he seemed to know Him.

That initial encounter with Dallas was so positive, so life-giving that I spent much of the next 20 years looking for excuses—a journal to establish, an institute to launch, DVD projects to film—for immersing myself and others in Dallas's ideas and presence. I am not sure I have ever stood in front of a class for more than an hour without referencing Dallas Willard; it is not unusual for me to do so while standing in the express line at a grocery store.

To speak boldly, it would not surprise me if Church historians of the future peer back through the centuries and judge Dallas Willard's contributions to the kingdom to be of equal importance to those of other reformers such as Martin Luther and Ignatius of Loyola. It also would not surprise me if future psychologists look back and see Dallas Willard as a giant in that discipline as well.

For the remainder of this article I will limit my comments to just three of the psychology lessons I have learned from "psychologist" Dallas Willard. These lessons are about (1) the components of the person, (2) the process of transformation, and (3) the implications to the field of Jesus' being very smart.

The Components of the Person

As we have discussed, modern psychology has had the tendency to ignore things that cannot be measured. It is rare to find the word "soul" mentioned in an American Psychological Association (APA) sponsored journal; or a *psyche*-ologist who would be willing to focus attention on that aspect (the *psyche*-logical) of his or her client.

Do not get me wrong; I am a huge fan of modern psychology. Most training programs in counseling or clinical psychology offer a curriculum that provides a breadth of exposure to scientific approaches to ameliorating dysfunction, including classes in the biological, cognitive, social, and relational aspects of behavior. However, the soul and its integrative functioning within the person is not part of APA's suggested course of study. So perhaps you can imagine my delight when I discovered a *psyche*-ologist who wrote and taught about the entirety of the person.

Examining the soul is not an easy task, even for a theologian. Even beginning with the Bible may not help. Attempting to understand what is written in Scripture about the *soul* or *spirit*—for that matter, about any of the components of a person—is confusing. But I have found Dallas Willard to be very helpful in elucidating matters of our inner world and navigating past three of the primary problems posed to our understanding: (1) He reminds us that the words *soul* and *spirit*, while often used as parallel expressions, should not be viewed as synonymous. (2) If you decide to lower the microscope to find distinctions between *soul* and *spirit*, you discover that in Scripture *spirit* can also refer to both *heart* and *will*.[6] (3) Hebrew and Greek conceptions of the soul's relationship to the body were very different. While Greek thought often presented a view of the soul as a separate entity from the body, Hebrew anthropology was more holistic than compartmentalized.

It seems that modern theology has gravitated toward the more unitive Hebrew view. It is no longer in vogue to debate as to whether human beings are composed of two parts (soul and body) or three parts (soul, spirit, body). For most scholars today, the *soul/spirit* is not considered to be "part" of a person's make up, but instead characterizes the individual in his or her totality. When asked in class if I am a dichotomist or a trichotomist, I will think of Dallas and simply say, "Either is a good start."

In contemporary usage it is safe to say that the terms *soul* and *spirit* refer to the nonmaterial aspect of a human being that gives individuality. In Christian theology these terms carry the further connotation of being the part of a person that has the potential to partake of divinity and survives the death of the physical body.

Against this slightly blurred background, I believe Dallas Willard offers more help than most in attempting to bring the entire "person" into focus. In *Renovation of the Heart: Putting on the Character of Christ*, Dallas Willard proposes there are six basic aspects of a human being, which together and in interplay make up "human nature."[7]

---

[6] Dallas Willard, *Renovation of the Heart: Putting on the Character of Christ* (Colorado Springs: NavPress, 2002), 33–35.

[7] Willard, *Renovation of the Heart*, 30.

- ✓ *Thought* (images, concepts, judgments, inferences)
- ✓ *Feeling* (sensations, emotion)
- ✓ *Body* (action, interaction with the physical world)
- ✓ *Social context* (personal and structural relations with others)
- ✓ *Spirit* (choice, will, heart, decision, CEO of the person)
- ✓ *Soul* (the factor that integrates all the above into one life)

Figure 1
WILLARD'S MODEL OF THE PERSON

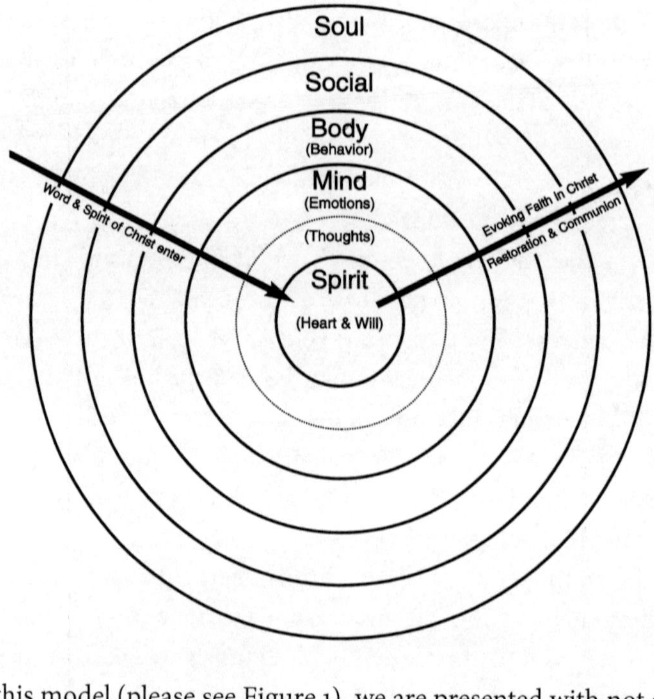

In this model (please see Figure 1), we are presented with not only the components of the person but also the only five things a human being can do. Humans can think, feel, behave, interact with others, and choose. *Spirit/will/heart* is the center or core of a person's life and may be called the "ego"—especially when functioning separate and apart from God as the source of life.[8] "Choice" is perhaps the best one-word encapsulation for the activity of this *spirit/will/heart* dimension. It underscores the most fundamental

[8] I hope I am not being confusing here; I believe that we both need a healthy ego and that as part of a Christian's journey of experiencing a greater sense of union with God, we need to lay it down. In this sense I am using "ego" to represent what has been called the "false self," or that aspect of the person which is holding on to the notion that a life separate from God is good and desirable.

decision faced by humanity. Like their foreparents, Christians awaken each day to the choice of living in an intimate, conversational, and communal relationship with God, or of initiating and maintaining a separate existence. The *spirit/CEO*'s critical decision is between willingness, surrender, and obedience versus willfulness, autonomy, and separation from the Source of life.

According to Dallas, the *soul*, as distinguished from the *spirit/CEO*, can be viewed as the invisible computer that keeps everything running and integrated into one person. The *soul* is the aspect that integrates all of the components of the person to form one life. The *soul* is not the "person." The person includes all aspects of the self, including the *soul*. The *soul*, Dallas pens, "is that aspect of your whole being that *correlates*, *integrates*, and *enlivens* everything going on in the various dimensions of the self. It is the life center of the human being."[9]

Why is this important? For starters, I have referenced being exposed to psychology at a time when many major universities saw the discipline primarily concerned with only one aspect of the entire person: behavior. It was very interesting for me to return to my alma mater a decade after my undergraduate graduation only to discover that the psychology department had been taken over by those who were lobbying for the primacy of cognition, a second aspect of the person. If you traveled far enough back in time, you would see that still other aspects of the person (emotional, relational) had been given their decade (or so) in the sun. The point is, I do not mean to be merely contrasting Dallas Willard's conceptualization of the person with behaviorism, but rather with any approach of modern psychology that is not both holistic and inclusive of the non-physical aspects of the individual.

What am I saying? I have found that Dallas Willard provides me with a more comprehensive model for understanding the person than what I was offered by modern psychology. And as an added bonus, it includes biblically and philosophically informed formulations about the soul (basic organizing mechanism) of the person and the spirit (or CEO) of the person and the importance of its moment-by-moment choices between willingness and surrender versus willfulness and independence from life and love.

I believe Dallas Willard's model of human functioning provides a holistic way of conceptualizing and working with individuals that easily

[9] Willard, *Renovation of the Heart*, 199.

embraces abnormal psychology, positive psychology, and the soul/spirit. That is to say, each component (let's think "cognitive" aspect as one illustration) can be focused on for the purpose of (1) improving maladaptive functioning (e.g., reframing and restructuring thought patterns that lead to negative outcomes); (2) increasing positive outcome (e.g., strengthening and enhancing existing thought patterns that support positive functioning); and (3) enhancing Christian spiritual formation (e.g., examining an individual's views and concepts of God for the purpose of facilitating the process of learning to live more moments "with" God). Now, that is a psychology I can be excited about.

Real Change Can Happen

Several years ago while I was producing a DVD for a small-group resource based on *Renovation of the Heart*, something very memorable happened. It had been a long day. That morning, Dallas had done a remarkable job summarizing each of the thirteen chapters from his book in front of a live studio audience. That afternoon he, John Ortberg, and Larry Crabb had been sitting around a small café table discussing the topics from that morning over coffee and on camera. The idea behind the casual recap was that since some people find Dallas painfully smart, it would be a good idea if a couple of colleagues helped him bring things down a few notches so the rest of us could get it.

We were two hours into the afternoon taping, and I was beginning to feel it was past time to take a break. I was moving to get the director's attention so he would call for a break in the action when I heard John begin to make a tearful confession:

"Dallas, I could take you to the time and the seat on the airplane when I read the words in your book that changed my life."

While I was not a seasoned producer, I knew that was not the time to yell, "Cut!"

John went on to quote the line from *The Divine Conspiracy* that states, "My central claim is that we *can* become like Jesus by doing one thing—by following him in the overall style of life he chose for himself."[10] There were

---

[10] Dallas Willard, *The Divine Conspiracy: Rediscovering Our Hidden Life in God* (San Francisco: Harper, 1998), ix.

tears in John's eyes as he went on to confess that these words impacted him deeply and filled him with hope because, even as a successful pastor, he had begun to doubt if real change, authentic transformation, was possible.

This cuts to the heart of the second indelible psychology lesson I learned from Dallas. Real change—not just alterations of thought and behavior but also a transformation of will and character—is possible. But it will require an inspired CEO.

The CEO of the Person

If God created the *spirit/heart/will* as the key influence (read, CEO) of one's life, then how the heart becomes transformed from "darkened and secretly idolatrous" (Deut. 29:18, 19; Matt. 15:8; Rom. 1:21) to "honest, good and open to God" (Luke 8:15; Rom. 10:9) becomes the most important question that can be asked in theology, philosophy, and psychology. To get a better grasp of the person in the context of transformation, I like to use the Dallas-inspired imagery of a Fortune 500 company.[11]

Picture an executive meeting of a large company. The CEO (*spirit/heart/will*), who makes the key choices, sits at the head of the table in a conference room. She is surrounded by five division heads representing research and development (thought), human resources (feeling), labor (body), corporate relations (social context), and information services (*soul*). In an ideal situation for your company, all essential parts are effectively organized around its mission statement—its purpose and reason for existence—that was put in place by the board of directors (the Trinity). The CEO (*spirit/heart/will*) seeks the higher good of the organization and its mission. In the best of worlds, the five division heads cooperate and comply with the administrative will of the CEO, which is one with the will of the board of directors.

The problem is, however, that most "companies" (or "human beings") are not headed by a CEO who operates in perfect alignment with the "board." The key question is how transformation can occur in me that will realign the vision of the CEO (*spirit/heart/will*) to comply with the mission statement of loving God with my whole heart and my neighbor as myself.

[11] I originally described this in my book *Renovation of the Heart: Leader's Guide* (Franklin Springs, GA: LifeSprings, 2003).

The biblical answer is clear. The *spirit/heart/CEO* is changed through a relationship with the Trinity—most specifically, Jesus Christ. When Jesus says as part of his commencement address to his disciples, "And this is eternal life, that they know you, the only true God, and Jesus Christ, whom you have sent" (John 17:3), he is pointing the CEO of our person to an intimate and interactive friendship with God. It is the CEO in relationship with the Board that produces singleness of purpose, willing surrender, and the ultimate organization of all the division heads around one purpose. Spiritual formation in Christ is the process leading to that ideal end where all essential parts of the human self are effectively organized around God. The ideal result is love of God with all one's heart, soul, mind, and strength and of one's neighbor as oneself (Mark 12:29–31; Deut. 6:4–9; Lev. 19:18).

Christian spiritual transformation involves "knowing" God at such a deep, relational level that one's *spirit* is progressively aligned to Divine Will while the *soul* is humming in the background like a well-functioning computer, integrating all the components of the person into one fully functioning organism.

From Fortune 500 Companies to the Desert Fathers

This all sounds almost too easy; most find the journey of transformation difficult to the point of seeming to be impossible. But it is precisely here that Dallas offers both hope concerning the possibility of real change and descriptions that seem to me surprisingly at home with the early traditions of the Church Fathers and Mothers and Orthodox traditions of Christian faith. Let me explain.

Kallistos Ware tells the story of a fourth-century desert father, St. Sarapion the Sindonite, who traveled on a pilgrimage to Rome. Once there, he was told of a respected recluse who spent all of her time in a small room. Sarapion was skeptical of her way of life because of its contrast to his own approach, which included much travel. He called on her and asked, "Why are you sitting here?"

To this she replied: "I'm not sitting, I am on a journey."[12]

To be a Christian is to be on a journey—from the pigpen of self-rule to the outstretched arms of a loving Father. Not surprisingly, one of the

---

[12] Kallistos Ware, *The Orthodox Way* (Crestwood, NY: St. Vladimir's Seminary Press, 1979), 7.

most ancient names for Christianity is simply "the Way."[13] It is possible that some Protestants have become fascinated with spiritual direction because of the partial loss of the richness and texture in viewing Christian transformation as a journey. Even though Reformers such as Calvin discussed three broad stages of the journey—conversion, sanctification, and glorification—in practice it seems that many modern Protestants are more likely to expect a microwave instead of a crock-pot approach to transformation.

As Rogers observes, one of the most striking differences between ancient and modern Christianity concerns the view of salvation. "At the risk of oversimplification," he states, "Protestants generally define salvation in legal, juridical, or forensic terms. Christ's death pays the just penalty for man's sin. We receive salvation (forgiveness of sins) by virtue of our faith in His meritorious sacrifice on our behalf."[14] While not denying the sacrificial aspect of salvation, ancient Christianity, according to Rogers, believes it is better to view salvation as a process of transformation and the fulfillment of the image of God in humankind.

Perhaps it should not be surprising to hear Christians described as "forgiven sinners" instead of "beloved children of God on a transformational journey that will lead to restoration of the *imago dei*, and spiritual union." Nor is it startling that someone whose identity is that of absolved reprobate might dance for joy at the notion of being offered a personal invitation to live in union with God.

Three Stages

The journey motif for spiritual formation was adopted by both Roman Catholic and Eastern Orthodox Christians and is conceived of as including three stages: purgation, illumination, and union.

Purgation is the process by which one's character is purified through confession of sin and a growing detachment from worldly values. Using the imagery of Dallas Willard's model of the person (see Figure 1), foundational to purgation is a *metanoia*, or a radical reorientation of all the dimensions of the person (thoughts, emotions, will, behavior, social interactions, life of the soul) toward God. It is here the seeker battles, along with the grace

[13] See Ware, *The Orthodox Way*, 7, and Acts 19:23.

[14] F. G. Roger, "Spiritual Direction in the Orthodox Christian Tradition," in *Spiritual Direction and the Care of Souls: A Guide to Christian Approaches and Practices*, edited by Gary W. Moon and David G. Benner (Downers Grove, IL: InterVarsity Press, 2004).

of God, against the passions and habit patterns of sin within the human body and soul that corrupt human nature. In the imagery of the parable of the prodigal son, purgation describes the stage of thinking things through again—leaving the pigs to begin the journey back home.

Illumination refers to a deepening experience of the love, joy, and peace of God, along with a growing desire to surrender the will to God. It is characterized as a time of becoming dispassionate for all things not God and passionately attached to God and his kingdom. During this stage, conversations with God increase and begin to deepen into communion and movement toward unceasing prayer from the heart.

With reference to Figure 1, illumination can be visualized as an increasing interior surrender to the presence and passion of the indwelling Spirit of Christ within each dimension of the person until the person's character becomes a better mirror of Christ. For the prodigal, illumination describes the time of staring into the eyes of the father, realizing the extent of his boundless love, and then becoming lost in his embrace.

Union with God is the final stage of spiritual formation. This state will not reach ultimate fruition until heaven. It involves complete interior surrender to the presence and will of God. As this stage is approached, there is little to distinguish the character of the believer from that of Christ. The mystery of "Christ in me" is realized as an interior surrender of all components of the person—thought, emotion, will, behavior, relationships, and soul functioning—is made to the transforming presence of Christ. For the prodigal son, union would mean a full re-entry into the family and taking on the mind of the father with such a deep appreciation for his love that he has become pig-proofed for life.

Willard describes the process of spiritual transformation as the renovation of the human heart. He believes that "*spiritual formation for the Christian basically refers to the Spirit-driven process of forming the inner world of the human self in such a way that it becomes like the inner being of Christ himself*" (*Renovation of the Heart*, 22, italics original). It also involves a progressive union with God that takes the form of a conversational relationship that is personal, concrete, and ongoing.

As the process of Christian spiritual formation reaches fruition, several things become evident: (1) One begins to awaken to her true identity and, with God's grace, dethrones the false self. (2) Conversation and communion with God increase and deepen into a sense of spiritual union. (3) The various dimensions of the person become united by the presence and love of the indwelling Christ. The truly important thing, the common thread of spiritual formation, according to Thomas Merton, is the journey of surrender to the will of God and his love.[15]

By way of summary, Dallas Willard rightly reminds us that the "The Spirit of the Disciplines" is "nothing more than the love of Jesus with its resolute will to be like him whom we love." He also reminds us there is but one "way," one "truth," and one "life." We must become like him and follow him in overall lifestyle, "and have put on the new self, which is being renewed in the knowledge after the image of its creator" (Col. 3:10).

Jesus Was Really Smart

The third psychology lesson I learned from Dallas is to always remember that Jesus was really smart. Let me explain.

I liked the title *Slums of Beverly Hills* more than I liked the movie. I think it struck a chord because it reminded me that many academics seem to think possessing Christian faith automatically relegates a person to the intellectual slums.

I recently received an invitation from the same psychology department of the major southern university I referenced earlier. They wanted me to send them some money. In a section of the appeal labeled "past milestones," a brief psychological history of the department was offered.

- ✓ 1800 Psychology first represented in the university's curriculum as "moral and mental philosophy"
- ✓ 1897 "Psychology" first appeared as a university course, but remained philosophically rather than scientifically oriented
- ✓ 1902 First laboratory course in psychology taught
- ✓ 1970s Department represents psychology as the "science of behavior"
- ✓ 1990s Major research grants awarded for achievements in neuroscience and the biological basis of behavior

[15] Thomas Merton, *Spiritual Direction and Meditation* (Collegeville, MN: Liturgical Press, 1960).

In just five lines taken from the history of the department, one can see an overview of psychology's evolution from "moral philosophy" to a "science" that can be used as a basis of reliable prediction and control of human behavior (*Knowing Christ Today*, 78). But in the century-long, cross-campus move, two very important things were lost: moral understanding and the human soul. And yet, in spite of this heavy tariff, psychology, for the most part, has existed for over a century in the slums of the natural sciences—physics, biology, chemistry, neurology—it has sought to imitate. As a psychologist interested in the integration of theology and a Christian worldview into professional practice, I am keenly aware of another slum. As Dallas Willard articulates so well in his most recent book, *Knowing Christ Today: Why We Can Trust Spiritual Knowledge*, faith in Jesus Christ and living life as his students has been repositioned outside the category of knowledge. "Serious and thoughtful Christians today . . . are urged to treat their central beliefs as something *other* than knowledge—something, in fact, far *short of* knowledge" (*Knowing Christ Today*, 1).

For most of my professional career I created a hierarchy of value for the various "schools" of psychology based on how closely they resembled the natural sciences. Neuropsychology and the biological explanations of behavior were at the top, closely followed by behavioral and cognitive approaches. I gave some credence to person-centered approaches as a safe way to spend time with clients before the "real psychology" could be brought in, and I tolerated the existence of Freudian approaches in a manner similar to the way I would tolerate a beloved, senile grandparent.

At the same time, I came to accept the Western view that the term "knowledge" should be reserved for subjects like math and the natural sciences. Religion—even Christianity—dealt in matters of faith, belief, and profession, but not knowledge. Indeed, how could one make a "leap of faith" if one's faith were grounded in actual knowledge?

For two decades, I have been a teacher and a practitioner of integration—integrating "knowledge" from the science of psychology with "beliefs and practices" from Christianity. Initially, I viewed Christians as an underserved population who could benefit from the knowledge psychology had to offer. I later began to view various soul-care strategies (e.g., practice with a variety of Christian disciplines) as outside-the-box techniques for some

Christian clients who might benefit in a variety of ways from participating in these "practices."

Recently, however, a slow change in my way of thinking has percolated to the surface and now causes me to believe that I have been dramatically short-changing what Jesus has to offer. I believe it is time for me—and perhaps others in the integration enterprise—to reposition faith in Jesus Christ and the ability to live interactively with him back within the category of knowledge.

Have I decided to join the ever-present band of psychology bashers who have dogged the integration movement since its inception? God forbid! What I am confessing is that before encountering Dallas's line of thinking, I had not given Christianity its rightful place at the table as a source of not merely belief and practice, but *knowledge*.

As just one example, consider afresh for a moment the following table, which presents the four most fundamental worldview questions in the universe: (1) What is real? (2) Who is well-off? (3) Who is a good person? and (4) How do I become one?[16]

1) The Reality Question: The foundational part of a worldview is always what it considers to be real—what is reality?	***Jesus' Answer:*** God and his kingdom; that is what you can count on and what you have to come to terms with.	***Skinner's Answer:*** The measurable physical universe.	***Freud's Answer:*** The physical universe—including the unseen subconscious mind.
2) Who has it made? The reality question is joined at the worldview level with the question of well-being. Who is well off?	***Jesus' Answer:*** Anyone who is alive in the kingdom: that is, anyone who is interactively engaged with God and the various dynamic dimensions of his reigning. Such engagement with God is *an eternal living, an eternal life.*	***Skinner's Answer:*** Anyone who is able to live with as many pleasant events as possible while living free from physical pain	***Freud's Answer:*** The person who is maximally in touch with his or her unconscious and able to live an examined life
3) The Character Question: Who is a really good person?	***Jesus' Answer:*** Anyone one who is pervaded with love	***Skinner's Answer:*** Anyone who on a personal and corporate level seeks to minimize pain and maximize pleasure for self and others	***Freud's Answer:*** A person who seeks to understand the self and help others do the same

[16] For a more detailed treatment of worldview and knowledge see *Knowing Christ Today*, 39–58.

4) The Development Question: How does one become a genuinely good person?	***Jesus' Answer:*** You place your confidence in Jesus Christ and become his student or apprentice in kingdom living. That amounts to progressively entering into the abundance of life he brings to us.	***Skinner's Answer:*** You learn to shape by your environment in such a way that you minimize the cause of pain in others.	***Freud's Answer:*** Analysis

In reviewing this table, I am convinced that Jesus offers a source of exquisite knowledge to life's most important questions and that his answers deserve—at minimum—equal attention as that received by psychology's pioneers. I also believe that profound psychological good could be accomplished by moving this knowledge from the academic slums to Beverly Hills. The mental health benefits of becoming a person pervaded with love are simply too enormous to ignore, as is the possibility of living more and more moments of each day in firsthand interaction (knowing by acquaintance) with Jesus and his kingdom.

Conclusion

I began this article with the statement that "one might find it odd that I would refer to the philosopher/theologian Dallas Willard as my favorite *psychologist*," and attempted to make the case that this "amateur" theologian and professional philosopher has made praiseworthy contributions in a third domain. In the chapter, "A Transformational Approach" (Moon, 2012), I have explored the application of these ideas in a clinical setting.[17] In conclusion I will simply say that when it comes to better understanding the person, the process of transformation, and the psychological implications for Jesus' being very smart; no one has helped me more with these matters of the *psyche* than Dallas Willard.

[17] Gary W. Moon, "Transformational Approach," in *Counseling and Christianity: Five Approaches*, edited by Stephen P. Greggo and Timothy A. Sisemore (Downers Grove, IL: InterVarsity Press, 2012).

CONTRIBUTORS

Darrell L. Bock is Executive Director of Cultural Engagement and Senior Research Professor of New Testament Studies at Dallas Theological Seminary. He has earned recognition as a Humboldt Scholar (Tübingen University in Germany) and is the author of over 40 books, including a two-volume commentary on the Gospel of Luke (1994), *Jesus in Context: Background Readings for Jesus Studies* (2005), and *Jesus the God-Man: The Unity and Diversity of the Gospel Portrayals* (2016). He was president of the Evangelical Theological Society for 2000–2001, is a consulting editor for *Christianity Today*, and serves on the board of Wheaton College.

Klaus Issler is Professor Practical Theology at Talbot School of Theology (Biola University). He has authored, co-edited, or contributed chapters to twelve books, including *Living Into the Life of Jesus: The Formation of Christian Character* (2012), *Jesus in Trinitarian Perspective: an Introductory Christology* (2007), and *Wasting Time with God: A Christian Spirituality of Friendship with God* (2001). He has published articles in journals such as *Journal of the Evangelical Theological Society*, *Journal of Spiritual Formation and Soul Care*, and the *Christian Education Journal*.

Catherine Looker, SSJ, a Sister of St. Joseph of Philadelphia, holds a master's degree and certification in Holistic Spirituality and Spiritual Direction from Chestnut Hill College, an MA from Villanova, and a DMin. from Lutheran Theological Seminary. She has published articles and chapters in publications such as *Imaging the Other: Essays on Diversity* (2009), *Sisterly Love* (2015), and the *Journal of Spiritual Formation and Soul Care*. She also serves as an editorial consultant for the *Journal of Spiritual Formation and Soul Care*.

Gary W. Moon is the Executive Director of the Martin Institute for Christianity and Culture and the Dallas Willard Center for Christian Spiritual Formation at Westmont College (Santa Barbara, CA). He has served as the Executive Director of the Renovaré International Institute for Christian Spiritual Formation and as Editor-in-Chief of *Conversations Journal*. Moon has also served as an instructor at Fuller Graduate School of

Theology, and Fuller Graduate School of Psychology and on the faculties of Erskine Theological Seminary, Regent University, Richmont Graduate University, Azusa Pacific University, and Westmont College. He conducts research concerning the theoretical and practical integration of psychology and theology and has published and presented over 300 professional and popular papers.

J. P. Moreland is Distinguished Professor of Philosophy at Talbot School of Theology, Biola University. He received a PhD in philosophy at the University of Southern California where he studied with Dallas Willard. Moreland has authored, edited, or contributed papers in more than ninety-five books, including *Does God Exist?* (1993), *Universals* (2001), *Consciousness and the Existence of God* (2008), *The Blackwell Companion to Natural Theology* (2009), and *Debating Christian Theism* (2013). He has also published about 90 articles in journals such as *Philosophy and Phenomenological Research* and *American Philosophical Quarterly*.

John Ortberg is the senior pastor at Menlo Church in Menlo Park, California. He graduated from Wheaton College with a degree in psychology and earned a MDiv and PhD in clinical psychology from Fuller Seminary. His teaching centers around how faith in Christ can impact our everyday lives with God. He has written several books on spiritual formation including, *The Life You've Always Wanted: Spiritual Disciplines for Ordinary People* (2015), *Soul Keeping: Caring for the Most Important Part of You* (2014), and most recently *I'd Like You More If You Were More Like Me: Getting Real about Getting Close* (2017). Ortberg is a member of the board of trustees at Fuller Seminary and is on the board for the Dallas Willard Center for Spiritual Formation.

Steven L. Porter serves as Professor of Theology and Philosophy at Talbot School of Theology and at Rosemead School of Psychology (Biola University). He completed his PhD in philosophy under the supervision of Dallas Willard and has contributed articles to *Faith and Philosophy*, *Journal of Psychology and Theology*, *Themelios*, *Religious Studies*, *Journal of Analytic Theology*, and *Journal of Psychology and Christianity*. He authored *Restoring the Foundations of Epistemic Justification* (2005) and has co-edited two books: *Christian Scholarship in the Twenty-First Century:*

Prospects and Perils (2014), and *Neuroscience and Soul: The Human Person in Philosophy, Science, and Theology* (2016). Porter serves as editor of the *Journal of Spiritual Formation and Soul Care* and Scholar-in-Residence at Biola University's Center for Christian Thought.

Aaron Preston is Associate Professor of Philosophy at Valparaiso University. He holds a PhD in philosophy from the University of Southern California and may be the only person to have studied under Dallas Willard as both an undergraduate and a graduate student. He also has a MTh in Systematic Theology from the University of Edinburgh. Along with Steve Porter and Gregg Ten Elshof, he has helped to complete Willard's last book, *The Disappearance of Moral Knowledge*. He has also written on the metaphysics of substance, personalism, religious epistemology, and on topics at the intersection of philosophy, psychology, and theology.

Gregg A. Ten Elshof is Professor of Philosophy at Biola University and Scholar-in-Residence at Biola's Center for Christian Thought. He has published articles in such journals as *Midwest Studies in Philosophy*, *Grazer Philosophische Studien*, and *The Journal of Philosophical Research*. His book, *I Told Me So: Self-Deception and the Christian Life* (2009) won *Christianity Today*'s 2009 Book Award for Christian Living. He is also author of *Confucius for Christians* (2015) and has co-edited two books: *Christian Scholarship in the Twenty-First Century: Prospects and Perils* (2014) and *Neuroscience and Soul: The Human Person in Philosophy, Science, and Theology* (2016). Ten Elshof studied under Dallas Willard at University of Southern California.

Kevin J. Vanhoozer is Research Professor of Systematic Theology at Trinity Evangelical Divinity School. He previously served as Blanchard Professor of Theology at Wheaton College and as Senior Lecturer in Theology and Religious Studies at New College in the University of Edinburgh, where he also served on the Panel of Doctrine for the Church of Scotland. He has edited and authored many books, including *The Cambridge Companion to Postmodern Theology* (2003), *The Drama of Doctrine: A Canonical-Linguistic Approach to Christian Theology* (2005), and *Dictionary for Theological Interpretation of the Bible* (2005).